MASTERING SENIOR LIFE

MASTERING SENIOR LIFE

Thriving and Surviving

JOYCE K. PORTER

Porter Publishing

CONTENTS

About the Author

Joyce Klowden Porter is a Chicago-area Professor Emeritus and actress (as Joyce Porter). She earned her Bachelors in Speech Education from the University of Illinois Urbana and a Masters in Theater from Northwestern University. She taught Humanities, Theater, Film, and Speech at Moraine Valley Community College in Palos Hills for over 30 years and accepted an early retirement offer to act full-time. Joyce has always enjoyed writing non-fiction. She was on the staff of her grammar and high school newspapers; she wrote a column for a neighborhood newspaper about her high school's activities; and she and her late husband were freelance journalists for *The Streak,* a short-lived theater newspaper. While teaching, she wrote two supplemental textbooks, *Humanities on the Go* and *Experiencing the Arts.* She was honored three times by the Chicago Tribune as one of their favorite writers of Letters to the Editor for the year. She has many loyal followers who read her daily Facebook posts, many of which are intended to help others. This is her first book intended for the general public, and like those posts, it offers helpful information.

Dedication and Acknowledgments

I dedicate this book to my late husband, Paul Porter, a man of wide-ranging interests and talents. We were lucky enough to be in love for 40 years. We were married for almost 39 years, most of my life, so it seems odd and lonely not to have him to talk to. During the first half of those 40 years, we were focused on work, buying a house, raising our son, and enjoying such things as acting together and taking trips every year. During the second half, much of our time was spent dealing with Paul's many health problems. He often was surprised at how much I knew about medicine and said I should have been a doctor. While this book isn't just about medical issues, I learned a lot from those experiences and hope they will help others. Paul would have been proud of this book. He kept a scrapbook of my many Letters to the Editors.

I am lucky enough to have many wonderful, supportive relatives and friends to help me through difficult times. I want to thank them for that. I am especially lucky to have a brother who is a retired doctor, who could act as my medical advisor. Every time someone at a hospital would call and ask for permission to perform a procedure, I would have them talk to Art, and then I wouldn't worry whether I was making the right decision. Thanks also to Art and my son David for the relief visits to Paul in the nursing home, and to my daughter-in-law Beverly for helping me to choose one.

I also want to thank those who encouraged me to write, and those who gave input on the results. These especially include Sharon Dalla Costa and my brother, Dr. Arthur Klowden. Sharon gave me excellent notes throughout the editing process. Arthur checked my medical information for accuracy.

Thanks to those who helped with the publication. Kevin Theis of Fort Raphael Publishing, Paul Stroili of Touchstone Graphic Design - who did cover - and Janis Clark Johnston and Marc Blessof, who read and commented on the book for the cover.

A special thanks to my niece, Ellen Klowden, who has always been a big cheerleader for me, and who put both her editing and medical social work backgrounds to use when she volunteered to edit my book. She even added some additional content, especially in the chapter on supports for people who are low-income.

Preface

I am not a doctor. I am not a lawyer. I am not a geriatric specialist. I am not even a professional writer. So, why should you read this book? I am someone who has been through so many new experiences in the past several years and has often said to herself, "I wish I had known *that* before." I'm hoping that, by sharing my experiences, I can make your life easier, by helping you navigate some of the problems and opportunities that I have encountered.

This book is a combination of facts, opinions, and personal narrative. It has its genesis in my Facebook posts. Partly because I am an actress, and partly because I like to write, I spend a lot of time on it. I have many people who read my posts regularly. At first, I was reluctant to post about the many medical problems that my late husband, Paul, was undergoing. I was afraid that people would think that such problems were my only interest, and that I was not available for castings. It was important to me that I managed to keep my acting career going while helping my husband through all his problems.

After he died in 2019. I found that people were very appreciative of everything I was posting, including both tips and personal experiences. I was amazed that sometimes, when I first met people with whom I am friends on Facebook, they were quoting to me their favorite lines from my social media postings. This floored me. One of my friends suggested that I write a book. Embracing this suggestion, I have found not only that writing the book gives me the satisfaction of knowing I am helping other people, but also that it is a form of therapy for me.

There is an adage that no one teaches classes on how to be a parent. Likewise, no one that I know of teaches classes on how to be a senior. Often, we enter act three of our lives without any guidance. In the past, we often looked to older relatives for guidance, but now we are less likely to live and spend full time with them. There are also new challenges today that people previously didn't have to face. For example, today, most people must be computer-literate. If you are the rare person who isn't, head over to a community college (or ask a grandchild to come visit) and fix that. Some of the information and suggestions I present will require internet follow-up to be effective.

This book isn't just about the challenges; it is also about the opportunities and joys of being a senior.

You are equally welcome to read this book linearly, or to pick and choose those chapters that interest you. As you look at it, you are likely to find that much of the information is already known to you. However, what is known to you might not be known to someone else; and I assure you that, in this book, you are almost certain to find some information that is new to you and beneficial to you and your loved ones.

I began this book before the COVID-19 pandemic, and I completed it as the danger seemed to be waning, only to have the Delta and Omicron variants upend our expectations. It was hard to predict then what the long-term effects would be. For example, would people want to return to cruise ships? In the first draft, I predicted that we would gradually return to normal activities, such as travel, and that this book would remain useful on that topic. That has proven to be true. I think we will actually have some long- term benefits from the increased use of technology. For example, religious services and life events will resume in person but will also be broadcast so that those who are unable to attend in person can participate by Zoom or other platforms. Those attending virtually will probably predominantly be seniors. Socializing or marking occasions, good and bad, with friends and relatives in other states might not happen as often but will probably continue.

You will need to do some customizing of the book's information to fit yourself. For example, I repeatedly refer to Medicare. Some readers might not have Medicare yet, or might not be eligible for it. Every private insurance plan, including every Medicare supplement and Medigap plan, is somewhat different; so, when I mention that something was covered by Medicare in my experience, it might or might not be covered by your insurance company. However, learning that something was covered for others could give you the basis for an inquiry to your company. Also, Medicare is considered the gold standard and Medicaid and other medical insurance plans use it for determination. Also, legal forms and procedures vary a bit by state, though usually not in a major way. It is a kind of shorthand throughout the book to simply say Medicare. In addition, there are always new products on the market, especially medical ones, and this book cannot address them all.

Feel free to contact me with your comments and suggestions, in case there is ever a second edition. You can email me at joycekporter@yahoo.com.

Here are some people I refer to repeatedly throughout the book and so may not explain:

Paul, my late husband

David, our son

Beverly, David's wife

Art, my brother who is a doctor and lives in the area

Judy, Art's wife

Ellen, my niece, who lives in Oregon and edited the book

Mike and Pat, my brother and sister-in-law in CA.

Part One: Thriving

Introduction to Part One:
Golden Years

Since much of this book deals with topics such as illness, it's important to point out that your senior years can be the best years of your life. My husband often said, "It's hell to get old". My response was always, "No; it's hell to be in poor health". If you are healthy, being older can be a real plus. A recent survey showed that 70 years old was one of the happiest ages there is. Just think about it. By the time you are in your 60s, if not your 50s, you have probably paid off your mortgage. Your children are probably grown, and you no longer have the responsibilities of financing their upbringing and education. IRAs were meant to be used at this point, so if you have saved for your retirement, you may find yourself in the best financial position that you have ever been in. If you are still working, you have probably worked your way up to a supervisory position. If you are retired, you have lots of leisure time. Why not enjoy all that?

In addition, there are so many discounts to take advantage of. Movie theaters, stores, hotels, drugstores, performance groups, and many others offer senior citizen discounts. Check with each store, restaurant, or whatever that you patronize to see what discounts they offer. Some offers are applicable every day, every time. Others are usable only on certain days of the week or month. For example Walgreen's has one senior day per month. Also, if you are under 65, ask what their starting age is for each discount. I remember the first time I was given a senior ticket to a movie without asking. I was only in my 50's and felt a bit insulted, until I found out they started their discounts at 55, not 65. You'll probably want to keep a list of which discounts are available and when. You will get a mailing from AARP when you are 50, offering you an inexpensive membership. Take it. You will receive an interesting magazine and additional discount opportunities. They also offer insurance plans, informational seminars, and driving safety courses that can get you an insurance discount.

Park districts offer special opportunities for senior citizens. In the case of my local park district, such activities are referred to as being for "active adults," and the age begins at just 50. Many workshops and trips are offered, and they are inexpensive, or even free, in many cases. They even offer a free lunch with a movie once a month for members. There is also a bank chain that offers senior trips; some religious institutions and various other organizations that do as well. These might simply be a trip to the zoo without the hassle of paying for parking or driving, or it may be to some place you've never been before. Some trips even include overnight travel. Those, of course, are not free, but they tend to be reasonable.

One of my favorite things about being retired is avoiding the crowds. I can go to stores and events during the week, travel off-peak, and generally be flexible about my schedule.

The whole point of this is to just enjoy your life, and especially, to enjoy your retirement. If you are in good health, or at least able to get out, this is your chance. Now, you're not bound by the restrictions of having to work so hard, raise kids, etc., and you have more time to enjoy life.

In the following chapters, I'll be talking about some of the other opportunities and choices available to you now in this part of your life.

CHAPTER 1

Your Real Age

It seems to me that there are three aspects to aging. The first is your statistical age, which you might call your chronological age. There's nothing you can do to change that, so there isn't much to say about it. The other two factors are your outward appearance, and your internal experience of age. All of them affect each other and can line up, but they are often quite different.

Generally, when people judge others in terms of age, it is based, in most cases, upon what we see of them. Have you been to a school reunion and noticed how some people seem so much older than other people, even though they are all the same age? Sometimes, this is beyond our control. Some factors that can affect your appearance include genetics, stress, health problems, and other factors we can't control. However, some of the things that affect the appearance of age we *can* control, such as drinking, smoking, using drugs, and cosmetic treatments, such as using tanning booths versus spending time in the sun with the correct amount of sun protection. I am not a fan of plastic surgery. In my personal opinion, I think most people look worse after cosmetic procedures, rather than better. There are exceptions of course. For example, my sister-in-law Barbara, had surgery for the area under her eyebrows, because it was drooping. Not only did this alter her appearance, but it was actually getting to the point that it made it hard for her to see. In a case like this, "cosmetic surgery" is *not* just cosmetic; it was indicated medically for her vision, and, as a bonus, also did improve her appearance. This is as opposed to something such as a major face-lift, which can, as we sometimes see in movie stars, significantly alter the patient's appearance or make them look unnatural. Excessive use of Botox can also look unnatural.

There are other ways we can keep ourselves looking younger. Meditation and facial exercises (yes, there *are* such things) may relax some stress lines. Many people choose to dye their hair to keep out the gray. In other cases, gray, silver, or white hair can actually make a person look distinguished or sophisticated. You have to see what works for you. Part of that difference is whether you keep your hair well-conditioned and find the right kinds of lotions or applications that will make your hair smooth and not frizzy. Your skin color may become more sallow, or your eyebrows more faint, so you may need to wear more makeup than you used to. I know I do. I strongly believe in using facial creams overnight. Some are specifically made for men. The way we dress also sends a message. Most seniors don't look good in mini-skirts, but in general, my wardrobe hasn't changed as much over the years. For both men and women weight makes a huge difference. A man with a beer belly, for example, is always going to look older than he would without it. Keeping your weight in check is very important not only for appearance but for your health.

Age is also partly how old you feel inside, which may not match the outside. For example, because I am fortunate enough to not have complications, such as arthritis, that would make me feel older, I actually have the same energy as, and I actually feel the same inside as I did 20 or 30 years ago. So far, fortunately, my only major health problem is osteoporosis, and that doesn't make you feel any different. It's only a factor if you actually have a fall. Since I exercise and I'm active, I sometimes feel as if I've been placed in a Time Machine and put in a world where people think that I'm older than I am. I'm still me. I believe I think about this more than most, because as an actor, I see the roles for which I'm considered, but I'm not the only one to have this feeling. I was once in a focus group about beauty products, and we began by going around the table, with everyone giving the chronological age and their inner age. I was surprised to find that, in every single case, people's inner age was significantly younger than their statistical age. Of course, these were all healthy people, or they wouldn't have been there. In general, baby boomers are staying younger, in terms of action and feel, than our parent's generation did. My mom never took an exercise class or wore blue jeans.

I think that you're better off feeling as if you are younger than your actual age, as long as you are realistic about knowing that others may not see you that way. There's no harm in using a little more makeup than you used to, and if you prefer not to have gray, dye your hair to a natural-looking color, if it helps your self-image. There are some people who go to extreme lengths to look young, and it can have the opposite effect, making their age more obvious. Examples include men who wear toupees which do not gray as the rest of their hair grays; and people who wear excessive amounts of makeup or dye their hair to very bright colors. I think it's important to feel good about the way you look without going to an extreme. You may have heard the phrase "aging gracefully".

While part of aging is beyond your control, part of it is up to you. An example would be that when I go up the stairs, I've caught myself starting to go up slowly when there's no reason I have to do that. So instead, I lightly hold the railing and go up the stairs quickly, and it helps me to feel young. In my exercise class, I sometimes look at myself in the mirror and notice that perhaps I'm not raising my arm or leg as high as I used to, so I correct that. On the other hand, you don't want to push your body to do things that hurt. Getting involved in satisfying activities, such as those listed in other chapters can help your state of mind and that can affect your overall health and feelings. Keep thinking young, as long as your body will allow it, and I think you will be healthier and happier.

CHAPTER 2

Enjoying the Arts

I remember once, many years ago, Paul and I were on vacation in lovely Myrtle Beach, South Carolina. The weather was perfect, and Paul commented that this might be a nice place to retire. I told him that retiring there wouldn't work for me, because I needed to have a lot of cultural activities nearby. "How often do you do that?" he questioned. I then said that I might not be going to a lot of plays and concerts now, but that, as soon as I retired, I planned to be doing that more often. In fact, that is exactly what happened.

If you enjoy the performing arts, once you retire you will have a lot more leisure time to enjoy them, or possibly even participate in them. This does not have to be extremely expensive. One way to enjoy theater is to purchase a subscription to a theater you like. I wouldn't do this unless you've been to the given theater, know that you like their productions, and find it fairly easy to get there. If you do like a theater and you subscribe, there are definite benefits to it. First of all, you will save money, compared to buying individual tickets for most or all of the shows. Second, if something comes up that you cannot attend on your scheduled day, you can exchange your ticket. This is something a box office normally doesn't do for people who buy individual tickets, but which they will do for subscribers. In most cases, all you have to do is call the box office a day in advance and tell them when you would like to attend instead, as long as the alternative date is not sold out. There might be an additional charge, if you move from a weekday to weekend, or from a matinee to an evening performance; but otherwise, generally, there is no additional charge involved. Having a subscription also gets you to see shows that you might not otherwise have seen, and which you will usually wind up enjoying. If you want to go with a friend, you can request that you be seated together. These subscriptions sometimes lead to real bargains. For example, people I know were paying over $200 for a single ticket to Hamilton in Chicago; but it cost me about $20 as part of my subscription package. It was in the second balcony, but it was still a fine seat. Subscribers sometimes get additional perks, such as access to a lounge or discounts on additional tickets.

If subscriptions are too expensive for you, there are other alternatives. There are websites where you can purchase tickets at a discount. Probably the biggest one of these is goldstar.com. Not only do they offer tickets for half price plus a fee, but sometimes I even receive notices about complementary tickets. Just sign up for their emails, and you will get notifications about opportunities. (If you don't yet have an email, or if you don't want to give companies your private email, there are many options, such as Gmail or Yahoo, for signing up for free email addresses just for public sites and subscriptions.) Another website to check is theatermania.com. There are half-price tickets available, in many cities, at many sites. In Chicago, we also have hottix.org. Sometimes this has the same tickets at the same prices as Goldstar, and sometimes not. Many theaters have "rush tickets," which are highly discounted tickets made available just an hour or two before "curtain" (show start time), if you're willing to wait until the last minute. In some cases that means taking the chance of going there and possibly not getting them, but some theaters do offer rush tickets online or over the phone. New York has a half-price ticket booth in Times Square. In Chicago, Hottix has 2 outlets Downtown, in the Block 37 building at State and Randolph and very nearby at 72 E. Randolph. Google "discount tickets" in the area where you live or are visiting, to find out more.

If you are really watching your budget, and if you are physically able to stand for at least an hour at a time, another possibility is to usher for shows (help people find their seats; give out playbills; etc.). In Chicago, there is an organization called The Saints for which you can pay a small yearly fee to sign up and join. You then get to select the shows which you would like to usher for and see for free. If there is no comparable local organization where you are, you could call the theaters and ask if they use volunteer or even paid ushers (or ask the ushers you see). If you usher, you will generally have to be at the theater an hour or so before curtain to volunteer, but then you will get to sit and watch the show.

You could organize a group. Most organizations have group discounts. The number of people it takes to constitute a "group" who can purchase at a discount can sometimes be as few as 10 people. In some cases, the group leader attends for free. It could be a one-time outing, or a regular group you organize. Of course, if you have to collect the money to pay in advance, you may decide it's too much effort. Some places will allow group members to pay individually at the box office. You could ask.

You could see if there are chapters of meetup.com in your area. People who share a common interest get together. You could organize a meetup interest group to get together once a month or so to see movies or live performances.

There are surprisingly excellent and inexpensive plays produced by universities, community colleges, and even high schools. The casts and orchestras are often larger than what you would see at a professional production, because they are not paid. Try one out, and you'll probably be surprised at the quality of the talent and the production. In Oak Park, Illinois, where I live, even the middle schools have impressive performing arts programs. One of them was actually featured in the New York Times, in an article about how they have worked with Broadway composers trying out school versions of their plays!

Many of the strategies that I just mentioned for theaters apply to concerts, as well. Most musical organizations have subscription packages, use ushers, are on goldstar.com, and sometimes even have free public outreach performances. During the summer, many groups perform outdoors for free, or for a very affordable amount. Many parks and malls also offer free performances. Check your local newspaper or its website for listings.

A Museum Bargain

If you go to many museums, and if you do some traveling, I have a tip for you about a terrific bargain. Probably, many of the museums you go to belong to the North American Reciprocal Museum Association, or NARM, as it is also known. If you enroll at some museums, and you join the institution at a certain level, it will include a membership in this organization. This is an association of hundreds of museums across the country that give reciprocal free admission to you. From their website (narmassociation.org): Be sure to check, before joining, if the museums you want to visit are members before you join, so you can't be disappointed.

The North American Reciprocal Museum (NARM) Association® network is a mosaic of 1,137 art museums and galleries, historical museums and societies, botanical gardens, children's museums, zoos and more. When you sign up with your favorite participating NARM institution you can receive reciprocal membership benefits across the United States, Canada, Bermuda, El Salvador and Mexico.

Here is another tip: you are best off if you do *not* join the local museum that you frequently attend, unless there are other activities in which you wish to be involved, or you just want to support them. The reason for this is that whatever your home-base museum is, you cannot use this free admission at member organizations within 15 miles of it. So, for example, if I were to join one organization in Chicago that is participating in NARM, I would not be able to use the free membership at other member museums in Chicago. On the other hand, if I join the museum that I visit on a Florida trip, I am able to use it, both in some other parts of Florida, and throughout Illinois.

Another tip is to go online to the museums and check the membership rates. The cost of a membership at the level that includes a NARM membership can double from one museum to the next.

I just looked at two museums that I was considering visiting. At one of them, a membership that included the association was $125, while at the other, it was only $60. Not all memberships at every museum included Membership in the Association. Be careful to get the right level of membership. If you do tour more than two or three member museums a year, you will come out ahead.

Virtual Tours

The best way to experience the treasures of a museum is to tour in person; but it's possible that, for various reasons, you might not be able to do that. Many museums today offer virtual tours. Not only does this allow you to enjoy your local museum when you can't get out of the house, it allows you to enjoy museums in other countries you might never get to. Here is a link to an article in Travel and Leisure Magazine that lists more information:

https://www.travelandleisure.com/attractions/museums-galleries/museums-with-virtual-tours

And another:

Collections or artsandculture.google.com.

You can also download thousands of books for free if you don't mind reading on your phone. The app is called SimplyE. There are other apps for free downloads of both books and audiobooks. Just ask your librarian.

CHAPTER 3

Rediscovering Your Creativity

I think everyone is born creative, though in most cases, we put that creativity aside as we become "grownups". We are forced to focus on practical matters, such as making a living and raising children. Sometimes we forget about our creativity. Your senior years can be the time to have the fulfilling experience of rediscovering it.

In my case, I was fortunate to be able to combine the practical and the creative by teaching theater, as well as film and humanities; working on curriculum development; and directing a play of my choice, every year. I also performed in some community theater, on the side. Many people, however, do not have such creative opportunities.

When I was 48, I got a very surprising letter, with a temporary offer to retire when I would be 52. Because this was unexpected and unplanned, and because I was enjoying my job, it took me several days to decide. Paul was instrumental in that decision when he said to me, "Just think. If you accept it, not only could we spend winters away, but I know you've always wondered what would have happened if you had gone into acting full-time, like some of your friends. Now, you can find out."

Your goals at this age may be different then they would have been at a young age. For example, if you are over 50 and you take your first ballet class, you have to realize that you have almost no chance of pursuing ballet professionally at that age. However, that does not mean that you cannot take a class and enjoy the experience of dancing, and perhaps even performing for friends, with your class.

If you've always wanted to act but never had the chance, there are many church and community theater groups out there that can give you a chance to perform. Some community theaters do very sophisticated work. Auditioning for them may be intimidating, but you could possibly start with a small part to get your feet wet and move on from there. Help with backstage work is always welcome. There are also community bands and choruses. Some of them require auditions, but others are simply open to anyone who would enjoy the experience.

If you don't know where to begin, try your local park district, which will almost certainly have classes in painting and sculpture and may have opportunities in the performing arts as well.

I strongly recommend checking out the offerings of your local community college. There is a reason why they are called community colleges. They bear little resemblance to the junior colleges of decades ago, where all the students were there to simply take the first two years of a four-year degree. Community colleges have broadened their scope considerably. Only about half the students enrolled in a community college are traditional students, who are there to take the first half of a bachelor's degree. Some are there for technical and career certificate programs, but many others are there for personal enrichment and the love of learning. Some community colleges offer highly discounted tuition for seniors. If you do not wish to actually pursue a degree, you can ask if it's possible to audit a class. That would mean you would attend the class but would not have to take the tests, write the papers, and get a grade.

An even better idea for most people is to check out the noncredit offerings that all community colleges, and in fact, even some universities offer to the community. These are normally quite inexpensive and do not have the pressure of grades or competing with younger students. They are meant strictly for enrichment. Offerings may include performing arts, visual arts, and writing classes. The community college at which I taught had a community orchestra and a community chorus, in addition to the student chorus and orchestra. Because community colleges are supported partly by tax dollars, they want to give back to the community.

Besides performing and creating art pieces, there are other ways to express creativity. You may want to go into writing. I have friends my age who have written poetry and short stories. Some of them have actually had small quantities of their writings self published, to distribute to friends and family. You could write about your experiences in your profession or life and share them with others, as I am doing in this book. Others compose memoirs for their families.

Your physical abilities may limit what you want to do, but that doesn't mean you have to put those desires aside. Instead, think about the possibility of modifying them. For example, instead of ballet, perhaps you could do ballroom or line dancing. Maybe you can't hit those high notes when you sing anymore, but you could join a choir as a mezzo soprano or even an alto.

Paul derived great pleasure from his hobby of model-making. When he began to develop Parkinson's and couldn't control his hands well enough to work on fine details, he moved from the detailed modeling of a miniature of our house and building a model train layout, to building a fountain in our backyard. This did not require intricate detailed work but gave him the satisfaction of creating and using his imagination. He was then able to sit out in the yard and have the double pleasure of not only listening to the running water but knowing that he had created that waterfall-style fountain.

Have a brainstorming session with yourself, and jot down all the things that you think would be fun to do, and creative activities that you think you might want to take part in, whether you are good at them or not. Then find out where you can pursue them.

CHAPTER 4

You Could Be in the Movies

How to Be in the Movies or TV

If you are a fan of the movies, you might have thought, "It would be so much fun to be a part of one!" If you are retired, participating in a movie is now a possibility for you. Even if you aren't retired yet, this is something you can do on your days off. True, if you have never acted before, the odds are that you're not going to become a movie star overnight. However, there are a few possible opportunities for you to be on a movie set.

The first one is to have a small part in a student film. There are so many film schools around the country, and the students are required to make a certain number of films. They mostly have access to young people to be in their films, so they are happy to get older people acting in them. Simply contact your local college, ask for the film department, and ask how to get involved. Usually there isn't any pay for this, especially in the kinds of roles you might get early on; but it is fun, and they will generally give you a meal. There may even be a premiere you can attend. It does require some patience, as the directors are not that experienced and sometimes don't use their time that efficiently. Make sure that you get the director's full contact information and the name of their advisor, to follow up after the film is completed, to make sure that you were invited to premieres, even if you have a small part. If you have a speaking part, you should be given a copy of the film or a link to it online. There is even a chance that the director may go on to be successful and you can brag that you were in one of their films.

Low budget independent (local, not studio) films vary widely but many use the student standard of "credit and copy" plus a meal as pay.

Being an Extra

There are many people who retire and become "extras". Other terms that are used for this position include, "background" or "atmosphere". These are the people you see in the background in movies, television shows, and commercials. Extras, by definition, do not say lines other than crowd responses. It is something that anybody can do. You do not need professional photos. All you need is a snapshot. There are separate agencies that handle nothing but background work. They do not normally handle speaking roles, though, occasionally, they do get to cast one. In order to register with them, simply Google "background casting" for your area, and ask what their procedure is to register. It does not obligate you to any extended period of time. Generally, the way that they work is that they will post their possible opportunities online, and if you are interested in it and available, you respond. That does not guarantee casting, but it means that you will be considered for that position. While there are such things as "core" extras who work on a regular basis on TV shows, such as the doctors we might see repeatedly in a hospital (core extras), most extra positions are for a single day or two. One word of warning. You should not have to pay to be an extra. It's possible that some company might ask for a very small registration fee, such as $10; but even that would be unusual. *If anyone is asking you for money, do not give it to them. Legitimate companies are paid by the producers, not the actors.*

In Los Angeles, there are agencies that do receive a fee for *calling* to get work for you. They do *not* do any casting themselves. They just help you get work. The downside, besides the fee, is that if they get you a casting, you *have* to take it, no matter what else you have planned for that day. This is only a good choice if you want to be a full-time extra.

In order to be an extra, you need to be able to stand on your feet for extended periods of time, eat at irregular intervals, and not have any obligations to get to that day, at all... oh, and have lots of patience. Occasionally days as an extra are short; but they can require as many as 12 or even 14 hours. Once you are there, you cannot leave, short of an absolute dire emergency. Once you are established as being part of the scene, they cannot shoot the scene without you.

The Perks and the Perils

If you are an extra, you may have the excitement of seeing some very big stars. I did extra work for about 30 years, on and off, since I was able to teach just four days a week. I have been in scenes with Robert De Niro, Dustin Hoffman, Jessica Lange and many others. I did not interact with them, but I had the fun of seeing them. Once in a blue moon, I did get to actually talk to them. On the other hand, you might not encounter anyone famous at all, or even get on the set that day. It still is interesting to see how a TV show or movie is made. With the exception of extremely large groups of people, such as spectators at sporting events, extras are paid. They're generally paid minimum-wage for the first 8 to 10 hours, and time-and-a-half after that. For example as of 2020,the rate as of this writing in Chicago for high budget projects is $124/8. That means if you show up on time, you will make $124 that day, even if you only work a few hours. If you work more than 8 hours, you get time and a half and can wind up making quite a bit for the day. In addition, you receive parking (if you park in their designated location), a meal, and snacks. Depending on the budget of the production and the size of the group of extras, your meal might be something very simple, such as pizza or sandwiches. But if you are lucky enough to be in a small scene in a large-budget production, you might be treated to the same food as the crew, which means dining very, very well. You can see why this becomes a regular job for some people.

You have to keep in mind the weather conditions, when you are an extra. *Be sure to ask if the shoot is indoors or outdoors.* If you don't want to work outside in January, don't accept an extras position for an outdoor shoot in January. Also, another thing to keep in mind is the wardrobe. I was once offered an August shoot for the parade scene for Miracle on 34th St. I thought about the fact that the parade is set during Thanksgiving, which means winter clothing. I turned down the August shoot. I heard from people afterwards that I had definitely made the right decision. In most cases you will have to bring several choices of clothes to wear.

There are cases where you get what's called a bump. The bump is generally for the use of your car. This is an extra $15 or so, on top of your pay for being an extra. You should ask if this is in addition to work-ing outside the car, or if you will simply be in the car all day, then decide if that is something you want to do. In extremely rare cases, someone may be "upgraded". That means they are given a line to say on screen, paid quite a bit more, and become eligible to join SAG-AFTRA, the union. Do not join unless you have an agent and a substantial resume, because once you join, you cannot do any non-union work. If you were to have union roles 3 times, you would have to join; but getting that single upgrade would be pure joy.

Always keep safety in mind. If you feel that you are doing something dangerous, just say no. There was a case, a few years ago, where a young woman was driving in a way that only a stunt driver should have been driving, and she ended up severely brain damaged. This is, of course, a very, very rare situation. Generally, work as an extra is fun, and you get to interact with interesting people between scenes.

When you get your first extra booking ask the company that books you for their guidelines, so you know what to do and not do. One tip that won't be on there. You can't ask when you will wrap (be done), but once you are on set you can see if there is a callsheet around. That is a list of the scenes that will be shot that day. You will get a rough idea by seeing how many other scenes, if any, are going to be shot after yours.

Do not say anything about the plot, or post photos, if you took any of yourself,(no pictures ever on set) until it has aired. Then feel free to post whatever you want.

This may all sound like a lot, but I used to enjoy extra work when I did it. I don't do it now, at least not for television, because I am auditioning for speaking parts; but in some ways, I miss it. It's a fun thing to do, and while I sometimes never even got on set, I had some interesting experiences. I still get comments about a nice shot I had on Prison Break years ago. I'm on the poster for Death of a President. I got to have a conversation with Morgan Freeman, spent a day chatting with Nathan Fillion, and Rod Steiger added a line he said to me. So, if you're lucky, it can leave you with stories to tell your friends for many years.

Another Option

Some seniors who do not have previous acting experience are successful as print models. Agencies are sometimes looking for older-looking people for ads, either live or in print, for pharmaceutical companies or others. In order to obtain this type of work, you do need professional photos, which might cost you hundreds of dollars, and it might take a fair amount of work to get an agent. If you know anyone who acts, ask them to recommend an entry level agency and then call and ask if you can make an appointment for an evaluation. If you don't know an actor, Google talent agencies in your area. If they ask you to pay anything or use their photographer leave.

CHAPTER 5

Additional Activities

There are many other ways to enjoy your leisure time besides the arts.

Physical Activities

We often associate retirement with playing golf. If you live in a warm climate, it's a way to get outside and get a little exercise, though not as much as when people walked from hole to hole. Most courses now require that you use a golf cart in order to speed things up. It can be expensive, and for most people, it is not a year-round option.

No matter what else you do, it is important to stay physically as well as mentally active. Every article that you will read about health and what's good for you will have different advice. You may be frustrated, because the advice about what foods to eat, for example, seems to change from year to year. The one constant, however, is the importance of exercise. Every time you read advice about what is going to help any condition, whether it be your heart, your bones, your breathing, insomnia, etc. they always say: Exercise!

Now, of course, it's also important to bear in mind that you don't want to do anything that is too strenuous, or too much of a sudden increase in the level of activity. Moderate exercise is fine. It could be simply taking a good, paced walk every day, and perhaps increasing the length of that walk a little bit each time. It could be taking an exercise class at a health club, or with your Park District. It could be taking a dance class. And for many people it could be swimming. Many hospitals, health clubs, and recreational facilities offer a pool where you can either free swim or do water aerobics. The resistance of water is really great cardiovascular and muscular exercise.

Silver Sneakers

Most Medicare Advantage plans include a membership in Silver Sneakers. There is no extra cost for this. Silver Sneakers has two parts to it. The first is a discounted or free membership at many fitness centers, where you would go in-person.

The second aspect is zoom webinar classes. While I do not want to switch where I do my in person exercise, I do take advantage of the Zoom classes on the days that I do not actually go to an in person exercise class. Once you have registered it is extremely easy. It's just a couple of clicks to get the link to attend the class. They are offered every day, several times of the day. Do be aware that the level of intensity is specified and it is probably best to start with the beginning level class and work your way up. Alternatively, since it is a webinar and no one knows what you are doing, you could always go to a small part of a class and continue or not as you feel best.

If you are exercising on a rug I suggest trying exercising barefoot as the shoes may catch on the rug, hinder your movement, or cause a fall. Of course, only exercise on a heavier rug that will not slip. There are also many exercise classes on YouTube and Zoom classes you can pay for if you don't have Silver Sneakers.

Sports

If you enjoy competitive sports, many sports will have a special category, so you are only competing against other seniors. There are seniors who run marathons. Frankly, I never understood why anyone would want to do that; but if you do want to do it, do it (perhaps check with your physician first, if it will be a new activity for you). Just be very careful to build up your abilities gradually. There are also much shorter races. Over-exercising, or exercising too vigorously, can be dangerous. The man who wrote the book about the importance of running died from a heart attack while running. So did one of my uncles. That's not to say that you shouldn't run, but as the Ancient Greeks liked to say, "All things in moderation". Another phrase you hear repeatedly is "talk to your doctor".

Combining the Physical and the Artistic

You do not have to choose between the artistic and the physical. There are ways to combine the two. For example, being involved in dance performances. I once saw a video of a group of seniors who found a teacher who would lead them in creating performances that they all could do through graceful movement. They walked in circles in time to music and waved scarves and it was lovely. I don't know if they had a live audience, but it was posted on YouTube.

 As I'm writing this it is still warm out and I am not certain what will happen when it gets cold out. The flowers will be gone and I don't like the cold. So my walks will probably be less frequent but I might occasionally take a picture of pretty snow or  whatever, but as someone with osteoporosis I will not go out if it's slippery. And next year my photos would pretty much replicate this year. Perhaps then I will consider an online store. Definitely if I were to get requests I would do that. If nothing else, it will have been a pleasant several months. If you are in a warmer climate this is a hobby you can pursue all year round.

Activism

Back in the '60s, protests were mostly limited to young people. After all, they were the ones who would be affected by the draft. Today, when you see television coverage of protests, you will notice that for many issues, there's a wide range of ages involved. Issues such as climate change, political corruption, treatment of immigrants, etc., are of interest to everyone, including senior citizens. As seniors, you have the time to work on issues that are of true interest and passion to you. This is another way you can use your time. You are also freer than younger people to express yourself, because you do not have to worry if your association with a particular issue might affect your job prospects.

Summing It Up

The most important thing is to stay active. It's especially important if you live by yourself. Sometimes people's identities are so tied-in with their work that when they retire, they feel lost, or they just sit home, watching T. V. If you are at least healthy enough to get out, you have to look at this additional time as the gift you have worked for all these years -- as a beginning of new adventures, not an end.

Volunteering

You don't have to wait until you're retired to be a volunteer, but the extra free time that you have in your golden years does make it easier to devote more time to it. There are many different ways that one can volunteer. You could be a docent, part of a volunteer corps, a member of a Board of Directors, or a general volunteer.

What is a Docent?

A docent goes through fairly extensive training in order to represent an organization to the public. They may have to study manuals, attend lectures, or even take tests. They use their knowledge base that they have gained in order to give tours, or in other ways provide information to the public. Friends I have known have done such things as give tours of historic homes, and even lead architectural tours on boats on the Chicago River. It's a great way to share your enthusiasm for a subject.

Volunteer Experts or Corps

There are various organizations that offer professional advice for free. For example, Lawyers for the Creative Arts offers free information on legal matters to arts groups. There are also Executive Corps that provide advice to businesses. This is a great way to utilize the expertise that you have gained over the years and pass it on to others. AARP organizes one. Other friends I have known have done volunteer tutoring or have recorded books for the blind. All of these ask for a regular, part-time commitment. It is a great way to pass on what you have learned over the years.

Boards of Directors

There are two kinds of Boards of Directors. For-profit organizations have a paid Board of Directors. However, each nonprofit organization also has a Board of Directors and those positions are not paid. Indeed, some organizations expect anyone on their Board of Directors to contribute substantially to the financial welfare of the organization. This varies very widely. If someone contacts you about being on the Board of Directors of an organization, this is a question you need to ask: "What is the financial obligation?" It might be very modest and one that you are glad to make. However, be aware of that up front. Ask both about the time commitment and the financial commitment. Boards are generally at least partly responsible for the financial welfare of the organization, help it with outreach, and offer advice. Being on the Board of Directors can be very satisfying and can offer perks such as free admission, social opportunities, etc.

Volunteering in General

If you would like to allocate only a limited amount of time to volunteering, simply think about what things you enjoy doing, or what organizations you enjoy. For example, if you really enjoy going to a particular theater, ask them about volunteer opportunities. If you enjoy your local public library, ask them if they need help with their annual book sale, or if they need help during the week. Do you contribute to an environmental, health, or other charitable organization? Virtually every nonprofit organization functions largely with the help of volunteers. If you have a gentle dog, you could look into what is involved in bringing dogs for comfort visits to health care sites and/or residences for people who are seniors and/or ill. Then there are political organizations. They are always happy to have volunteers, especially when there is a campaign in progress. Some of the volunteer opportunities involve a specific schedule, but others simply let you drop in whenever you have some free time. Some are very short-term, such as sorting books before the library book sale, or helping with an event. Some local newspapers list volunteer opportunities in a special column or page. You can look at that. Personally, I think that everybody should volunteer to improve the world, in some way, for at least a part of their lives. That's how the world becomes a better place.

Almost every volunteer opportunity will offer social activities and a way to meet new people. It can be one of the most satisfying things you can do.

My Story with Volunteering

I was on the Board of Directors of Oak Park Festival Theatre (OPFT) for 22 years. OPFT is the oldest professional theater in the Midwest that performs classics outdoors. Because of the vagaries of the weather, and the professional salaries that must be paid no matter what, it has always been tricky to support the theater financially. I contributed simply as a member of the Board, for many years, while I was working. As fate would have it, right as I was about to retire, the theater had a financial crisis, and there was a vote to cease production. I am rather amazed that I was able to convince the Board, not only that we shouldn't cease production, but also that we should actually expand production from the single outdoor Shakespeare play we were producing each year and add modern classics and indoor productions. I became both President of the Board, and after a little while, also became the Acting Managing Director, since we did not have the money to pay for one. For three years, I performed both those functions. After that, I remained as Board President for another four years.

Because I was retired, I was able to work a full-time, unpaid job for the theater. The Artistic Director and Board worked with me to implement my idea of broadening the scope of programming and finding new sources of funding, and new programs such as college interns. It all worked, and the theater is still producing. When I go to a performance today, there's a great sense of satisfaction in having played a part in its continued existence and increased success. That's the sort of thing you can do when you're retired, and you have fewer time restraints than someone working full-time.

Whether it's a major project or a few hours here or there, I hope you'll consider volunteering for the cause of your choice.

CHAPTER 6

Travel

Preparing to Travel

Many of you are probably very experienced travelers, but I have a list of suggestions, and some may be helpful to you.If you don't travel frequently, it's easy to forget some of these points. Here are some suggestions that will help make your travel departure go smoothly.

A General Tip for Saving on Travel

Book everything months ahead of time, and then keep checking back, once a month or if you get an email about a sale. I recently booked a flight to New York at what I thought was a good rate. When I got emails from Southwest, saying they were having a sale, even though fuel rates were skyrocketing, I doubted it would do any good, but I figured it couldn't hurt to check. I reduced my fare, then reduced it again, and I wound up saving enough points for another entire flight. Don't call. Just make changes online-- it's super easy. Other airlines have become more flexible than they used to be, as well. I have also saved on car rentals by checking last- minute. You are not stuck with your original rate. Generally the best day to book travel is Tuesday.

A Month Before You Travel

If you are going to travel internationally, be aware that unfortunately, electronics standards are not universal. You will need a converter kit for any electronic items that you bring. Not only are the currents different in Europe and other parts of the world, but the configuration of the plugs are different. If you bring any electronic items whatsoever, you will not be able to plug them in. However, you can buy a kit that has the American version on one end and the European version on the other, so you can plug in. A good converter kit will cover other continents, as well. (One place to check for such products, and ask about comparable products for other parts of the world, is your local AAA store, if you have one nearby.) The alternative is to not bring electronic items; but realistically, you are likely to at least have a cell phone with you, or an Apple watch, or something that needs recharging.

Talk to your cell phone carrier about how you can make international calls. You used to have to change SIM cards or purchase special phones when you travel, but companies have now made it easy and relatively inexpensive to use your phone in other countries.

Start preparing two lists. One would be the list of those things you need a helper to do while you're gone, such as water the plants, and shovel or mow. You will need to arrange a neighbor to do these things as a favor or hire someone to do them. The second list would be a packing list. If you add things to your lists as you use them, as ideas occur to you, you will have much more thorough lists to look at, the week before you leave.

If you will need a wheelchair in the airport or have other special needs, be sure to let your airline and car rental places (and/or train lines, bus lines, cruise lines) know.

When you purchase suitcases, most have wheels, these days, but make sure that they have the kind of wheels that rotate. It can make it so much easier to push that bag down the aisle or other places. Also, before you buy a wheeled bag, check out how easy or hard it is to extend and retract the handle. Especially if you are in a hurry at the airport or during boarding, an unwieldy handle can be quite a problem.

Speaking of bringing bags down aisles, if you have a free bag check because you're flying Southwest, or if you have a special credit card or status that will give you free checked bags on another airline, take advantage of it. Only bring on the plane a very small carry-on bag that can fit under the seat in front of you. Why clog up at the aisles as you try to find space in an overhead bin? The only exception, in my opinion, would be if you were only going away for 1 to 2 days. Another advantage of checking your main bag is that if you decide to walk around the airport and not just sit at the gate, you don't have to trust a stranger to watch it for you or schlep it around with you.

Another advantage of checking a bag is you can pack items that aren't allowed in carry-on bags, such as a Swiss army knife, which is always handy; and liquids, such as shampoos, of which, when you pack them into carry-ons, you are limited to only bringing a few ounces in a specific size of a Ziplock bag. Make sure the caps are tight on any liquids. Encase them in something stronger than just a Ziplock, such as a makeup case. You don't want them accidentally drenching or staining your clothing.

A tip: When the bags are on the carousel, it can be hard to pick yours out. A simple solution is to tie a ribbon or other noticeable, colorful item around the handle. I always see that my bag is approaching when I see the ribbon. I also put a business card in the outer compartment of each bag, including my carry-on, in case it gets misplaced and the airline tag comes off.

When I am flying on Southwest and am allowed 2 free bags I take one, but also put a lightweight flight bag without wheels that folds flat, inside the suitcase. I can use it as a tote bag while on the trip and then if I buy souvenirs or other items that crowd my suitcase I check it as my second bag. Or if I have too much to pack in one I pack clothes in one bag and other items in the other one. That protects my clothes and helps organize my unpacking.

When packing, there is a cliché that you should get packed -- and then take half the clothes and double the money. There's some truth to this. Probably, any place you stay will have a washer and dryer available, so you only need a little more than a week's worth of clothes. Keep in mind that, when you travel to warm places, they can have a very cool evening. I have two or three sweatshirts that I purchased on trips to warm places that turned out to be not so warm. A winter jacket that has a removable hood can be usable for an evening jacket, without its hood. A scarf can substitute for a jacket, if you're just a little cool, and it can be added to your jacket, if you are arriving home to a cold climate. When I am traveling to other countries I pack a couple of washcloths, as they are not usually provided.

An Item You May Want to Purchase and Pack

Even if you are perfectly able-bodied, if you are either going to be hiking or traveling to other countries, you might want to purchase a folding cane. I just did. It has a carrying bag, weighs only 3/4 of a pound, and costs less than $20 online. The reason I bought it is because I am a spoiled American, used to things like handrails on stairs. If you visit a centuries-old castle, for example, do not expect such safety measures. If it turns out the area you are staying in is easy to navigate and it stays in your suitcase or tote bag (don't forget to pack one), it won't be much of a loss; but there might be that one day trip to some ruins where it gives you reassurance. You don't want to spend part of your vacation dealing with an injury.< Also, keep in mind that some old cities have cobblestone streets. Pack shoes with good soles, so you don't feel the stones as you walk.

The Evening Before You Leave

Wash all your dishes. If you have a dishwasher, run it and empty it. You don't want to come home to not only dirty dishes, but dishes that may smell stale because they've been closed in the dishwasher for weeks.

Arrange for whatever ride you are using to the airport, such as ordering a taxi or Lyft, if a friend isn't driving you.

Make sure whoever is helping you with your home has a duplicate set of keys. You will want your own key to get into the house immediately when you come home, rather than have to wait for someone to open up for you; so, you will have to have a duplicate key. If you have a burglar alarm system, make sure that they have either a remote, or the codes to set and end the alarm.

Change all your linens. When you get back, you may be tired, and it will be enough to deal with simply getting home and getting your suitcases inside, and you may want to just slip into a clean bed. The unpacking can wait. Try to arrange your bags in such a way that those things that you will really need when you get home, such as your medicines, your phone charger, your toothbrush, and your night clothes, are in one specific place, and you can unpack just those and save the rest for the next day.

Make sure that you have packed any medications or over-the-counter drugs that you need or may even want.

I like to pack a nightlight and a small flashlight to keep on the bed stand. If you must get up during the night, for any reason, you will be unfamiliar with the layout of your room.

If your basement gets flooding or seepage, assume the worst, and move area rugs or other objects that you would normally move if it did flood.

Place all your bags by the front door, if you are being driven to the airport (or train station, bus station, cruise port, etc.), or put them in your trunk, if you are driving yourself.

Most airlines will want you to check in the day before. They will often send you an email to that effect. If you are flying on Southwest, set an alarm for 24 hours before your departure to check in. Your boarding number will be first come, first served. The number will determine when you board and how much choice you have in seating. As an alternative, if you care about where you sit, you may want to consider paying for Early Bird Check-In. It costs about $20 or $25. The airline checks you in automatically the day before, and you get a higher number and therefore a better selection of seats.

On the Morning That You Leave

The first thing you should do, if you are flying, is check to see that your flight is on time. I usually forget to do this, and I am taking the chance that I could arrive at the airport only to have to sit there for hours. Fortunately, that hasn't happened to me yet, but you never know. Of course nowadays the airlines generally contact you if there is a change. The same is true if you are taking a bus, train, or cruise. Check whether departure is reported to be on time. If you are driving on a road trip, check the traffic reports and/or Google Maps, to see if there are any construction sites or accident-related delays that suggest altering your intended route.

Do not leave any appliances running. The lint in dryers can catch on fire, and clothes washers and dishwashers can malfunction and flood. The chance is very remote, but you don't want to take any chances.

Pack your phone charger, computer charger, watch charger if you have one, and toothbrush, including toothbrush charging base, if applicable.

Lower the thermostat, or if you have one that automatically lowers when you are away, lower your away temperature for that.

Take out the garbage and recycling, and if applicable, the compost and the yard waste.

Run the garbage disposal.

Do one last check of the refrigerator to make sure that there is nothing in there that will spoil while you are away.

Set the burglar alarm, if you have one.

However, while all these things will help, there is almost nothing that can't be replaced when you get to your destination; so, other than, perhaps, your chargers, don't worry about it too much. Also, if you are staying in a hotel, many hotels can provide you with a small toothbrush, toothpaste, or other toiletry items, if you forget them.

If you are flying, then when you arrive at the airport, you're going to want to check to make sure that your flight is still on time, and to see how far away the gate is. I strongly recommend curbside check-in. I don't know why so many people go inside the airport to stand in long lines, when it's so much quicker to check your bag outside. Yes, it is expected that you will tip, but you don't have to, and it's worth a dollar or two to me to avoid waiting in that long line.

Be careful about using public Wi-Fi. Try to use it only for short periods of time, and do not open any financial applications while using it. It is fairly easy for someone to hack in and steal your information. **When you get on the plane, put your electric devices on airplane mode just before takeoff. Not only can the signal interfere with the plane operations, but your battery will be drained searching for a signal that isn't there if you don't.** You can switch them off of that setting as soon as you land, even though you haven't reached the gate yet. With airplane mode, you still have the phone on and can still take photos, and you can use your computer to write things down and view entertainment.

Very Important Health and Safety Precautions for Flying

Blood clots are a serious threat when you fly. If you get one in a vein, it can break off and go to your heart, or other vital organs, and block the flow of blood. They can be caused by injury, surgery or illness, but most controllable are blood clots that are caused by inactivity. This can happen anywhere, and in fact, I know someone whose husband almost died from sitting in one position with his legs crossed too long at a meeting. However, this dangerous condition, also known as DVT or deep vein thrombosis, most commonly occurs on long flights. Be sure to stand up and either walk up and down the aisle every hour or so, or if it is too crowded, simply walk in place. If you cannot get up because of turbulence, be sure to move your legs around. Raise one and then the other, and flex and point your foot every once in a while.

Also, don't drink too much alcohol, as the different altitude and pressure may increase the effects. Be sure to stay hydrated. However, I have read some articles that contend that the water on airplanes isn't really safe. If you are worried, that means that not only should you either bring your own water or stick to canned beverages, but you should specify no ice. Of note: If you bring water from home to an airport, TSA security will make you pour it out. However, you can keep the empty plastic or, preferably, empty reusable, bottle, and fill it at an airport drinking fountain after security. Filling your own bottle both helps you save money, compared to expensive airport bottled water, and helps reduce use of plastic, as well as helping protect drinking water sources. Remember that both alcohol and caffeine are diuretic and can be dehydrating on flights, and that drinking a lot of any beverages will mean waiting in line for one of the few bathrooms on the plane.

Do not wear sandals, or especially flip-flops, when flying, both because you may wind up barefoot in a TSA Line, and also because if there is an emergency evacuation, they could catch as you slide down a chute.

Leaving the Place You Are Staying

It's so easy to be in a hurry and leave something behind in a hotel or other place you might stay. It has been my experience that it's very hard to retrieve those items. Not only could they be taken by someone, but their importance might not be recognized, and they may be thrown out. For example, I lost the diaries that way, for both the year I was married and the year I gave birth. I was very upset, and I was especially angry with myself for making the same mistake twice.

The night before you leave, check everything very carefully, so you don't run out in a hurry and leave anything. All you should have to pack in the morning should be your night clothes and toiletries. Lay out the clothes you will be wearing. Be sure to fully charge any electronic items, such as computers, phones, and mobility devices. As soon as they are charged, immediately pack the chargers in your flight bag. The single item most commonly left behind in hotels is a phone charger. You may have them plugged into a low outlet and not be able to see them and thus remember them. Phone chargers, of course, can be replaced, but it's difficult to replace a computer charger or mobility device charger. While it is tempting to pack the charger for the mobility device in your suitcase that you will be checking, because of its weight, I would think twice about that. What if your flight is delayed and you spend a lot of time going around the airport? What if your mobility device battery needs charging when you arrive at your Destination? You might not need it -- but you might; so, why take a chance? After all, nearly all suitcases have wheels, now, including flight bags.

Put everything that you will need right away when you get home, such as toiletries, in one particular bag, or on top, if you only have one bag. That way, if you are tired, you only need to unpack that one area. The rest can wait till the next day.

If you think there is any possibility that your suitcase might be over your airline's weight limit, which is usually 50 pounds, be sure to actually weigh it, if at all possible. The fees for being over the weight limit or checking extra bags can add up to as much as your fare. I can tell without a scale. If I can lift it straight up without really straining, it's fine. If the piece of luggage is over the weight, you can either take something out, transfer some weight to your carry-on, or wear the heaviest clothes. While this is also something to check the night before your trip begins, it is more often a problem on the way home, because of souvenirs, whether purchased or found, such as seashells, gifts, new clothing, and mysterious expansion of the contents of your suitcase, or so it seems. Even if you aren't going to be charged, it's just a real bother carrying that extra weight around. So, on several trips, we have stopped at the local shipping store or post office and shipped those seashells or whatever home. If you don't include anything you will need right away, you can send via a flat-rate box or other cheap methods.

Another thing you'll want to do the night before you leave is verify your way back to the airport (or bus, train, or boat terminal). If you are setting up a ride, whether from a pal, Lyft, taxi company, or hotel shuttle, you will want to set it up before you go to sleep, and to verify both the time you have reserved, and the next available time (in case you miss your shuttle). A lot of people might check out at the same time as you; you don't want to risk missing your flight by just showing up expecting a spot on the shuttle. You might want to time your shuttle so that you can take advantage of any free breakfast available at your hotel, motel, or B'n'B. Some websites also let you check the approximate TSA wait time at your airport. This will, naturally, vary with whether you have something that expedites your processing through security, such as TSA Pre-Check, which is a really worthwhile investment. It's savvy to take into account how far in advance of your mode of transport you have to arrive, when planning your ride and meal.

When you are about to leave the hotel, put all your possessions out in the hallway, and then go back and check. Make sure you look under the bed, and check in the bed linens. One mistake I have made is to not look on the hook on the door in the bathroom. I lost a beautiful night-gown that way. So, when you go into the bathroom to look around on the sink and in the shower, make sure you also check on the door.

If you stay in multiple places, you'll have to repeat this procedure each time you leave one.

If you have used valet parking, allow extra time for them to get your car. A lot of people may be checking out at the same time, and it may take 20 minutes or more for them to get your car. Likewise, there may be a line to check out. If I do not receive an itemized bill slipped under my door before I leave, I do like to look at the bill. Sometimes the clerks will ask if I just want them to just leave it on that charge card, but I always insist on seeing the bill itemization. It's usually fine, but I have caught errors, such as being charged the wrong rate, or I've been charged for the use of the safe I never used and never agreed to pay for. It will be much harder to dispute those charges once you get home.

Travel: Planes, Trains, and Automobiles

One of the best things about being retired is that you have time to travel a lot. Also, you can travel off-season. Of course, you don't want to go to Europe in Winter, if you don't like the cold; but just waiting a week or two, until after the kids are back in school, can make a huge difference in the amount of money you pay for something, and in the size of the crowds. This is especially true at family attractions, such as Disney World. While some people like to take the kids out of school to go on vacation, or go with toddlers, the crowds are markedly smaller than during school vacations. Also, your rates will go down. We used to own and rent out a condo near Disney World, and the rates during school holidays were almost twice what they were at times such as in October.

Tour Discounts

If you love to travel, but you don't think you can afford it, there are many travel discounts that are available. One way you can save a lot of money is to contact a tour company and ask about group travel. Very often, it only takes as few as 10 people to form a group that will give you a free trip. Then it's up to you if you have a totally free trip, or you divide the discount among your friends. I suggest you enjoy the fruits of your labor. When I was single I once offered a trip to England and Scotland to my students. Even though I was only able to sign up 6 students, rather than the 10 required for me to earn a free trip, the tour company did give me 60% off my trip, and everyone enjoyed the experience. So, it is worth inquiring about incremental discounts for group travel plans.

Another possibility is to get a discount for sharing your lifetime of experience by lecturing. You don't have to be an experienced teacher to give lectures to groups, or to teach a craft, in such situations as on a cruise or at a resort. While there is preparation time involved in getting your PowerPoint presentations ready, once you are there, it really doesn't take that much time. I did lectures on a couple of cruises, and I only had to give a few lectures on each cruise. The negatives were that I had to pay a daily fee, and that I was only allowed to have an inside cabin on the ocean cruise. There was not an extra charge, however, for the second person. I went with Paul, but you could go with a friend and split the cost. When I lectured on a river boat cruise, all the cabins were outside. Unfortunately, that line dropped their lecture program. If you are flexible and don't have to plan ahead, they sometimes waive the fee, if they don't have any lecturers close to departure. I've even seen offers for free airfare. The one challenge is that sometimes, when you apply, they will ask for a videotape of you giving a lecture. You could volunteer to do a free lecture for a local club or other organization and record that. Even if it's just a few friends to whom you are lecturing, if the camera is on you, no one will know. Some cruise lines hire directly, but many use services that provide lecturers to several lines. The best bet is to Google information about lecturing on cruise ships.

You could also look into an organization called Road Scholars, which is a pun. These are trips that are organized around learning. This may interest you, either as someone who wants to participate as a traveler, or as a lecturer. You can Google more information about it.

You could contact the tour company that operates tours that interest you and ask what you would need to do to go with them on a tour and be a group leader.

Of course, if you aren't worried about the cost, you could just sign up for a tour and have your arrangements taken care of for you, or you could just travel independently. Budget Travel and Travel Zoo sometimes offer great deals on tours. Always check the fine print and look at online comments about the company. For example, I have seen some incredibly cheap trips to China. When I researched it, even though the cost doubled with the fees it was still cheap. However, I saw in the comments that most of your time was spent shopping and you could not opt out of that. I did not go. Also, be sure to ask if a package requires you to attend a sales presentation. Then decide if you are willing to do that. If you don't go you will receive significant charges.

Planes

I don't know about you, but I hate baggage fees. In fact, I hate paying extra fees, in general. Therefore, my favorite airline is Southwest Airlines. They do not charge for your first two bags, and they do not charge if you need to change your ticket (if the fare is the same). When you travel internationally all airlines allow a free bag, but the fees for domestic flights can really add up. Also, check to see that your bag is not overweight. If I'm not sure I step on a scale holding it and then put it down. The standard acceptable weight is 50 lbs. If you are over, maybe you can put a heavy item into your carry on, wear your heaviest shoes, or just take something out and leave it at home. Some people ship a box ahead to where they're going.

The other way to cut down on your fees is with some of the credit cards that are offered by some of the airlines. With the United Explorer card, for example, not only do you get enough miles for a free round trip or two, if you charge enough money in the specified length of time, but your first checked bag travels for free. Getting the airlines' credit cards is a great way to fly for free. Some of them don't charge any fee the first year; and even if they do, it is usually worth it. You can always cancel after a year, when the renewal fee is going to kick in. Even if it appears on your statement, if you call up and cancel right away, they will refund that fee. You will not lose the miles you acquired.

Don't let your miles expire on any airline. In many cases, they expire if you don't have any activity on your account for a year and a half or two years, though Southwest recently made them permanent and others may follow suit. **Tip:** If you live in a major metropolitan area, there is an easy way to keep those miles active. All you have to do is link a credit card to their dining program, and dine at one of the restaurants in the program, at least once a year. That's all it takes to keep your miles active forever. It doesn't have to be an airline credit card. Eventually, your miles, even if they're only from an affiliated credit card and not from flying, will add up to a free flight. Many of the cards give you so many miles as an enrollment bonus that you can immediately have a free round-trip.

I recently booked my round trip to Cannes France with my American Airlines Aviator card. It was 30.000 points each way for economy. I had that much from my enrollment bonus. Out of curiosity, I checked the cash price. It was $800 outbound, and for some reason $2200 for the return! And this was months out. I was glad I had the card. I would not have gone on the trip otherwise. Also, I was offered good priced travel insurance and told I could change my date without a special fee. An all around good deal. Be sure, though, not to apply for cards very often or you will hurt your credit score.

Most airlines sell some nice snacks and cold meals at a reasonable cost, typically $10. If you are on a longer flight and flying first class, a hot meal is included. You may even be offered a choice of entree ahead of time. If you want to bring your own food, try not to bring something smelly or messy. You don't want to annoy your seatmate, and you might not be able to get to the bathroom to wash up. If you are on an international flight, you will be provided with a complimentary meal or meals.

I just heard about dollarflightclub.com. They notify you when there are bargain flights from your home airport. It might be worth checking out.

Many airlines have lounges in airports. While these are usually expensive to access, there are ways to have access. The Explorer card I mentioned above gives you 2 passes per year. You can go twice as an individual or once with a companion. The higher-level American Express Hilton card I have provides unlimited access to a set of lounges that aren't tied into flying on a particular airline. It's called Priority Pass. The negative is that it could mean that the one in your airport is not in the same terminal as your gate. This is something to check out ahead of time and consider in your timing. The positive is you can use a lounge if you are flying an airline, such as Southwest, which doesn't have their own. The other positive is that you can use it a greater number of times. Small airports generally do not offer lounges, and there may not be one in the airport to which you are traveling. Check ahead of time. If there is one you can go to, you might want to arrive extra early. Not only will you have a comfortable place to sit, you will have a light food buffet and free beer and wine. If you go, be sure to keep track of your time so you get to your gate on time. I was recently told that if you are flying First, or even Business Class, you can go to the lounge. I did not know this. The last few times we traveled together, Paul would only go if we flew First Class. By booking early and using points, this was doable. Too bad I didn't know about the lounge. So, if you're considering upgrading your flight, be sure to ask.

If your flight is long, you might benefit from bringing eye shades for a nap, and/or an inflatable pillow for your neck.

If you haven't flown for a long time, you might not realize that the entertainment options have changed. Instead of the airline projecting one movie for everyone, each customer is offered many options from among which to choose. Sometimes it's on the seatback in front of you, but sometimes you watch on your personal device. That means that if you don't want to watch on your phone, you might want to put your laptop in the personal bag that fits under the seat in front of you, so you can access it, and not in a bag you are putting in an overhead bin, where it has a greater chance of being damaged, anyway. Download the airline's app to your phone and laptop before you leave, as that is how you will access the entertainment during the flight and you won't be able to do that on the flight. Once you have the app you can use it even with your phone on airplane mode. Pack some earphones for entertainment, so you don't have to wait to get some, or headphones or earbuds if you want to be more comfortable. Noise canceling ones are best, in case you wind up sitting near the engine. Even if you just want to read, I suggest setting airplane mode in your controls, instead of turning off your phone, in case you want to take a photo. Some airlines provide electrical outlets at each seat, for charging devices, but not all, so make sure to top off the charges in the waiting areas or lounges before you board.

Check with your cell phone carrier before you leave. They may provide free internet access on your flight. I know T mobile allows a certain amount of time, depending on your plan. Also, they can set your phone so you can use it in other countries inexpensively.

Documents

Currently you may not be able to board even domestic flights without either a passport or a Real I. D. To get the Real I D., which would be easier to carry around than a passport, you need to bring several forms of identification to the same place that you get your driver's license. Go online to find out which forms of identification you can use and bring extra ones. I had to make a second trip to the driver's license facility because one of the ones I presented the first time was rejected.

There are wonderful opportunities to save yourself a lot of time waiting in line at airports, by purchasing a type of expedited access to the TSA security checks. There are two available through the government, and one that is private. There are TSA Pre-Check, which saves waiting in long lines, removing your shoes and worrying that you might miss your flight; Global Entry if you travel internationally; and the private "Choice" package. Look them up and see if they'd work for you! Certain credit cards will reimburse you for the fee, up to $100. Be sure to check which ones before charging it. Especially if you are traveling with a service animal, a grandchild, a person with a mobility impairment, or a lot of luggage, these options can save you a huge amount of time and inconvenience. Allow extra time getting to airports so you don't have to feel tense. Arrive at least an hour and a half before your domestic flight and two hours before an international one.

Please note: If you are applying for one of the above programs, start the application process well ahead of time. I recently filled out a Pre-check application and made an appointment for the required interview for the day before a trip. I then found out that after the interview, they check your background, which can take a few weeks. I canceled to focus on packing and rescheduled when I was not pressed for time.

Another warning: Be sure you use the exact same name for all IDs. I did receive pre-check confirmation and my number while I was on my next trip but was unable to use it for my return because my middle initial did not match my ticket. I have sometimes used my maiden name for my middle initial. I had that on my driver's license and ticket, but my pre-check went by my passport, which uses my birth name. I have now made sure my passport, Pre-Check and my Trusted Traveler number on file with the airlines I use.

Here's a tip that will save you time money and effort. The government website about Global Entry (https://www.cbp.gov/travel/trusted-traveler-programs/global-entry) implies that you should apply when you are about to go on an international trip. Don't worry about that. If there is any possibility that you will travel outside the United States in the future, apply for it. It turns out that Global Entry includes TSA Pre-check and Real ID. If I had known that, that would have saved me all the hassles I went through to get both of those. Also, even though the application for Global Entry requires that you enter all your passport information, be sure to bring the physical document with you when you go for your interview, even though their confirmation email doesn't say so. If you can't get an interview soon enough keep checking back, as people do cancel. Once you have the number, be sure to enter it on the airline websites in your profile right away.

More information about passports: it is best to renew them several months ahead of their expiration date. You can go to a special office and pay for expedited handling, but if you are sending in through the mail expect it to take two months. Initial applications can be done at some post offices. Passport photos can be taken at drug stores, the post office when you apply, or for free at AAA offices with higher level memberships. Some travel companies require that your passport is good through six months after the beginning of your trip.

Trains

Trains are not the most efficient way to travel, but they can be the most pleasurable. If you have the time to spare and are not in a hurry, trains allow you to walk around and view the scenery much better than traveling by car or airplane. Trains in Europe are much more commonly used and efficient than in America. However, if you remember in your youth how it was so common to get a Eurail Pass and travel around Europe as I once did, you should know that it is not as inexpensive as it used to be. If you were thinking about taking trains in Europe, you should investigate whether you will be better off with something like a BritRail pass, which is only good for that country, or just single fares.

See the chapter on snowbirds for information on a special Amtrak train that will allow you to bring your car along with you.

Automobiles

I've never seen such a wide variance among prices as I have with car rentals. Be sure to do a lot of shopping around. You may save hundreds of dollars, especially if you're renting for a long period of time. Here are some tips:

- If you own a car at home, and therefore have auto insurance, it will transfer to your rental car. Bring your insurance card with you, because there is a chance they could ask for it. If you don't own a car, ask about purchasing temporary insurance. I suggest calling the national number for the rental company to get the rate, rather than trusting the location. You can also call a separate insurance company to see if they sell temporary insurance and compare rates.
- Even if you have basic insurance, rental companies sometimes try to sell you CDW, which covers your insurance deductible, to make money. You don't need to pay for CDW, which stands for collision damage waiver, in some cases. Your credit card might cover that. It used to be all of them, but that isn't true anymore. Call and ask to determine which card you use to pay for the rental.

- If you are traveling for more than 30 days, the CDW coverage may expire at the end of 30 days. Talk to your credit card company and see what period of time they will cover, and then consider your options. Ask the rental car company if you can pay for collision damage waiver after that time, or treat the next 30 days as a separate rental.

- Unless you have no choice, because the other locations will be closed, such as on a Sunday and/or a holiday, consider not renting at an airport. It is almost always well worth the price of a taxi, Lyft, or Uber to go to an offsite location and rent there. When you are comparing rates, you should enter both the airport you are flying into and the city you are going into, to compare rates. Keep in mind that every city is different, and that you need to compare companies for each trip. I have sometimes rented in a city and returned the car to the airport at no extra charge, which was convenient and saved a transportation fare back to the airport. However, I recently was checking Los Angeles rentals and got quite a surprise. I forgot to check the box on the comparative rental site near the top that says "return to a different location". I then called the rental company directly and asked about returning to the airport. The agent told me that my $450 rental would be over $2000! I literally laughed out loud. I kept the original rental, and went back to the website, only to find similar figures for all companies. So, the next task was to see which of the possible city sites would be closest to the airport and require the shortest, cheapest transportation from the return site to the airport.

- If you are renting at an airport, which in some cases doesn't add much to the cost, call the rental company ahead of time, and ask about check in. Sometimes, it will be a matter of going to a desk in the airport itself, and then taking a shuttle; sometimes, walking to cars in an airport garage; and sometimes, taking a shuttle to check in offsite. If you are going to be taking a shuttle, ask where to wait and how to recognize the shuttle. It can be confusing, because some serve more than one company.

- Carrentals.com is a good source for comparing the various rental companies. There are others, but that is the one that I like to use, though I recently got an even better rate from rentalcars.com, which is owned by Priceline. Generally, what I do is I rent from them at their rate, and then call the car rental company and see if I can add onto it an additional discount, such as the AARP discount. If you are a member of a major union, check to see if they have a discount arrangement with a company; some do. The AARP discount usually works and gives you a very good rate. Another excellent source for renting is Costco, through their travel program, if you are a Costco member. I actually found this to be best for two of my most recent rentals, but not best another time. Another is the Entertainment Book and the coupon codes that they have in there. In any event, get the best rate you can, and then ask if you can add on the AARP or senior citizens' discount on top of it. Usually, you can. The cheapest rates are often if you pay when you book rather than after use. I never do that. If your plans should change and for some reason you didn't cancel you would not get a refund. Even more important is that even though they say free cancellation if you read the fine print you will almost always find it to be deceiving. While the rental itself is not charged you are given a substantial cancellation fee.
- Schedule your rental as early as possible. The great thing about car rentals is that you can cancel with no penalty. Be sure to read the details. Of course, the trick is to keep track of where you rented from, and especially if it's more than one, to cancel the extra reservation. It isn't fair to others if they can't get a car that winds up not being used. I have a folder for travel in my emails, and confirmations get forwarded there. I also use tripit.com to keep track of my itinerary. When you get a confirmation email, you just forward it to plans@tripit.com. You want to be sure to cancel all of your reservations, so you do not get any penalty charge. Be sure to check the arrival time of your flight, and put in that specific arrival time, plus add extra time to deplane, get

luggage, and get to the rental location. There may be a default on the rental site for, let's say, 10 AM, and if your plane doesn't arrive till 4 PM, your car may have been given away.

- If you will have a second driver, ask if there is an extra charge for that. They will have to be present at the rental counter and show their license. And they must be at least 25. If you are picking them up later, you can stop at any branch of that company to add them. Costco does not charge for a second driver, but if they arrive separately you will have to stop at one of your rental company's locations with them when they arrive.

- If you are going to be driving anywhere that there are tolls, ask if the company has a transponder, and what the fee is to activate it, or you may get fines. Some places don't have manual toll collection. Some states have reciprocal agreements, and you can bring the transponder from your car. You can usually check this online. To find out if your route will have tolls, put the route into a directional app, and it will tell you. If so, go to the part (3 dots on Google Maps) where you can pick route options, and set it at "avoid tolls". See how much time the tolls save you, and see if it's worth it. One company I rented from charged you a daily fee for the rest of your rental once you paid a single toll even if you never used one again. Be specific in your questions on this topic. When you get directions on google maps you can click on route options and say avoid tolls and see how much time that adds.

- If you have a handicap placard, be sure to pack it, and find out what that state's regulations are. For example, some states require you to feed meters, and others do not.

- If you are renting off-site, the one difficulty is that many of those small locations are closed on Sundays and holidays or close early. What I do is I schedule my flight, if I know I can cancel it within 24 hours, and immediately book my rental company; or, rent the car, and then book the flight. Don't cut things too close. If, let's say, you are arriving on Christmas Eve, and your flight arrives at four and the location closes at five, you might not make it on time, and you may have a problem. You will have to come back the next day that they are open to rent.

- Be sure to join whatever frequent user program that company has. It may give you certain privileges, such as making it easier to pick up your car. So, it's worth it, even if you won't be renting often enough to get a free rental. My niece just rented with Enterprise Plus, and even though it was her first rental in years, they still gave the perk of 5% off the rental fee. If you belong to a union or other organization, they also may have discounts; and if you go to the website of the airline you're using, they have rental partners, which may give you points on the airline. However, compare rates. I just tried to add Budget's Fastbreak to my reservation, and the agent warned me that it would raise my rate over $50. I didn't do it.

- Try to think of every aspect when you rent. If you make the smallest change later, it will often be considered a new rental and invalidate the discounts you have arranged. I suggest that if you are not sure of your return date, for example, you reserve for both dates, and then cancel the reservation you won't be using, when you decide. I once actually ran into a situation where the rental company would have charged me more if I had returned the car a day early and taken the hotel shuttle to the airport.

- Never prepay for gas. You may wind up returning the car with half a tank and you will not get any compensation for that. Be sure to fill up the morning you head to the airport. If you don't return the car with a full tank they will charge you roughly twice the going rate for the gas they have to put in. Don't worry about the drive to the airport if it is 20 miles or less. It won't really show. In most cases there are lots of gas stations right by the car rental return, but my friend and I once drove around for what seemed like forever looking for gas when we were returning a car in Salt Lake City. Since then I have tended to get gas before getting on the highway to the airport.

Safety Precautions

When you go on a trip, there are certain safety precautions that you're going to want to take. You were probably taking some of them already. First, tell your neighbors on either side of you, across the street, and behind you, if you're in a house, that you will be gone, and who, if anyone, is allowed access to the house during that time. Then, if they see anyone else going in or out, they hopefully will call the police. They should also have your cell number, if you're going to be traveling domestically, and your email, if not. **Speaking of the police, you can notify them about your plans and ask them to keep an eye on your house as well. Do let them know if someone will have access.**

You should have at least one light on a timer, ideally. If, for some reason, you can't put one on a timer, then, unless you have someone entering your home to feed pets, water plants, etc., who can put a light on for you part of the day, you might consider leaving one on all the time and having spare bulbs available near it. You want your house to look, and perhaps even sound, as if someone is home; so, if you have an alarm that is set to play music, you might want to just leave it as is, rather than turning it off.

It would be safest to not post information about your trip on social media until you return. You can ask for travel advice, share your excitement, etc.; but don't give the exact dates of your trip. If you are totally secure about your burglar alarm, etc., you might want to do a travelogue; but at the very least, do not name the day of your return, so no one will feel comfortable breaking into your house.

One thing people sometimes don't think about is your garbage can. It's very easy for someone to go down the alley and lift the lid of a garbage can. If they notice, day after day, that it's empty, then that is a dead giveaway that no one is home. Ask a neighbor if they wouldn't mind throwing an occasional bag of garbage into your garbage can.

Of course, if you have newspapers delivered, you're going to want to put a hold on the papers. Be sure to think about not just daily papers, but weekly ones as well. And then, of course, there are free papers that get thrown on your porch and will pile up after a while. You can't stop them, but you can have someone recycling them.

No matter how you look at it, you're going to have to hire a kid or have a friendly neighbor or someone else look after your house while you're gone. Someone has to check to make sure that those papers did stop coming and collect the mail, and if you have plants, they need to water your plants. They should have a key to your house; and, even if your plants are all outside, they should go into your house at least once a week, to make sure that there aren't any problems. We once came home to find that the furnace had broken, and the house was at about 35°. Since it was much colder than that outside, it obviously must have happened very recently, or else the house would have been below freezing, and then we would have had a serious problem.

The problem you really have to watch out for, if you travel in Winter and live in a cold climate, is frozen pipes. Frozen pipes can completely destroy your house. I know someone to whom that happened. They came back from a wonderful trip to Disney World, only to find that a pipe had frozen and burst. To make matters worse, it was not a pipe in the basement; it was a pipe upstairs, which then flooded the entire house. Their house was virtually destroyed, as well as most of their possessions.

To avoid frozen pipes, there are a few things you can do. First of all, do not set the thermostat too low. You might want to leave it in the upper 50s. Second, leave a tiny bit of water dripping from a faucet. And if it is very cold, have your house caretaker flush all the toilets when they come in for their visit. Make sure they know if you have more than one toilet.

If you have an electronic thermostat connected to the internet, check the temperature every couple of days, so you can alert your caretaker if there is a drop in the temperature. I recently made a mistake and put not only my cable, but my internet on vacation hold without thinking about the thermostat. The batteries went out and there were problems

I had to deal with. After that I stopped trying to save money with vacation holds. Of course, make sure your caretaker has your cell phone number in case of emergencies.

The other winter problem is making sure you have arranged for someone to shovel snow. Not only is lack of shoveling an indication that you're away, but also, there is often a legal requirement to shovel. You could hire a service or an individual. Have them shovel the back as well, so it isn't obvious that no one is home. Be sure to have them keep track of how many times they had to shovel, so you know how much to pay them. I suggest discussing the price ahead of time. If you are going in summer, you may want someone to mow and water.

Mail is a big concern when you're traveling. You can't let it pile up. If you're only going to be gone for a short period of time, such as a week, you could have a neighbor collect your mail each day or ask the post office to hold it, though they will only save First-Class mail, which might be all you want anyway. You don't want anyone to see that the mail is piling up, which definitely would indicate that you were not home. If, however, you were going to be gone for more than a week, you may have a problem with your bills and other mail. Try to put most of your regular payments on automatic payments. Pretty much every-thing that I have to pay, such as utilities, is linked to either my checking account or a credit card. The exception is credit card bills, themselves, because the amount varies so greatly each month. However, I do have most of my credit cards set up so that the minimum payment is taken out automatically from my checking account. This prevents the possi-bility of a late fee and keeps my credit rating intact, if I should somehow miss a bill. Most companies offer this option.

If you pay your bills online, then you're going to take care of the biggest problems. However, if you're going to be gone for a few weeks, you're really going to want your mail. There are a few ways to do this, none of which are perfect. If you are going to be staying in one place for the entire time you are gone, that is the easiest situation. You can go to the Post Office to get a form to temporarily forward your mail. If you're going to be moving around from place to place, it gets more complicated. What I have done, when we used to take longer trips, was that I would get flat rate boxes from the post office or FedEx, and pre-address them to where I knew we would be staying each week, and put the mailing date on the box. My helper would collect the mail and, once a week, send out a package. Of course, you have to backtrack. If you are going to be somewhere from the first to the eighth, for example, you want to make sure that your package is mailed by the end of the previous month, to be sure that it gets to you. It gets very complicated if you've moved on and have to travel back to get the mail that arrived too late. Do not have anything sent to you the last week of your trip. Just have the mail collected and waiting for you at your house. A friend of mine uses a service that the post office offers to forward her mail once a week. You could ask for details on that. Having your mail forwarded not only means that you're less likely to miss bills or other important mail, but it also means that when you come home from your vacation, you are not faced with a humongous pile of mail that you have to deal with. It's difficult enough getting back to normal life and unpacking without having to deal with that.

Finally, do all the planning and precautions well ahead of time, so that when it comes time to travel you can enjoy it, without worry.

Cruising

If you are a cruise regular, you know the many benefits. If you've never taken a cruise before, give one a try. When you schedule your cruise, be sure to avoid school vacation times, unless you are planning to bring your grandchildren. Otherwise, you may wind up on a cruise that is full of teenagers and is pretty noisy. Also, some companies tend to cater more for particular ages of people or types of people. For example Carnival often attracts a young crowd, but Crystal Cruises does not. You might want to talk to a travel agent when you book your cruise. This will not cost you anything extra. There are agencies that specialize in cruises and know the information well.

A lot of people love cruises because you only unpack once, and you don't have to look for restaurants or hotels or figure out where you're going. Everything is done for you. You do have options about which excursions you will take. The cruise lines will tell you that there are advantages to booking the excursions through them rather than on land. The two main advantages are that you know the quality is going to be good, and that the tour providers are safe and legitimate and insured; and that if for some reason the tour is delayed, the ship will wait for you. If you take a private tour and something goes wrong, you could literally miss the boat. It would be your responsibility to get yourself to the next port. If, however, you do have a long time on shore, and you're only thinking about taking an excursion for part of that time and not the whole day, you can probably get a better deal on shore. There will be people trying to get your business as soon as you land.

Dining times on cruises tend to be fairly late in the evening. We used to always ask for the first seating, because Paul would eat on a schedule. If you are diabetic, or if you have medications that you have to take with food on a regular schedule, you will want to talk to your cruise director or banquet captain to see how to time your seatings. We did not ask for a private, two-person table, because we thought it would be interesting to meet other people. Generally speaking, it was. All cruise ships have premium restaurants, and a meal at one of these may be part of a package that is offered to get you to book, but the food on cruise ships is so good that you won't be missing a lot if you don't pay extra to eat at one of the premium restaurants. There are always a lot of choices about what to do for your meals. If you don't feel like table service, there is always a buffet. It's easy to gain a lot of weight if you're not careful. Always pack a variety of sizes of clothes and wear the tightest ones first!

I personally think that it's worth the extra money to get a balcony. This is especially true in the case where you go close to land for multiple days and there are a lot of things to see, such as in Alaska. You can enjoy the sights from your balcony. If you don't want to spend the money, I definitely recommend an exterior cabin rather than an interior cabin.

Paul enjoys a view of the Panama Canal from our ship's balcony.

Many cruises offer guest speakers and many different activities. I recommend taking advantage of at least some of them. Be sure to get a schedule as soon after you board as possible. There may be one about your first port. Even the shopping events are worth going to for the giveaways, if nothing else.

You will generally get the best prices on cruises by booking either very early or very late. If you are flexible, many cruise lines offer discounts at the very last minute. Of course, you cannot count on this. Those discounts only apply when they have the spaces available, which they might not for your specific week, if you have a narrow travel window. This is something that a lot of people do who are already in Florida, from which most cruise ships set sail. After all, you don't want to fly to an area and then not be able to take the trip you planned on, unless you have alternative plans. Many cruise ships give you a package where you fly in on the same day and they rush you to the ship. I personally have never done this, because there's always a chance that something could happen with the flight. And in Winter, of course, there is concern about weather delays; but even if it is not Winter, there can always be a mechanical problem or storm. We always flew in at least the day before, enjoyed the area, and made our own way to the ship.

One very important consideration when taking a cruise is mobility. There is a lot of walking on a cruise ship, no matter where your cabin is. You have to get to the various dining rooms, the decks, etc. The last cruise we went on was filled with mobility scooters. The cruise ship is one of those places, like airports or zoos, that even if you don't normally use a mobility device, you may want to consider one. The cruise ships have deals with companies that deliver the mobility scooters and wheelchairs right to the ship. You don't have to worry about arranging delivery if you rent through one of their approved vendors. On the other hand, if you are concerned about mobility, this would be the perfect time to purchase a mobility scooter. That is exactly what we did. Paul's first mobility scooter had broken, and we were thinking about buying a better one. We decided that it made total sense to buy it before our cruise and not after. That saved us hundreds of dollars in rental fees. Renting isn't cheap. A tip: If you rent a scooter and don't bring a fold-up one, book early, and get a handicap-accessible cabin. They are roomier, and you don't want to keep tripping over the scooter.

I personally avoid the super large cruise ships. Even if the company does a good job with boarding, dining, etc., they make the ports super crowded when they dock. Larger ships also mean more walking and longer times getting to things. If you are wealthy, you can afford a very small ship, but all the cruise lines have a range of sizes for their ships. I think it's one of the big factors to consider when booking.

Cruises tend to be very nice, as long as you avoid the bad weather season, and don't have rough seas. There is wonderful entertainment on them, and it is a very enjoyable time. If you are retired, you can go in the off-season and get some good discounts. Do some comparison shopping before booking. Talk to agencies that specialize in cruises, and they will usually have some nice incentives to get you to book through them.

Keep in mind that, whatever the published cost is, it's only a portion of what your total cost will be. There is usually a mandatory gratuity to the crew that will go on your charge card. You may have to pay for alcoholic beverages, internet, excursions, etc.; so, plan on doubling whatever your cost is, and have a good time.

There is always a chance of contagion onboard, most commonly noroviruses (which affect the digestive tract), and in rare cases something more serious, as most notably recently happened with the coronavirus. So that is a consideration for the elderly. I have never had a problem, and my son worked on cruise ships for four years and never got sick. All cruise ships do have a clinic with a doctor onboard. In the case of serious health problems, such as a heart attack, they will airlift a patient to shore. It could, however, take several hours for the helicopter to arrive.

If you have known health problems, I suggest limiting yourself to river cruises, as you are always near a port and can get to a hospital quickly if needed. There is special insurance you can purchase that will transport you home if needed. Transportation home from travel is not covered by standard travel insurance. Google "medical evacuation service" to compare companies. Even just using that helicopter I referred to can be quite expensive.

Communication Tips

Put your phone on airplane mode. It's possible that if you receive a text from someone, you may incur roaming charges. If you plan to actually make calls when in port, talk to your carrier about getting an international SIM card, or look into buying an international phone. Using the wi-fi on ships is usually expensive, so find out where the crew goes to use the internet on shore, and wait until you dock to check emails. If you don't think you can wait for that, buy a larger package from the ship, so your per- minute cost isn't too great.

My favorite cruise that we ever took was a river boat cruise. Do consider taking one of these, whether foreign or domestic. There are several advantages to them. For one thing, there is no such thing as an inside cabin on many of them. The state rooms are large and have large windows. The capacity of the ship is smaller, so events, corridors, and dining areas are not crowded. Generally, the excursions are included, and there are few hidden charges in river boat cruises. You do not spend a lot of time at sea getting from place to place. You generally are at a new port every day. And because you're close to shore, it is sometimes possible to go on and off the boat into town.

With large cruise ships, you may have to take a tender (a small boat) to get to shore; but with river boat cruises, you generally can just walk out onto shore and back again. You can, for example, come back for a meal. The whole atmosphere is relaxed and luxurious. It may be more expensive, but if your excursions and beverages are included, the cost difference may not be as much as you think. We took a wonderful river cruise from Amsterdam to Budapest. Another advantage is that, while there can be flooding in some rare cases that could prevent bridge clearance, you generally are not as affected by waves and weather conditions. It's something to look at, anyway.

Both ocean liners and river boat cruises have a limited number of themed cruises. For example, I lectured about music on our river boat cruise. I've seen listings for cruises in France that focus on wine or food. One I would like to take someday is one of the Playbill cruises that feature Broadway performers. So, with all the options available, do a lot of looking before you book.

CHAPTER 7

Becoming a Snowbird

What is a Snowbird?

The term "Snowbird" refers to those who flee winter cold for warmer climates for an extended time period on a yearly basis. While some people go to different places each time, the majority return to a favorite area, if not a specific place, each time. Being a Snowbird can give you the best of all possible worlds. For example, I've often said Chicago is a great place to live except for January. When I was considering my early retirement offer, one of the arguments that Paul made in favor of it was that we could become Snowbirds and spend our winters in a warmer climate. We did do that, and we alternated between Florida and California when we couldn't quite make up our minds between the two. We have family in both states whom we enjoyed seeing while we were there.

Being a Snowbird can give you the advantage of experimenting with what it is like to live in a given area, before you actually commit to moving there.

Purchasing a Second Home

Some of my friends have purchased condos in Florida or elsewhere. There is a great advantage to this. You don't have to spend time each year looking for a place to stay. Furthermore, you can store some of your possessions there and not have to pack so much. You also get to know the area and your neighbors, and you can feel more at home than you would in some place such as a motel or an extended-stay hotel. It can also be financially advantageous, if you rent out your condo for part of the time that you are not there and have someone else paying part of your mortgage.

We actually purchased a condo in Kissimmee, next to Disney World. We thought this would be an easy area to rent out a condo. We were considering retiring to Florida, and we wanted to get into the market and take advantage of prices that we thought would go up. It took a few years to get the rentals going steadily, and to get the recommendations that make people want to book it, but it did wind up eventually paying for itself each month.

A second home is a different tax status than an investment property. Legally, if it is an investment property, you can't spend more than 2 weeks per year there. If it is an investment property, as ours was, the disadvantage is that you can't spend much time there. The advantage is that you can deduct from your taxes almost every expense involved in its maintenance, including the cost of flying there to visit it to check on it once a year. Of course, you must also declare the income, as well. If you're going to rent out your property at all, you absolutely must have a local professional management company that checks on and keeps up the condition of the property, arranges cleanings, etc. If it is an investment, you also need to keep careful income and expense records for tax purposes. Also, discuss with your tax accountant the merits and necessity of depreciating your property (saying it has gone down in value). I was recently hit with a huge capital gains payment from the sale of our condo, because my accountant had depreciated it for 15 years; so, when I sold it, I paid a lot of deferred taxes. I was concerned about that possibility, but I had never discussed it. Of course, there were years when the savings came in handy along the way. This is something to go over with your accountant, rather than to go into in detail here.

Your management company will probably do rentals for you. They will, of course, keep a commission, which can range anywhere from 10 to 50% of the revenues generated. Be sure to ask about the level of commission before signing with them. However, if you have the time, you will probably come out ahead if you orchestrate some or all of the rentals yourself. Your management company may charge you a fee for entering each rental into their calendar. Be sure to ask them about that. Some people set up their own websites, but your individual website is unlikely to be found in searches, unless you hire a search engine optimization company. I found the best site on which to list is TripAdvisor, also known as Flipkey. There's also VRBO.com. The sites are not cheap to list on. You will have to pay several hundred dollars per year. However, a single rental can pay for the entire year's fee, and I did the majority of the bookings myself through these websites. They also offer free listings, where they take a commission. Find out if your complex has its own rental site. I was able to get a few rentals through the site that someone had set up for our complex, and that was cheaper. There is also Airbnb, which does not have to be just bed-and-breakfasts; you can use Airbnb to rent your condo, but be very careful about the way you list how your property is available and how it may be booked. If you're not careful, they will go ahead and book rentals for you when you might already have booked the property for those dates. Check the parameters of your listing very carefully. You can set up a master calendar with the rental sites. Having one master calendar enables you to copy it into the other sites, to avoid the horror of possibly double booking your dates. Of course, your management company will receive the dates immediately, because they have to arrange cleaning and inspection; and they would let you know if you had double booked the dates. In addition to rent, you have to charge for cleaning, and you have to collect a damage deposit, which is returned a week after checkout if no damage occurs.

If you can afford to only stay there yourself and not rent it out, life is a lot easier. You don't have to deal with the work that's involved with rentals, tax reports, damage, etc. I did enjoy my correspondence with the almost universally nice renters, but it did take time. I was actually relieved to sell the condo a few years ago while Paul was in the nursing home and my time was limited. I was extra fortunate because I would have lost a lot during the pandemic when I probably wouldn't have had renters.

The view of the Gulf of Mexico from our timeshare's deck

Alternatives to Purchasing

What if you were going to an area for the first time, for an extended time period, or returning and don't have the ability or the desire to purchase a property? You don't want to stay in a hotel room for over a month. There are ways of staying in an apartment, instead.

Most apartment complexes require a lease of 6 to 12 months, but there are ways to stay someplace for a month or two. Google "corporate housing" for the area where you want to reside for a while. There are companies that specialize in providing furnished apartments for people who are traveling for business and staying in an area for a month or two. For example, actors who are coming to LA to shoot a film will often stay at the complex that used to be known as the Oakwood. If you stay in corporate housing, you will receive a fully furnished apartment, which includes linens. Many of them quote a rate that includes maid service.

Enjoying an informal concert

Tip: You will save a lot of money if you ask if you can rent without maid service. My experience is that they will quote the rate with it, but you can ask for a lower self clean rate. They will usually have a recreation hall. Recreation halls have activities, and they often have a swimming pool, and they are very comfortable. They are not cheap, but when you compare it to what you would spend on a hotel plus food, it really doesn't cost much more to get a home-like atmosphere.

Tip: Ask how long you would have to rent to avoid paying sales tax. At our Florida condo, it required a year's lease, but the duration in Los Angeles was only 4 or 5 weeks. If you stayed a little less than that, it would actually cost you more, because of the tax.

If you go to TripAdvisor or some other sites, they have condos for rent, and there are also any of the sites that I mentioned could be used by you as an owner, which are TripAdvisor, HomeAway, and Airbnb. They do charge fees, so you may just want to Google "long-term stays" in the area where you are going and contact an owner directly. What's ideal for some people is that they can work out an arrangement with the owner of the property to come back every year. While we owned our condo in Florida, we had a couple that rented from us on a regular basis, for 2 months at a time, for 6 years. They are now renting from the new owner. It was nice to know that they would always be coming back, so I gave them a bit of a discount, and I turned down other offers. This way they always knew not only the general area where they'd be staying, but also the exact location and the specific features of our unit. Engaging this kind of recurring long-term rental can be an excellent alternative to purchasing a property.

Timeshares

What about timeshares? With timeshares you are buying a stay in condo-like accomodations a week at a time, and therefore, you don't have to invest nearly as much money as for a condo. Traditionally, timeshares were sold by the week, but today, most use points. The advantage of points is flexibility, if you want to go to different places each year. However, there is an advantage to the week system. Even if you purchase two or three weeks of points for a timeshare, you cannot be guaranteed that you will be in the same unit each week, nor that all the weeks will be available. If it's a large complex, you could be moving to a building blocks away if you want to stay in that same resort. There are exceptions to that, if you purchase specific weeks in a specific unit. For that reason, there is a very active resale office at our favorite resort.

As weeks become available, people try to line up a continuous stay and not have to move around. The office gets a commission for handling the paperwork. One couple from Scotland kept buying a week each time they came, until they accumulated a stay of almost 2 months each year. Many timeshares offer activities for the guests, and sometimes the people who come at the same time every year become friends.

Purchasing Timeshares

The main reason timeshares have gotten a bad reputation is because no one enjoys sitting through the timeshare sales presentations. If you do agree to go to one, you have to keep in mind that they invited you, you didn't request anything from them, and you are not obligated to buy. The incentives for attending a timeshare presentation can range from a free breakfast or a ticket to an amusement park, all the way to saving hundreds of dollars on a vacation package. Usually the presentations that are offered last minute, when you're already in a location, involve something such as a ticket to an amusement park. But you may get phone calls offering a discounted package. Typically, these packages are three days, two nights. While it can be a good deal, you have to keep in mind that two out of the three days are spent traveling, and the third one, you're going to spend half the day at the timeshare presentation.

They may tell you that the presentation is only an hour and a half, but you can count on it being at least two hours long. I recently attended one, because the inexpensive stay offered did save me hundreds of dollars, and it was with the Hilton Grand, not an unknown company.. What I did was I asked if I could purchase one additional night, so that I had some time to enjoy New York. If you are already in the area, attending a presentation for a gift is not as much of an issue. If you accept any package, you must attend the presentation, or you will be charged a penalty and be hounded with phone calls for years.

If you are offered an incentive to attend a presentation, don't take the first offer. If you seem interested, but hesitate, they will throw in something else to get you to agree to participate. Likewise, if, at the end of the presentation, you do think you actually might want to buy the timeshare, be sure not to take the first offer. Inevitably, the salesperson will say they'll see if they can talk to their manager, and the manager will find some way to make the package more attractive.

If you do buy, you might want to think twice about using the company's financing. This is one of the ways that they make money. You can probably get a better rate with your own home equity line of credit or personal loan. Do not look at the *monthly* cost; look at what the *total* cost will be with the interest you will be paying.

An alternative is to buy on the secondary market. There are websites that deal with timeshare resales. If it is a weekly purchase at a specific property you want to know that you like that exact property, as it might not be easy to exchange. If it is points, it doesn't matter. I've never been to the property where I have my points timeshare. That doesn't matter because I have a set number of points I can use to stay at any property in the system. One of the questions you should ask is how large that system is. That is, how many properties will accept your points for a stay? If you buy from someone who already owns a timeshare unit, you will get it at a highly reduced price. Sometimes it is next to nothing. Of course, you have to look at what the yearly maintenance fees are. The one thing you would have to be concerned about is how the actual deed of sale and clearance of title will be handled. It's possible that it might be the website that takes care of those things; but you want to be sure that everything is legal and on the up-and-up, that you're not stuck paying somebody else's unpaid maintenance fees.

If it should come time to try to sell your timeshare, do not sign with a company that asks for a substantial fee to list it. If you can find one that is commission-only they will have an incentive to actually sell your property. You don't want to go into default and hurt your credit rating. Some management companies will allow you to turn in the deed to your timeshare and not give you any compensation, but at least it doesn't hurt your credit record.

I know that all this might sound rather daunting; but I have to re-iterate that I am very, very glad that I bought the timeshare units that I did buy, and I have really enjoyed using them for a number of years.

Never think of a timeshare as an investment. Timeshares never resell for more than what you paid, and you may have difficulty selling them, at all. In fact, the selling point that you can hand them down to your children might not actually be doing your children a favor. However, timeshares are really great to use, and they are probably worth whatever you invest in them. Keep in mind that you must consider not only the purchase cost, but also the yearly maintenance fees, which have the potential to be increased each year. However, the accommodations in timeshares are so superior to staying in hotels that I regret that we did not buy our timeshare years earlier when we were still traveling with our son. We had too many arguments about staying in the same room together. They are also great for traveling with grandchildren.

The Car Rental Problem

It's one thing to rent a car for a week's vacation, but another to rent one for a couple of months. Obviously, it is going to cost more. So how do you deal with it, if you are going to be a Snowbird?

Some people drive to their destination, so they don't have to deal with car rentals at all. I never chose this option, for a couple of reasons. First, if you are driving in Winter, you can encounter some terrible driving conditions, even in places that would seem to be warm. You can encounter, for example, ice storms which are treacherous. Second, driving isn't free. When you factor in the miles you are driving, the wear and tear on your car, and the cost of gas or diesel and potentially tolls, it can be quite significant. Plus, on the way, you're going to have to spend money for food and lodging. All this may add up to more than the cost of airfare to get down there and is considerably more work. If you are not traveling in Winter, which obviously is the most common time for Snowbirds, then you can turn a road trip into an experience, in and of itself, by stopping at various tourist destinations. However, driving in

Winter does not make being a tourist very pleasant. The other question would be whether you have more than one driver and can switch off, so that it does not become too tiring, and so you do not have to worry about falling asleep at the wheel.

Some people who are regular Snowbirds find it convenient to purchase a second, used car to keep at their Winter residence. This can be the most economic method, if you know you will be using it for several years. Of course, you have to have a place where you can store the car when you are not there, ideally for free. Some municipalities have nonprofits that coordinate car-sharing resources. You might see whether where you would like to reside part time has such a service.

Another possibility is to use a service that will drive your car to your destination for you. There are several of those. They would take the car either a couple of days before you leave, or you would arrive and take a taxi, and then your car would be delivered to you. You can Google those. Obviously, you do have to pay for this service, but it may be well worth it.

Amtrak offers a service on one line where you can actually ship your car on the train with you. Our Winter renters in our condo did this every year. They lived in the Eastern United States, and there is an Amtrak line that goes directly from Washington D. C. to Orlando once a day, which allows you to bring a car or even a van. This is a great service, but it's only available on that one route. There is more information available at Amtrak.com.

We always opted for car rental. Since we did not go to the same location every year, we could not keep a car at a second home. We did not want to deal with the risks of driving long distances in Winter. So, the best solution seemed to be flying and renting. This was not as expensive as you might think, as some car rental companies do have monthly rates. For example, Enterprise has a special division that only deals with rentals that are a month or longer. They do give special discounts on these rentals, and in many cases, you can still add on additional discounts, such as an AARP discount. The first time you try a long term stay, it's going to take some real research; but after that, you'll have a better idea of what you want to do, and it will become easier. Be sure to rent very far ahead of time. I recently checked and found a car rental I had reserved a few months ago would have cost me twice as much, had I initiated the rental now.

The final option would be not to have a car at all, if it is the sort of place that has good public transportation and you only have to take a taxi, Lyft, or Uber occasionally, or if you plan to spend most of your time at the pool. However, that will not be true in most cases, and the cost of paying for rides frequently might add up to more than the cost of a car rental.

Precautions

If you are a Snowbird, you will have to pay even more attention to the safety precautions that I mentioned in the travel chapter. The longer you are gone, the more likely that it will be obvious that the home is empty. You may want to rent a safety deposit box and have an alarm system installed in your house.

Another possibility is to either do a house exchange or hire a house sitter. This is especially advantageous if you have a pet. Your pet(s) get to stay in their own home, and you don't have to pay for their care. Most house sitters will work for just the free place to stay; some may charge a small fee. You also wouldn't have to worry about leaving your home empty. If you do this, be sure to let your neighbors know and give them a picture of the person who will be staying there so they don't call the police. Obviously, you would have to check references carefully. There are sites that specialize in matching people up. The problem is I don't know how many people would want to come to a cold climate in Winter. It's worth a try, but these positions are very competitive. The one time we successfully did it we got our position through craigslist. It was great. We stayed for weeks in a house with a deck for free just for watching a cat. If you do create a listing for your house, be very specific about your house and animal(s), to avoid wasting time on incompatible inquiries.

Saving Money As a Snowbird

Going away for weeks or months is an expensive proposition, but there are some ways that you can save a little bit of money while you are out of town. These are not worth bothering about, if you're only going to be gone for a couple of weeks; but if you're going to be gone for a month or more, they can realize some savings for you.

As already mentioned, you will be suspending your newspapers. This can add up to a significant amount of money. You can always read the larger newspapers online. I don't cancel my weekly papers, and they are forwarded with the mail.

If you have a cleaning service or a housekeeper, suspend their service, and give them sufficient notice, so they can plan around it. If you do that, they should not charge you.

Walk around the house, and look for all those little "ready" or "standby" lights, which are red or other colors that stand out on electronics. Those are the lights that tell you that something is plugged in and ready to be used. Try turning off the lights in a room sometime and look around, and you will see a lot of them. I once read an article about how much electricity they draw, and I was really surprised. You will want to unplug most of them or turn the switch off if they are plugged into a circuit breaker; but in some cases, you will have to decide if it's worth it: for example, whether you are willing to reset your clocks. Do not unplug things such as motion detector lights and your light that's on the timer. But you can unplug ready lights, for such items as space heaters, humidifiers, radios, etc. Be sure to have a light you can readily turn on when you come home, if it will be at night, or have your helper come in earlier that day to turn on lights and raise the thermostat, if you aren't doing that remotely. This is an advantage of a digital thermostat. My thermostat is connected to my phone through an app and automatically lowers or raises the temperature if I am in or outside a certain radius, which provides year-round savings. When I am more than 3 miles away, it goes to the away temperature I have set. If I am going to be gone for days, I lower that base temperature.

If you have cable or satellite service, contact the company and see what the minimum time is for a vacation hold and what the different options are. For example, with my cable service I once inquired, when we were still doing long trips, and I found that if I totally suspended the service while I was gone, I would lose all my recordings and settings; but they had a basic service without internet that they could maintain for a lower fee during my vacation, so that I was not paying as much as usual. It was a significant savings. However, you may have read my earlier entry about that disabling my access to my electronic thermostat, so it is complicated. Every company will be different, so you will need to talk to a representative --and not to a computer-- to see what your real options are.

Not using your refrigerator as much means that it will not keep drawing electricity to make up for every time you open the door. You can lower the temperature a little, but not too much, because you probably have items in the freezer, as well as things that don't spoil easily, such as condiments, in the refrigerator. Of course, be sure to check your refrigerator very carefully before you leave, to make sure you do not leave dairy or meat products in there to spoil. Don't forget to check the produce drawers as well. You don't want to have a smelly refrigerator when you get back. You can also lower the cost of the use of refrigeration by filling your refrigerator. It may seem counter-intuitive, but refrigerators work most efficiently when they are full, not empty. Since you don't want to leave a lot of food in there to spoil, what you can do is fill containers with water and place them in there, or place items such as boxes of cereal, crackers, and cookies in there. Not only will that help the efficiency of the refrigerator, but also, those items will be fresher when you return, and won't run a risk of attracting ants or worse.

If you have a membership in a gym or health club, ask if you can suspend that membership. If you can, ask if, for the time that it is suspended, you may receive either a financial credit, or an extension of your membership. If it is a national chain with locations in various places, ask if they have a facility in the area to which you are traveling, and if your membership can be used there. If so, it will save you from having to purchase a new membership or getting out of shape.

Not using your car will, of course, save you money, but be sure to have someone start it occasionally, and run it for a few minutes with the garage door open, if it's going to be very cold out. You can also ask your insurance company about suspending your car insurance, if you are not going to be driving while you're gone. If you are going to be driving, you will want to have that insurance to cover your rental car or your second car that you keep at your snowbird destination. If you want to take the time, you could inquire what it would cost to get insurance for the rental car through the rental company and compare the rates, but I would venture to guess that you would find that it's better to keep your own insurance.

Simply the fact that you were not using your utilities as much as you would if you were home will, of course, lower your utility bills in general. All this will not add up to a lot, but why not save what you can?

CHAPTER 8

Sharing Your Life with Others

Spouses and Partners

Most couples feel that being retired together will create a great opportunity for them. And it can. It can give new life to an old marriage. However, in many cases, it actually winds up causing quite a bit of friction. The problem is that sometimes one spouse expects the other spouse to spend most of their time with them, and the first spouse can feel resentful when the second spouse doesn't want to do that. In every marriage, whether you are retired or not, people need to have time together, but they also need individual time. Sometimes it's difficult to find the right balance.

One thing that Paul and I always did was that we had Saturday night scheduled as Date Night. Unless there were circumstances that absolutely prevented it, Saturday nights were set aside for each other. Usually we would go out, but if not, I would put the computer down, and we would order out dinner and watch a movie or listen to music together. My friends knew that if they wanted to do something with me, they could not ask me to do it on a Saturday night. This was a bond in our marriage. If something, such as work, came up that couldn't be moved to another night, we would select a substitute Date Night for that week. I also tried not to be gone more than two nights in a row, unless I was rehearsing a show.

While we spent a lot of other time together, we had our individual interests, as well. For example, I knew that Paul pretty much just liked musicals; so, when I subscribed to theaters, I would arrange to do so with a female friend. Sometimes I even went by myself, but of course it was more fun to go with a girlfriend. As long as I spent a certain amount of time at home, that worked. Paul knew that he had the option of going with me, and about once a year, there would be a show he actually wanted to see, and I would purchase an extra ticket.

If I had limited myself to only doing things that Paul also wanted to do, I would have felt that I was missing out on a lot of things. He understood that. It also proved to be beneficial, after he died, that I already had friends and activities established, independent of our relationship as a couple. Sometimes men have a harder time dealing with being widowed than women do. One of the reasons is that some of them don't develop as many friends as women do. So, spouses should be happy if their spouses go out with their friends once in a while, too.

Do try to find at least one activity you can enjoy together. For us, it was classical music concerts. We had a subscription to the local symphony, and we sometimes went to hear the Chicago Symphony Orchestra. We also had various family gatherings. It was important to see that Paul, who had to give up driving, had things to look forward to. You have to balance your needs and those of your partner.

Trips are a great way to spend time together and not be distracted by other activities. If you want to have a girlfriend trip or a fishing trip with the guys, balance it out by having another trip as a couple. You will have memories to share for a long time.

The Joy of Grandparenting

So many people I know say that grandparenting is the greatest joy they've ever known. There is such love between you and your grandkid(s), without many of the arguments and responsibilities that parents have to deal with. I feel blessed that I am now a grandmother and have experienced joys such as a grandchild falling asleep on my shoulder or proclaiming "Welcome back! . Of course, you don't have very much say as to what your children do, and you may never become a grandparent; but if you do become a grandparent, whether by childbirth, adoption, step-parenting, or fostering, consider yourself very blessed.

Another thing that I found with people I know, is that in so many cases, the children live far away. While that is a bit of a difficulty, it isn't as difficult as it used to be years ago. Not only can people travel more easily than they used to, but also, technology is a great aid. If you don't already know, be sure to learn how to use Skype, FaceTime, Gchat, Facebook Messenger or any other live video chat. Skype enables you to make a phone call on your computer, using its camera to see whoever is at the other end, and Facetime does the same thing on an iPhone. Just ask your friends for help. If they are grandparents, they most certainly know about it already. Then not only can you talk to your grand-children, but also, they can see you as a person, and you won't be a stranger when you go to visit. You can also see their progress as they change. Their parents can show off their children's early steps and other achievements. Weekly Facetime during Covid let me see my grandson grow and change. I am thankful for that technology. Now I can visit him and his little sister in person.

If you know you're going to be a grandparent, there are things you need to do to prepare for the blessed event. I strongly suggest that you take a grandparenting class or workshop. Yes, you did raise a child or children, but that was so many years ago; and even if you remember what you did then, the techniques and equipment that are used today have changed quite a bit. These classes are available at many hospitals. Simply Google them and you will find out. I took a class at a hospital not too far from my house and paid just $10 for a two-hour work-shop. I was, I have to admit, surprised at how much has changed. For example, when the instructor was talking about soothing a crying baby

I suggested checking for a diaper pin that might be sticking them. As a younger woman, she was pretty surprised I mentioned this, because it turns out people haven't used diaper pins for years. Just goes to show.

Another class or workshop that you should take is one in CPR, that is, cardio-pulmonary resuscitation. These are offered both by fire departments and hospitals. There may also be schools nearby that offer them. When you are selecting a class, of course you are going to look at how the scheduling works for you. However, note that there are different kinds of CPR classes. While there were some that were specifically for babies, I chose to take one that dealt with both babies and adults. After all, you never know when you might be in a position to help someone. This could be your spouse or a stranger. These classes will teach you not only how to do CPR but also how to use the defibrillator. It only takes a couple of hours of your time, and what you learned could save a life.

If you are considering ever having an infant in your car, you're going to want to get a car seat base that is compatible with the car seat that your children are buying. You must have the exact same model to know that it is compatible. Getting just the base, rather than an entire car seat, will still serve the purpose and will save you some money. It will also be easier for the parent(s), as they can transfer the baby without unbuckling and waking them up. Bases are still quite costly. It's not like the old days, where you just would strap car seats in with the seat belt. Nowadays, car seats must be installed by your local fire department. Call their non-emergency number, and they will make an appointment for a specialist to install the car seat base for you, at no charge. This is the only way that it is safe. There are also very specific rules about when the car seat faces forward or backwards, depending on the age and weight of the child. I'm sure the parent(s) will be aware of this and let you know when they switch from back- facing to front-facing. When the child reaches toddler age they will need what is called a booster seat. That does not use a base, so it does not have to be the same one the parents are using.

If you ever have a child in the car, you must become aware of a horrible danger. I know everyone thinks it could never possibly happen to them, but it happens to many children every year. The baby is forgotten in the car seat and dies of heat exposure. In 2018, 52 children in the United States died this way! I know that is unthinkable, but you don't want to have to be worried about that. There are safety precautions you can take to make sure this never happens to you. Because the car seats for infants face towards the rear, you do not have a view, when driving, of the baby themselves, and so it is a possibility that, if you're distracted, you might forget that they are in the car. An easy way to prevent this from happening for women would be to place your purse right next to the car seat, so you have to go back there to retrieve it and have to see the baby. For men it is a more challenging situation, but one thing that I would suggest that you can do is to remove your car key from your key ring, and leave the rest of the keys next to the baby, so you have to go back there to retrieve your house keys or office keys or whatever. If you use your cellphone a lot, place that there. It's crucial not to distract yourself with a cell phone while driving, anyway. You could also work out a system with a sticky note on the steering wheel, when the baby's in the car or set an alarm on your phone for around the time you should arrive. One other safety precaution is never, ever, ever leave your keys in the ignition when you get out of a car. This would be true even if you didn't have a child in the car. There have been several cases where a car was taken with the child inside because someone left the keys in the ignition and stepped out for just a minute or two.

The good news is that Congress has passed legislation that new cars must have a detection system that will alert you if a child or dog is left in the back. 2 cautions though: it may only work if you lock the car and I'm not sure if the system can be installed in current cars. It is worth checking into. My new 2022 car has this system. The one problem is that it senses the seat itself, especially if an item is placed on it. Sometimes when I turn off the motor it dings and a notice appears on the dashboard to check the rear seat. I hope I don't get so used to it that I start to ignore it. Still, it does get my attention and is reassuring.

Also, you want to baby-proof your home. One thing that hasn't changed too much is the plastic plugs that you can put in sockets to prevent a child from putting a finger or something they're holding into a socket. Medicines can look like candy to children. That's why child-proof caps were invented. Toddlers can be ingenious about reaching things they want, so be sure to keep medications way out of reach or locked up. A new danger is medical marijuana. Unfortunately, some of the medications look very much like candy and could put a child in the hospital. There are other dangers in the house. The most obvious of those would be stairs. Once the baby is able to crawl or walk around, you want to be sure to keep the doors closed at all times while they are there. Modern buildings which are designed to be ADA (Americans with Disabilities Act) compliant are in some ways more dangerous, because the door handles are easier for a small child to reach and turn. Therefore, you may want to install a bolt on the door, or some other device, in order to prevent them from opening it. This is also true for your outside door. This is especially true if you happen to have a pool in the backyard.

When you think about all the baby-proofing required where you live, you may decide it is easier to go to their house. There, they have all their toys, their crib, etc. I bought a stroller, and I might buy a highchair for when they visit me, but I did not get a crib, since luckily the family lives just 40 minutes away. If they were coming in from out of town, it would be a different matter.

One of the most dangerous places for a small child is any pool of water. For an infant, it could be a bath. For an older child, it might be a pool. You never want to take your eyes off of kids when they are by water. If the phone rings, ignore it.

One other precaution is that you should get some vaccinations in order to safely handle the baby. See the chapter on vaccinations.

I am sure that you look forward to spending time with your grand-child(ren). You don't want to just be a visitor. You want to spend some quality time with them. While it's a lot of fun to shop for toys and clothes for a baby, there isn't any greater gift you can give your children than to offer to give them some time out to themselves, while you watch the baby. Scheduling, of course, can be a little tricky, and if you do agree to babysit, you need to set that time completely aside.

There are responsibilities that go with grandparenting, but the most important thing is the pleasure. Of course, you are going to take, receive, and show off photos with your cell phone, but I suggest that you also buy an old-fashioned brag book for in-person show-and-tell. That is a small, little album that you can carry with you and pass around. I bought some at Dollar Tree. It's just much easier to show people photos that way, than on your phone. It can sometimes take a while to locate what you want to show people on your phone. It's very easy to have photos printed. Just go to the Walgreens or CVS website, or some other place such as FedEx-Kinko's, and upload the photos, and then pick them up the next day (at a pharmacy) or print them immediately (at FedEx-Kinko's). There are always coupons available online or in the Sunday newspaper, so it's quite inexpensive and easy, and it's a pleasure to have and show off.

When it comes to parenting and grandparenting, one of the most important pieces of advice is, "Zip thy mouth, unless asked for thy thoughts." It's so tempting to offer advice, but how the parent(s) choose(s) to raise their child is completely up to them. The only time that would be an exception would be if they are doing something that is hazardous to the child's health, such as not getting them vaccinated or having something dangerous in their home. Also make sure you are clear on any requests they have about sharing on social media, such as Facebook. You will notice there aren't any photos of, or even the names of my grandchildren in this book, because I honor the family's requests.

Some grandparents do daycare for their grandchildren on a regular basis. I've known several friends and relatives who do this, and the situation can vary a lot. In some cases I know, it is a pure joy. In another, there is some pay involved and it is a financial help for both parties. However, in some cases, it can take more of their time and energy than they are comfortable with, but they are reluctant to say so. Before you agree to a regular schedule be sure to be upfront about your feelings and needs and consider what the backup would be if you cannot do it on a particular day. Perhaps specify that the first 2 weeks are a trial and adjustments may be made after that.

Your job as a grandparent is to be supportive and to enjoy.

CHAPTER 9

Pets

Few things can bring greater joy and health into your life than owning a pet. We were lucky enough to have Athena, a smart, loving dog for over 15 years. She was a part of our family, and when she passed, we missed her for years. We did get a second dog, but unfortunately, she developed serious health problems after just a couple of years and had to be put to sleep. Pets are a great responsibility, and they are not for everyone. If you already own a pet, please do not give it away simply because you are too old to take care of it. If you need help, hire someone to help take care of your pet. To give them away would be emotionally devastating to both them and you. There are services that walk dogs, but they can be expensive. You can always just ask someone who lives in the neighborhood if they would be willing to do it for a reasonable rate. Or perhaps you can do an exchange of some kind of service, or barter for goods with someone, if you are healthy but just aren't up to three walks a day. Even if you were to let your pet out into the yard, you would need to pick up after it. Please find a "godparent" for your pet. By that I mean a designated person who will take in your pet(s) if anything should happen to you. Make sure that your designee and your pet(s) meet each other, so that you know they are compatible, and so the designated person knows what to do if for whatever reason you cannot care for them, whether it's for a short while or permanently.

There are several advantages to owning a pet. First, of course, is the benefit of the animal's companionship. However, there are other benefits . An article I read online recently said that pets are the surest way to increase your lifespan. Why is that? I have read studies that show that when you pet an animal, it releases healthy hormones into your system and lowers stress levels. That, of course, can help you stay healthy. Another way in which animals help your health is they keep you active. Even taking care of an animal other than a dog involves feeding, grooming, etc., which can help keep you active and keep you from doldrums. If you are missing having structure in your life because you've retired, setting regular times for pet care can give you the reassuring sense of having a daily routine. If you are missing having unconditional love and daily cuddles in your life as a widow/widower, having a pet who sleeps in your room with you can help you feel less lonely. Most especially, if you have a dog, you have to take walks. The walks are good exercise and force you to get outside and not become a shut-in. In addition, while you are out on your walk, you are likely to have social interactions with other people who want to pet the dog, if it is friendly, and maybe even make friends. Some cities have special designated "dogs off leash" parks. Those are great places to make new friends, both for yourself, and for your dog(s).

Finally, dogs, especially those trained as helper/care animals, can make noise and attract attention if you have a medical emergency, and they can detect health problems. If you have a dog and they keep sniffing at a particular area of your body (other than your butt), you would want to talk to your doctor about that and have them check that area. Dogs can smell cancer and other problems. If you have certain problems, such as seizures, you can get a specially trained support animal. Any dog, even a small one, will help protect your house. If burglars hear barking they will probably move on. But of course, the main reason to have a pet is because of the unconditional love that they provide.

If you are considering getting a pet, you have to think about everything that is involved. For example, pets are expensive to take care of. I feel they are well worth the expense, if you can handle it. I strongly recommend pet insurance, which helps cover the cost of trips to the veterinarian and any emergencies that arise. In some cities, you can even find "mobile vets," who do house calls. There is a surcharge for the house call, but if you are homebound, if you don't have transportation, if you are disabled, if your pet gets car-sick, etc., a mobile veterinarian can be a godsend, and all but the house call portion of the vet bill can still be submitted as expenses for your pet insurance. If you are thinking about getting a cat because they are lower maintenance than a dog, please bear in mind that many people are allergic to cats. If you've never had one before, I recommend spending an hour in the house of a friend who has one. If you don't have an allergic reaction, a cat can be easier to have than a dog. Some people like having bunnies instead of cats or dogs, and while they aren't cuddly, fish can be relatively easy to take care of, once you have everything set up. Do not buy a young parrot, because they will probably outlive you, and then where do they go? One thing you have to think about, if you have any pet(s), is what will happen to them if you go on vacation. One reason we did not get a third dog is because we knew we were going to be retiring and spending winters away, and we didn't want to have to deal with the problem of finding a place for our dog to stay. Many dogs are miserable in conventional dog motels or boarding kennels. The worst experience was when we went away for the Independence Day weekend, and Athena was surrounded by dozens of terrified, barking dogs. When we picked her up, she was obviously the worse for wear for our lack of foresight. If you do have to leave your dog somewhere, the best place is someone's home. We were lucky. After a couple of bad experiences with commercial boarding, we put an ad in the local paper, and a nice woman saw it, and her house became Athena's second home. If you are willing to drive into the country, there are some places that have large areas for the dogs to run around. There are also places that board cats, and cat sitters that come to your home.

One other possible solution is to have a dog walker come into your home. There are pros and cons to this. It is generally costlier than boarding, if you want 3 walks a day; and while the dog is in familiar surroundings, they have to sleep by themselves, and they can get lonely. I think it's fine for a short trip, but not for a long one. You can have someone come in for other animals, as well. Paul used to do dog walks, and one time, he was asked to take care of a rabbit while the owners were gone. Not only did he feed the bunny, but he also was asked to let it out of its cage for a while, and he would spend an hour or two there to keep it company. By the way, he stopped walking dogs, because sometimes the dogs got very protective of their homes when the owners were gone even though they had met him before. That can be a problem.

I have a good friend who is a difficult combination of a Snowbird and a dog lover. When her dog died recently, she was taking a long time to find a replacement. She explained that one of the reasons she was being very particular is that she wanted a dog who would fit the airline size requirements to fit under the seat. Putting a dog in the cargo hold can be traumatic, and even dangerous for the dog. By being patient, she found a dog who could be with her year-round and travel in her reassuring presence.

With all that being said, I have thought about everything involved and chosen not to get a dog at this time. It is a big responsibility.

Alternatives to Adopting

If you are not willing to make the commitment to have a dog full-time, year-round, there are alternatives that still give you some companionship. One possibility is to board dogs in your own home, as we did for several years. The woman who watched Athena that time wound up doing this with other dogs as well. When Paul went on disability and couldn't work I suggested this as a part time business. Not only was he contributing to the household income, but he had companionship when he was home alone. We always required that the dogs come for an interview, and that the owner leave the house for 10 or 15 minutes so we could see how the dog reacted when they were not around. We would also take them for a short walk to see their behavior. I suggest that, even if you were considering adopting a dog, you take them for a walk and see their reaction. We would not accept for boarding dogs who were under a year old, because of their tendency to chew. We had house rules as to what dogs could and could not do, and they learned them pretty quickly and remembered them whenever they came back for another visit. We allowed them on furniture, but not the bed. We checked with the owners about whether they could have scraps at the end of a meal. I'm proud to say we did have regular customers who were happy to have a good place for their dog to stay. It was very satisfying. We only stopped when Paul's back problems made it hard for him to do the walks.

Another alternative is fostering rescue dogs while they are waiting for adoption. I have a friend who does this all the time. It can be emotionally hard to see the dogs leave, but you are doing a very good thing by taking care of them, and she gets great satisfaction seeing them going to good homes. She did wind up keeping one of them, and that dog has decided it's her job to help take care of the dogs that come and go.

One more alternative is to volunteer at a pet shelter. They are always looking for people to come and spend time with the animals and walk them. If you are mobility impaired, there are cats and bunnies at shelters in need of cuddling by volunteers.

Pet Safety

If you choose to adopt a pet, do some research beforehand. Did you know, for example, that dogs should never eat chocolate? That certain plants can be poisons to dogs and/or cats? Read up about these things. The ASPCA publishes an informative list, "101 Things You Didn't Know Could Harm Your Pet." https://www.aspcapetinsurance.com/101-things-you-didnt-know-could-harm-your-pet/.

Make a list on your computer for pet sitters, shelters or boarders that includes eating, sleeping, and other habits and restrictions, as well as contact information for your vet, a neighbor, and yourself. If your pet has insurance, and/or a microchip for identification, you will want to include this information. Also include current photos of your pet, that your pet sitter could use if, G-d forbid, they need to put up Missing Pet posters or go out searching. Serendipitously, my niece helped reunite a calico kitten and her owner by recognizing the fur patterns in the photos on the Missing Kitty poster with those on a Found Kitty poster – while we were editing this chapter! You may be distracted when packing and not realize until too late that you haven't prepared this, if you save it for the last minute. Do it now, while you're thinking about it, if you have a pet or immediately after adopting. If it's ready, you can just print or email it. If you remember, print a copy and adhere it to your refrigerator with a magnet before you leave for your pet sitter if they are going to care for the pet in your home.

Our dog used to love to put her head out the window on car rides, but there is some risk to that. You can now buy special harnesses for dogs that will hold them in place, in case of a sudden stop or crash, and keep them from distracting the driver. There may even be a local law that requires that. If you crack their window, they can still enjoy the sounds and smells that they pass, as well as looking out the window. My niece has a cat and recommends putting them in a cat carrier, with the carrier strapped in by seat belt, positioned such that the cat and you can see each other's faces, when driving. She also recommends using the child window lock function, if your car has one. Once, before she owned her own cat, a pal asked her to drive his cat about an hour into the country where he was living, on a hot summer day. She had her window open about 3 inches, for ventilation. The cat tried to feel the breeze, stepped on the window-opening lever, and leapt out the window once it was down about a foot. It took about 20 minutes to find the cat in the bushes on the side of the country road. Fortunately, the cat was ok, but don't take any risks!

A crucial warning: Never leave a dog, or any living being, without competent, awake, human companionship, in a car on a hot day, especially with the windows up. You are not doing them a favor by taking them along on your errands if they will be left for more than a minute or two (and on very hot days, in full sun, even that can be dangerous). The solar heat in cars is intense. Every year, dozens of dogs (and other living beings) die this way. Just leave them at home, or if you can't do that for some reason, take them out and attach their leash to something close to the entrance of the store and keep the errand short. If you know you will be leashing a dog outside a store in hot weather, consider carrying a bowl and a bottle of water, so you can leave that for them. If you do leave them in the car, even if it will just be a few minutes, even if in the shade, crack the windows a few inches so they get some air. With our dog, I had an experience similar to my niece's experience with her pal's cat. The first week we got Athena, I had her in the car when I went to the grocery store. I didn't want her to be hot, so I left the window open about a foot. A few minutes later, there was an announcement over the P.A. system that there was a dog outside the door. After that, I left her at home when I ran errands.

If you happen to see an animal left in a car in very hot or cold weather, look to see if they seem distressed. It may not be a problem, as the driver may have just run inside to pick something up. However, if you check back several minutes later and they are still there, or if they seem distressed and you can't locate the driver, call 911. If they don't arrive quickly and the animal is definitely distressed or unconscious, there is a Good Samaritan Law in most places that allows you to break a car window to save them.

Be sure to microchip your dog, cat, or any other animal that might get out and get lost. When animals are found, the information stored in microchips has sometimes reunited owners and pets, even miles and months apart. Also be sure to keep a collar and tags on them at all times. Do not just have the rabies tag. Be sure to order a tag with the animal's name, your address, and your phone number. A couple of times, I have been able to return pets with that information. I would not know how to read a microchip. A final point: If you move, be sure to get the information on the microchip updated.

CHAPTER 10

Vaccinations

Here is some very important vaccination information. The focus of most of us in recent times , appropriately, has been on Covid vaccinations. I, personally, am a strong proponent of being fully vaccinated and boosted. Other vaccinations are associated with children, but adults need to consider their complete vaccination status, as well. This is crucial information.

If you were born before 1957 you never had an MMR (measles, mumps and rubella, which is also known as German measles) shot because you actually had the diseases. I had measles and rubella, and apparently, I am immune to mumps, because not only did my brother have it when I was 2, I am told I put some of his discarded gum in my mouth! (Don't try this at home!) I was told I have lifetime immunity to these diseases and do not need a shot. I also do not have to worry about being a carrier. If you never had either the diseases nor the shots, get the shots now. Not only are you a danger to others, but childhood diseases are much more dangerous when you get them as an adult. If you are not sure whether you had the diseases or are fully vaccinated, talk to a doctor about being tested. If you are going to be cuddling newborn grandbabies and great-grand-babies, you will want to be sure you are immune to measles, mumps, and rubella, for their sake.

Likewise, the chickenpox vaccine did not exist when I was a child, and I had the disease. On the plus side, it is very likely that I will never get chickenpox again. But the virus stays in your system, and a large percentage of people who have had chickenpox eventually get shingles. The CDC estimates that one-third of adult Americans will get shingles. For those who live to age 85, that percentage rises to one-half. In fact, I already had it at the young, for that disease, age of 29. Fortunately, I had a mild case; but it can be devastating and cause years of pain. It really is much worse than chickenpox. When I saw the doctor who was treating me for the last time, he said, "Now that you're over it, I can tell you that some people have committed suicide from shingles." I replied, "Well, at least I don't have to worry about getting it later." Unfortunately, he told me, no, this is one of the diseases that do not provide lifetime immunity, and I could get it again. That was a shock.

Fortunately for everyone, since that time, scientists have created a shingles vaccine. Several years ago, I had a shingles shot. Since that time, they have developed a new and better vaccine. I checked and was told that if you had the old shot, you should get the new one; so, I did. In actuality, it was the first of two you have to get. Depending on your insurance, it can be fairly costly. My doctor warned that I would get a sore arm from being over-vaccinated; but we agreed it would be worth it. If you never had chickenpox or its vaccine, I do not know whether it is better to have the chickenpox vaccine or the shingles vaccine. Ask your doctor. Even if you don't think you will be around children, if you ever had chicken pox, do not fail to get the shingles vaccine. I'll never forget what my doctor told me.

If you are going to be around babies, I was told you want to be sure to get 2 shots to protect them. First, the shingles vaccine, because infants do not get the chickenpox vaccine immediately; and even though you had chicken pox years ago, if you have shingles (which you might not realize, at first, as it creeps up and doesn't always strike quickly), you can give them chicken pox. Second, is the DPT (diphtheria, pertussis, also known as whooping cough, and tetanus) shot. Adults do not normally have to worry about whooping cough, but it is still common and a threat to children; . If you think you might be around children, and you have not had the vaccine, it would be a good idea if you did, as well. I remember my son having whooping cough, and I am glad children don't have to go through that anymore.

The cause of death, for many elderly people, is pneumonia. You might be aware of this, and you might believe you have protected yourself by getting a pneumonia shot. However, this is more complicated than it may seem. First, there are many different ways one can get pneumonia.. Not all of them are infectious and covered by a vaccine. Second, there are many different strains of bacteria from which you can protect yourself by getting vaccinated. So if you are considering getting a pneumonia vaccine, ask your doctor which one is right for you. If you have had one before, ask which one it was, and whether you also need the second one. You might also check with your insurance to see which they cover.

You probably already get a yearly flu shot. Just be aware that if you are over 60, unless you request otherwise, you will be given an extra-strength dosage. The first year it was offered to me, I declined. I thought the only difference was strength. I didn't realize that the stronger dosage actually covers more strains. The second year, I tried it, and I did not have any problems. However, this year I learned that my doctor could give me a shot that covered the increased number of strains (4 instead of 3) without the extra strength. I opted for that.

One more word of caution: Most shots are one and done. However, others require 2 or 3 doses, at specific intervals, or they wear off after a certain number of years. Be sure to ask when you get your shots, and find a way to create a reminder when you need to get a booster or second shot. The shingles shot is an example of a two-parter.

Hopefully you have all received the Covid vaccines and boosters for the protection of you and others.

Most vaccinations are available at pharmacies, as well as at doctor's offices. In fact, my doctor told me that her office could not get the shingles vaccine because the drug stores had purchased all the available doses. Even though there may be a sign advertising the vaccine, they may be out of it at that location. Call first. Some vaccinations are covered by insurance, some not. If you have multiple insurance carriers, such as a separate one for drugs, etc. bring all your insurance cards with you, as you don't know which one will cover it. I'm amazed that not all vaccines are covered, as the treatment for the disease would cost so much more. Frankly, it makes no sense. My two shingles shots cost over $160 with the Medicare Part B discount. Some Medicare Complete plans do cover it. Call all your insurance carriers before going for your shots. If you itemize on your taxes and have a lot of medical expenses, save your receipts.

CHAPTER 11

Discounts and Safety

Home Electronics - Television Discounts

Cable television bills can be thousands of dollars per year, but there are ways to reduce those costs. There are at least four ways you can save money on your television bill and still have a wide variety of channels to choose from. The first is to eliminate cable TV and switch to free antenna TV. Antennas are very inexpensive and easy to connect to your television. They are no longer rabbit ears. They are normally a flat panel that screws into the back of your television. You'd be surprised at how many channels you can get with them. Of course, it won't help for premium channels, such as HBO; but you can get all the broadcast channels, plus some you might not expect. I opt to have only free antenna TV on my kitchen TV, as I mostly watch it when I'm preparing dinner. I'm simply watching the news, so that's all I need. That saves me the extra monthly fee for another receiver from my cable company.

The second way you can save money is to use a streaming device, such as AppleTV or Roku. It's a contraption, such as a mini-box or thumb drive, that gets plugged into your TV. Streaming devices might be advantageous for you; albeit that, when you add up the individual costs for any premium channels that you'd like to stream, you might find that the amount of effort and the financial cost are about the same as maintaining cable. Nonetheless, it is often worth buying a streaming device, to see what is offered in your area, as the devices, themselves, are relatively inexpensive, and it's just a one-time purchase fee, if you don't add on specific premium channels.

The third way to save money is by asking your cable company for a discount. You'd be surprised. You might think that everyone would be charged the same rate for the same bundles of services; but that isn't true, at all. I called AT&T and complained, in September, when my monthly charges increased substantially; and the agent with whom I spoke let me in on a secret: At the beginning of each quarter, the company disperses discounts -- but only a certain, small number of them. The agent instructed me to call back on October 1. I did, and with the seasonal offer, my monthly cable TV was reduced by $55, and my monthly internet bill was reduced by $20! A very remarkable savings. I encourage you to check to see whether there might be some services in your bundle, for which you are charged, that you don't actually use, and then ask to remove those unused services. For example, if you are not a fan of watching sports, you might be able to cut some unused channels from your package, and save that way. My experience has been that, while it doesn't save that much, it's worth checking out. If they won't give you any discounts, let them know that you are considering canceling your subscription altogether; and they will connect you to a special department, Customer Retention, that may have special offers.

Finally, you can try following up on special offers designed to get you to switch providers. If you pursue transferring services across companies, be sure to request clarification about the minimum time you have to maintain your subscription with your current company to avoid change fees, and make sure you have met that requirement; and ask if there are any installation fees. I personally think this is more bother than it's worth, and you would also have to change your password to connect to your internet.

Phone Discounts

Some of the same techniques that I mentioned for obtaining discounts on your cable bill can be used for obtaining discounts on your cell phone bill, as well. It never hurts to ask if there are any discounts available. Watch the ads, or browse the internet for special offers.

Most companies allow you a new free phone after 2 years, but I know many people who don't take advantage of that offer. If you are intimidated by smart phones and their technology, ask a young person you know for help. Once you get the hang of the light touch needed to successfully utilize the phone's keyboard, you will love it. For those who find using their fingertips a challenge, such as those with tremors from Parkinson's, as my husband Paul had, you might benefit from using a stylus. This is something that looks like a pen, and you hold it like a pen and push keys or write on screens with it, instead of your finger tips. There are also some actual pens that have a stylus tip you can use. There are also ways to use your phone "hands-free" by dictating numbers and text messages. All recent smartphones have a microphone button, usually in the bottom right corner. If you press that you can talk and it will type for you with pretty good accuracy. You have to say punctuation commands such as "period". If you have an older model it's possible you may need to download an app.

Another option is to get a prepaid phone. Instead of signing up for an automatic, monthly fee, you can get a Trac Phone or similar that allows you to purchase minutes. This is what Paul had, because we have a landline and he only used his cellphone on rare occasions, such as if I had to meet him somewhere. It cost us less than $10 a month. These are the so-called "burner phones" that you can get at 24-hour convenience stores. You can also look into family plans.

I saved some money on my landline by eliminating long distance. I still have the landline to answer calls from anywhere in the house, and if I want to make a long distance call I use my cellphone. Landlines are easier to hold, easier to hear, and will work in a power outage. A tip: Be sure to have one phone that is a traditional, corded phone, not one that uses batteries, in case of a power outage. Also, I won't put my landline on my cable service, no matter how many times the cable company encourages me to do so, because if the cable goes out, so does the phone.

Cell Phone Protection and Safety

One way to save money with your phone is to decline any insurance that the manufacturer or your carrier offers. Be sure to get a good screen protector that comes with a guarantee that, if the screen shatters, the screen will be replaced. This warranty may be offered to you by your carrier as a package when you get your new phone, or you may have to go to a store to buy it. Shattered screens are expensive to fix. Also, get a protective case for your phone. If you do obtain both of those things, I don't think insurance is needed. If you review phone insurance policies, at least the ones that I've seen, you will find that they have high deductibles, as well as a monthly fee; and that adds up to doubling the cost of your phone in the long run. So, unless you (or those sharing your phone, or your kids, or your pets) have a history of accidentally destroying your phone, you will come out ahead by not buying insurance. You might be able to add your phone to your renters' or homeowners' insurance at no extra cost to you. If it is stolen from or broken in a crash of your car, it should be covered under your car insurance.

As for theft, be vigilant about using your phone in public, especially on public transportation, and especially at stations, where thieves sometimes run in, grab phones or purses, and run out. I try to not sit right by the door. When you are walking, put your phone away. You shouldn't be looking at your phone when you walk, anyway, so that you don't trip or walk into things, especially when crossing the street. People have even fallen off train platforms because their gaze has been too fixated upon their phones. If you are using something such as Google Maps for walking directions, you can just listen for the directions.

If you purchase your phone outright, your credit card company might cover the cost of replacements. If you have an iPhone, be sure to download the "find my iPhone" app and activate it. If you have an Android phone, check to see if there is a similar app available. If you simply lose your phone, have someone call it for you. You might want to attach a business card to the back with your email or alternative phone number. Some phones have a feature whereby you can list your emergency contact(s) that can be visible, even without unlocking your phone. In addition to the fact that this might help a Good Samaritan return a lost or stolen phone to you someday, this could potentially save your life, or help people know whom to notify if you are unconscious someday.

My best recent discovery is that some credit cards offer free cell phone protection, if you pay your cell phone bill on their card. As soon as I found that out, I switched my payments. Call your card company and ask if they have that coverage.

Why You Should Buy an Apple Watch

If you aren't familiar with Apple Watches, here's a quick description. An Apple Watch is made by Apple and is a larger-than-average wristwatch that, in an amazingly small space, is a computer that not only tells time, but also, if linked to your phone, can receive emails and other information and even answer phone calls. It reminds me of Dick Tracy, and I wonder if it might have been inspired by that comic strip, just as some other inventions, such as automatic doors and cell phones, were inspired by Star Trek. It recharges like a phone, so you don't need to keep replacing batteries. It is similar to smart watches made by other companies, such as FitBit, but it is a little larger, because it does more. I recently read an article that Apple was surprised at the proportion of their purchasers who are seniors. Now that I have an Apple Watch, I am not surprised. *Please bear in mind that any endorsements in this book are strictly from my own experiences, and not based on any reimbursements from anyone.*

I recently purchased an Apple Watch for $300 from Best Buy. I bought it for one reason, and one reason only: I read that it has *sudden fall detection*. Since I now live alone, and since I do not work a regular schedule where I would be missed if I don't show up, there is the danger that I could be hurt or ill, and no one would know it, for an extended period of time. My great aunt once slipped in the tub and was unable to get out of it for a day and a half. She was only rescued when a neighbor noticed the newspapers piling up in front of her door. No matter how healthy you are, you could always slip, fall, and hurt yourself and not be able to get to your phone. Yes, there are medical alert devices, but many of them require you to push a button. What if you were unconscious? There are some more sophisticated ones that can detect falls, but they require a monthly monitoring fee. A single purchase of an Apple Watch, which has no monthly fees, will pay for itself in a single year. If you do fall, it will automatically call 911. It will ask you if you want to call 911, and if you don't need the help, you can stop the device from making the call; which is good, because you could fall and not be seriously hurt, and you do not want to incur an ambulance bill or needlessly alarm anyone. That does bring up one issue I have not resolved yet, which is the question of whether it's a good or bad thing to lock my front door. Probably the best thing to do is lock it and talk to the fire department in my village about a neighbor who has a key.

Another important safety and health feature is that an Apple Watch monitors your heart rate. If it detects an arrhythmia (irregular heart beat), it will sound an alarm, and if you do not stop the alarm, the Apple Watch will call 911. A friend's friend found out he was having a heart attack because his Apple Watch detected an arrhythmia , and he was able to get to a hospital. It may have saved his life! The model 6 will even sound an alarm if it detects a fever.

The one criticism I would have is that there is very little included in the way of an instruction booklet, when you receive the watch. There is a very simple diagram that comes with it, which will get you started, and you have to go online or ask a friend if you want more information. It was a little while before Apple emailed me and told me there is an app to download that gives you instructions. Now you know. I'm constantly learning new things about my watch and being surprised.

One morning, I was reading the newspapers and on my computer, and after a while, my watch buzzed. When I looked at my Apple Watch, it told me I've been sitting too long and that I should stand up for a minute. It was right! Sitting for too long of a time can cause varicose veins and affect your blood pressure. It isn't healthy. I'm thinking, too, that this feature might wake me up when I fall asleep watching TV, as I sometimes do in the evening.

If you are in a theater, you scroll down to the tragedy and comedy masks and click on them. Not only will the theater mode silence your phone; it also will dim the illumination on your phone, so that if you look at it to check the time, it will not disturb your neighbors. If you have your linked phone with you and put that on the Do Not Disturb setting, your Apple Watch is automatically silenced as well. I'm sure there are other positive features I will keep finding. It's actually much easier to use than I thought it would be, and it seems to do pretty much everything your phone does that doesn't involve having a camera.

Another plus: If your iPhone is misplaced, there is a button whereby it will ping your phone for you. The Apple Watch can be bought independently, but it is best when paired with an iPhone. Then it will pick up calls, emails, and other things from the iPhone. Yesterday, I didn't hear my phone ring, because it was in another room; but it rang on my watch, as well, and I was actually able to answer the call on the watch. I wondered how people could reply to emails on such a small surface, but you can hit the reply button, then hit the microphone button, and speak your reply, then press done and send.

If you are going to buy an Apple Watch, be sure to get an Apple Watch Four or later. The earlier Apple Watches are cheaper, but they do not have the safety features. When you first set it up, you are offered the option of using a password or not. I opted for no password, so all I have to do is rotate my wrist and I instantly see time, weather, and the next activity on my calendar. It is a different situation than my phone, as I'm not going to set my wristwatch down somewhere where someone else could use it. I initially thought I would only be using it at home. I'm liking it so much, though, that I am wearing it outside, if not dressed up.

If you forget your phone at home your watch cannot perform a lot of functions. If you are concerned and have a late enough model you can add a line for the phone with your cell company for a monthly fee. I do not do that.

The Apple Watches are also waterproof, so that you can wear them in the shower or bathtub, which of course, are very risky places for anyone prone to falling. It's all very easy to set up, and very easy to pair with your iPhone; so, it's a strong recommendation. Even if you don't live alone, you are alone at times, and this could literally be a lifesaver.

I read that other companies are planning to add similar features, so by the time you read this they may be available for the Android operating system, and the price may have dropped. Keep in mind that once you have purchased an Apple watch you have to keep buying I Phones. If you don't think you will do that look into FitBits or other kinds of smart watches.

CHAPTER 12

Where to Live

Considering Moving

There are several reasons why you might want to move when you're older. Once you are an empty nester, you may feel that your house is larger than you need or want. Maybe you aren't concerned about the schools anymore, so you want to move back into the city, or to somewhere with lower taxes. Perhaps you no longer want to deal with the constant work a home requires, so you'd prefer to be in a condo or apartment. Maybe you're considering moving to be closer to your kids, or to move into some kind of facility that is especially for seniors, whether simply a retirement community or a facility that provides helpful services, from just dining and housekeeping to actual nursing, social work, or activities.

If you are over 50 and healthy, you may not think about the future too much when you are moving, but you should. That three-story townhouse may be beautiful and seem perfect, but will you be able to climb those stairs in 20 years? If you are renting, it isn't that much of an issue; but if you are purchasing, and then you suddenly need to move because of a disability, what if the market has hit a downturn and you can't sell?

Likewise, even a one-level condo in a vintage building could be a problem. How many stairs do you have to climb to get into it? If you later become dependent on a cane or walker, the presence of even one stair, to enter and exit your home, or within it to walk between rooms, can pose a trip hazard. Are the doorways, including to bathrooms, wide enough to accommodate a wheelchair and/or scooter, if you need one later? How would you get a wheelchair up the stairs?

In general, I'd say if you are over 60 and moving, at least consider the possibility of renting instead of buying. That way, in case of sudden illness or growing disability, you can move more easily. Take the money you made selling your property and put part of it in a CD that isn't too long-term, and part in the highest-paying FDIC-guaranteed account you can find. I recently moved much of my money from an account earning 0.25% to one earning over 2%. That's 8 times as much! Of course, you do have to pay taxes on it; but home ownership isn't as advantageous for taxes as it used to be anyway.

One bright spot for owners is that, at least in Illinois, as a true senior, you are entitled to a discount on your property taxes, and if low-income, you are also entitled to the "senior freeze".

Here is a little-known tip: In Illinois and probably other states, if someone in the household is officially disabled, not only can you get a handicap parking permit, but you can get an additional deduction on your taxes. Paul was officially disabled the last 20 years of his life, and no one had told me that. When I did find out, the township was able to go back just 4 years to get me refunds, but that was hundreds of dollars lost forever because I didn't know. Now you do.

As a senior, when you do sell your home, you do not have to pay capital gains tax for the full amount of sale. You get a significant one-time reduction. Talk to your tax attorney or consult the free tax help available through AARP at libraries during tax season. Also, save receipts for significant improvements to the property, because that may help your tax base, as well.

A phrase that I hear as a growing phenomenon is "aging in place." That means that even though you begin to have physical challenges, you choose to stay in your home. If you do stay in your home and don't want to sell, there are ways you can make it more accessible. The easiest and least expensive is to add grab bars in critical places, such as at corners of rooms where you may be turning, and in bathrooms. There are companies that specialize in this, and it may be covered under Medicare (check your plan's Durable Goods provisions), but you can also have a handyman install them. Do not waste your money and time or risk your health with grab bars that use suction cups. Grab bars need to be screwed into the wall, or they may make a fall worse, if they disconnect under your weight. Yes, when you go to sell your house and remove them, that will leave holes; but those holes can be filled in. Grab bars in showers are helpful for everyone and should be left in place.

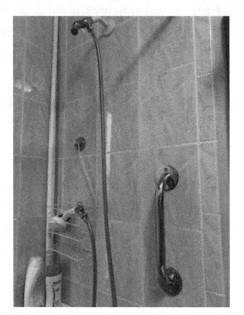

Think creatively. My husband was having problems going up our stairs because of an arthritic back and difficulty balancing. One possibility we considered was Acorn Stairlifts or similar. You might have seen ads where you sit on a seat and ride up the stairs. They have versions that work outside and are weatherproof. Naturally, they cost a considerable amount of money. Paul realized that his main problem was that our front stairs are so wide, you can't reach both sides at the same time, and you either have to hold on with just one hand or go up sideways. He hired a handyman to build a center railing that matches the side railings. It actually looked as if it were part of the original structure. He found that, once he could hold on with both hands, he was able to navigate the stairs without any help. It was easy to remove later.

If you have to use a wheelchair, it is a problem to get it upstairs. Some weigh 50 pounds. Traditionally, people have built ramps for this purpose; but ramps have disadvantages. Because the incline has to be gradual to be safe, ramps can take up and eliminate an entire yard, and they might have to be removed before putting a house on the market.

Another possibility is installing an outdoor elevator or chair lift. I was actually looking into this possibility right before Paul died, and I found out that it costs about $8000. Not cheap, but I would think it might be tax- deductible; and if you have home health coverage, it might be paid for with what you don't pay for a nursing home. If the person could be cared for at home (Paul was not at that point yet), it would be worth it to them.

Wheelchairs present other challenges. In an older house, the door-ways may not be wide enough to get through all of them with the chair. This is especially a problem with bathrooms. If the person can stand and walk a couple of feet, you can leave the chair outside the room. If not, you may need to have a professional tell you if it is possible to widen your doorways and what the cost would be. If renovations are not possible, you might have to move to a modern elevator building.

Another big question that you have to deal with is not only the kind of housing that you will be in, but also where it will be. Many people plan on retiring to a warm climate, such as in Florida or Arizona. Some-times it works out well, but many times, cross-country relocation is an area of great regret.

Be sure to investigate an area very thoroughly before considering actually packing up and moving there. I would suggest that you check out the chapter on being a Snowbird and consider being a Snowbird, at least for a season or two, before you decide to actually move to a place. Just getting away for a few months may be all you need.

If you do want to try out a place, don't go during the ideal season, such as visiting Florida in winter, but instead visit it at the worst time of the year. For example, spend the month of August in Florida, and see if you are happy dealing with the heat and humidity. If you are, fine. But at least give that a try. Consider such aspects as hurricane season and other types of impactful weather.

Another consideration is, do you have friends or family in the area? If you do, that is a definite plus. It isn't easy at any age, let alone when you're older, to move to a strange area where you probably aren't even making associations at a workplace, and develop a new set of relationships. I've heard of many cases where people regretted their decision and ended up moving back to the area they know and had to start a housing search.

Selling your home is a very big and final decision. Don't do it unless you are very sure. Once you have moved out-of-state, it isn't easy to move back.

If you think you might want to move soon, start working on decluttering. It's going to take months to do it. Odds are that wherever you move will be smaller. If you think you are saving things for your kids, ask them if they really will want those things. Odds are they won't. There are people who specialize in this process. If you want help, Google for one in your area.

Senior Housing

If you decide to move and are at least 55, you might want to consider senior housing. There are many options, and they often have different names associated with them. It is a big decision. One service you can use to explore options is A Place for Mom. I talked to them once and the person was very pleasant. They don't do much with nursing homes, so I didn't use their services. Here are some types of living situations to consider if you are considering moving.

"55+" or "Retirement Communities"

Senior, or age-restricted communities: Del Webb and similar communities are intended for seniors who are in good health. They offer attractive housing at reasonable prices, loads of amenities, classes, entertainment, etc. Some are spread out over many blocks and consist of individual homes. One major factor of some of these communities, which some might consider as too strict a restriction, and others might consider a relief, is that children can only come for short visits. Additionally, many of these residences are fairly far from city life.

There are senior residences for active seniors in cities, as well. Many of these are mid- to high- rise buildings. It depends on the lifestyle you want. Many require that you have a meal plan for at least one communal meal a day, even though you have a kitchen. These types of residences and their meal plans are not cheap. Some require a "buy in". That is a lump sum, up front, that can be quite substantial. A portion of that "buy in" might be returned to you, if you move out, or to your estate, if you die. Be sure to ask about the "buy in" terms before signing a lease.

Continuing Care Communities

There are a few different terms used for this type of housing. It might be continuing, life, or other terms, but generally they are called CCRCs. That is, Continuing Care Retirement Communities. The attraction of these communities is that it is the last time you ever have to move. They offer 3 levels of care in one location. You enter as a resident of Independent Living, which is like the 55+ communities I described. The difference is that you don't have to move out, if you can no longer live independently. The second level is Assisted Living. If you begin to need help with daily activities, such as dressing and bathing, or taking your medications, they have people at the facility who can help you. In some cases, they simply come into the residence that you were in independently and help you. In others you may have to move to another building. But if you move, you are still in the same general community, you are still close to any friends whom you may have made, and you may continue to participate in activities.

The third level is Skilled Nursing Care. Once again, if you need more care than can be found in Assisted Living, you can stay in the same general community. Once you get to the point of needing Nursing Care, you probably will not be able to remain in the same apartment you moved into originally, but you'll still be in the same general community in a nearby building.

This can be a very attractive alternative to traditional retirement housing. This would especially be advantageous if you had a situation where you and your spouse or partner require different levels of care. One of you may need assistance before the other, and you would still be walking distance from each other, even if one is in nursing.

These facilities can be quite expensive, but some much more so than others. Once you receive assisted living, your long term care insurance should help with the cost. If you are considering this possibility, you'll have to do a lot of research and contact several facilities in your area and ask a lot of questions. I know I have a good friend who moved into a continuing care community, who is still in an independent living situation, who is really enjoying all the activities that the facility offers. She picked a place in a location that allows her to participate in the city's activities, as well.

Subsidized Housing and Health Facilities

For subsidized housing information, see the chapter on low-income support.

If you have health problems that make it impossible to stay in your home, because you are living alone and can't afford 24-hour assistance or cannot be treated sufficiently in a home setting, **see the chapter on Health Facilities.**

CHAPTER 13

Support for Low-Income Seniors

While many seniors are financially secure, there also are many people who are subsisting simply on Social Security. This is barely enough to get by on. Other seniors have low incomes for various reasons. If that is your case, you need to know more than simply how to save money on leisure activities. You need to save on the basics.

Food - Dollar Stores

You probably already know this, but I have been amazed at some of the items I have found at Dollar Tree and other dollar stores. Many are the very same brands you pay twice as much for at grocery stores. I have even gotten a small portion of wild caught salmon from the freezer and a good bag of coffee. You can get a loaf of day-old bread for a dollar or so. When I went to the 99 cent store in L. A. they even had some fresh produce.

Food Pantries

It is worth it to look into food pantries in your area. Food pantries are all over the place, not just in poor neighborhoods. The offerings have become more sophisticated. In my local community, some working poor qualify to use the food pantry but have little time to go and pick up the food. For this reason, some pantries have now started allowing online ordering of food. Check with Senior Services in your area or local congregations to see what might be offered.

Senior / Community Centers

My local township offers weekly daily lunches at their center for just a few dollars for seniors. Menus are available, and it is a chance to socialize, while eating a balanced meal. They also have a Dine Out program where you get coupons, and for four dollars, you can have a complete meal at several different restaurants. Obviously, your local situation may be different, but it is worth asking around in your local community for comparable options.

Senior Discounts at Restaurants

There are many places such as Denny's that offer them; it never hurts to ask. Be sure to look on the back of the menu when in a chain restaurant, because they will often place senior specials there.

Free Delivery and Curbside Pick-Up from Grocery Stores

Some grocers now offer free delivery to your home, within a certain radius, for their regular customers. It's worth asking, as it might save you time, money, and effort, especially if you are mobility impaired and/or don't have your own car or can't drive yourself. In most cases, you need to be able to get online to order, but you might be able to order by phone. Other places provide options both for delivery, and for free curb-side pick-up; you pay the same prices as you would inside, but you don't have to take the time off work, or hire a caregiver to help you, or expend the energy to roam the aisles and fill a cart. For example, Fred Meyer's Grocery Pickup (formerly known as Click List) is available up and down the whole West Coast, as well as delivery. There are also online food ordering/delivery services not associated with a particular store, which vary from area to area. They may charge a fee, but it may be worth it to you. Google for one, and you can then compare offerings and prices to your local store.

Soup Kitchens

Many communities offer places where people can go get free hot meals. In many places, there are religious institutions that offer breakfasts one day a week. In some places, there are private nonprofit or activist groups that serve food, primarily for people who are homeless, but available to everyone, if you are open to standing in line in a public place. Other places, municipalities, or counties have upscale versions of soup kitchens, deliberately structured inside and out and marketed to provide a clean, safe, dignified experience, and to resemble and be run like a restaurant. You sit at a table, there is a menu, wait staff take your order, just like a restaurant; except it's all free. If you are vegetarian or need to restrict cholesterol intake, it is often possible to request vegetarian options (and sometimes those are all that are offered).

Food Stamps

There are programs at which you can apply to see if you qualify for the electronic benefit transfer (EBT) cards that are now used in place of what used to be paper "stamps". Your local Adult and Family Services or Senior Services office can help you apply. Application processes, financial qualification standards, and quantities of benefits offered can vary by state (especially for Alaska and Hawaii). Some, but not all, noncitizens are eligible to apply. There are strict requirements as to what documentation of your resources and identity will be necessary to apply. Many states have work requirements for most applicants; one must be working or be able to document actively seeking employment by documenting jobs for which one has applied, to qualify. There presently is the possibility of massive cuts to this program. If you are able to get enrolled before the cuts are enacted, that will be beneficial. Especially if you have a microwave or toaster oven for reheating food, it can be really convenient to buy cold-packaged food from the hot bar of your local grocery. Just heat and eat.

Gleaning Groups

My niece out in Oregon participates in a gleaning group. Many seniors are involved.

Gleaning is when someone has more food growing in their garden, orchard, or farm than they need, and they invite neighbors to come and harvest the excess.

a. You might be a senior who has a tree, and you can no longer climb a ladder to harvest your fruit or nuts.

b. You can contact your local gleaners. They will come for free. They will harvest it for you, give you half, and give you a tax receipt for the portion that you donate.

c. You might be a senior in need of food. If you are fit, you can join a glean. It's a great way to get outside, get some exercise, and make new friends.

d. The gleaning groups often need other types of volunteers. If you are not up to the exercise, but have some time, and are computer-savvy, they often need people to help with member lists and with organizing gleans. They have web pages for sharing recipes. That can be a fun way to learn how to make new dishes or share your favorites from your culture and your family recipe book, especially if you don't have kids or grandkids with whom to share them.

Canning Groups

There are places you can take, or teach, classes on how to preserve food. These can help stretch resources.

Barter Groups

If you have something that grows in your garden, and more of it than you need, another option is to find the local group that encourages bartering. You might, for example, be able to trade flowers, or even herbs grown indoors, for fresh eggs from a neighbor's chickens.

Meals on Wheels

There are some places where the funding is cut, but if it exists in your neighborhood, it can be a godsend. My brother's mother-in-law, who became legally blind, was able to live alone in her apartment as a widow into her 80s with the help of Meals on Wheels. In some areas, the program even delivers pet food. For those of us who love animals, that can be a huge help.

Clothing

Recycled clothing has become very fashionable and is now widely available and purchased by all classes. Yes, you can get a real bargain at a Salvation Army store or Goodwill, but there are also consignment stores that carry selective merchandise. The trick to getting a bargain at one of these is to check the tags to see how long they have been there. It is common to reduce the price if they have been there for an extended period of time. Another option is that there are often local "Free Stores," or free bins, sometimes run by churches or other organizations. This is a movement that began in the 1960's in San Francisco and has now spread around the world. I know I was surprised to learn about this. Some offer not only clothes but also household items, all for free. Dollar stores also have a surprising amount of clothing, such as gloves and T-shirts for only $1.25.

Shelter

Almost all communities offer some type of subsidized housing for low income seniors. Qualifying for subsidized housing depends, of course, on your income. They typically do not charge a set monthly rent, but rather a percentage, typically 30%, of your income. The apartments are on the small side but usually are pleasant, and in some cases, certain services, such as a weekly visit to the building by medical personnel, are offered. The worst aspect, if you are able to qualify, based either on your being low-income and/or having some forms of disability, is that the wait to get into one of the nicer buildings can be months or even years. If you are even thinking of moving into one of these buildings, get on the waiting list right away. You can always say no later. Paul's sister lived in one for a year or so until she had to go to a nursing home and had a nice one bedroom apartment several floors up with a view of a park.

Medical Care

Medicaid is a very important asset for those people who are low-income. Medicaid can be even better than Medicare. Medicare does not cover such things as long-term care, hearing aids, eye glasses, and dental services, but Medicaid sometimes does. A friend of mine has official custody of her grandchild and told me that Medicaid is even paying for his braces. Not surprisingly, you may have fewer choices than if you are paying for things yourself. Not all providers accept Medicaid. In order to qualify for Medicaid, you have to have a small amount of income and savings (or none). If you have more than that amount, you go on what is called a spend down to get down to that amount. You are allowed to keep your residence, if you or your spouse lives there. If you have to go to a nursing home, and if your home is unoccupied, you must be expected to return to it to keep it. Likewise with your vehicle. You or your spouse must be expected to use it.

Do not think you can qualify by giving your money to others. In order to qualify, you might be asked to provide tax and other records, for an extended period of time, to prove income and that you have not done this . Since Medicaid varies from state to state, you will have to check to see what the requirements are. You can call your local Medicare office for more information.

If you do not have Medicare or Medicaid, and you receive a medical bill, you can contact the provider and ask for a reduction in or a waiver of the bill. Nearly all hospitals, and some long-term care facilities, have programs to reduce the bills for those who cannot afford them, and they work out a payment plan. I clearly remember, several years ago, when we were paying for an assisted living facility for a few months for Paul's sister while she waited to get into her low-income housing, I went to talk to the financial person for clarification about the bill. She told me I was making a mistake, and that I should never pay a bill in full. I think that is an exaggeration, but it never hurts to ask if there is a discount available. Don't feel bad about asking. Many hospitals make big profits, and many of the most profitable chains of hospitals are run by religious institutions and pay no taxes. They build into their budgets the expectations of some charitable write-offs, and they include how much free or reduced-fee care that they provide into their publicity for their funders/shareholders. Most especially, remember that you are important, and that your self-care is important. Please don't ever skip out on any aspect of health care for fear of a bill.

Your community might also have one or more clinics that operate totally for free or on a sliding scale for uninsured or under-insured patients. These may be run by private secular or religious non-profits; by schools training their students; or by federal or county governments or indigenous nations' clinics. Government clinics that take sliding scales and/or provide some services for free include Health Care for the Homeless Clinics; Ryan White Act programs for people living with AIDS or HIV; tribal clinics for enrolled members of indigenous nations; and Community Health Centers. There are some programs that provide some specific screening services for free, such as the BCCP (Breast and Cervical Cancer Project); county and private HIV and STD screening services; etc. There are sometimes free vaccination outreach programs.

Academic institutions are a special opportunity for additional low-cost care. At some community colleges, attending for even one credit per term gets you access to a lot of benefits. For example, at the one my niece attends and works for, it only takes attending one academic credit of on-campus class (around $100-150) to get 3 months' worth of free access to the health clinic, a free bus pass for 3 months, as well as access to a weekly food box and a weekly allotment of 5 pieces of clothing for adults and 5 pieces of clothing for kids. Plus, you can keep your mind active, learn new skills, and meet new friends. Many academic institutions and trade schools provide various types of health and other types of care at no or low cost, even to community members not affiliated with the school. For example, dental schools offer free evaluations of dental hygiene, and phenomenally low-cost dental hygiene services, as well as discounts on restorative care, when it is provided as part of the education of their students. Cosmetology schools offer haircuts and other hair services for free or very low cost. The trade-off is you have to be open to it being relatively inexperienced students doing the work, and to it taking much more time to get scheduled and for the appointments to last. Many seniors find the trade-off worth it to save that much money.

Another potential source of free or low-cost health care and health education is the set of support groups that meet at hospitals. There are often support groups for people who are grieving, for caregivers, for people with certain diagnoses (such as specific cancers, hearing loss, Alzheimer's, prosthetics, etc.); nutrition groups/cooking clubs; even Tai Chi or Qi Gong classes. It's worth looking into.

The V. A. (Veterans Administration)

If you and/or your spouse served in one of the branches of the military, you may be eligible for veterans' benefits. You do not need to have served overseas or in a combat situation. You merely need to have received an honorable discharge.

Some of the services that are available to you include medical care, prescriptions, low-interest rate mortgages, and burial benefits. Even if you have Medicare, you may be able to receive some benefits it does not cover, such as dental care, for free or at a reduced cost. I was kicking myself when I learned that we could have saved thousands of dollars by getting Paul's hearing aids from the V. A. In order to receive these benefits, you will need to have or obtain written proof of service. If you cannot find the discharge papers, contact the V. A. and ask how you can replace those, before you ask for the benefits.

Low-Income Heat & Energy Assistance Program (LIHEAP)

This is a locally administered, federal fund to which people can apply for grants toward the utility bill (electric or gas) that pays for their heat. This fund prioritizes applications from people who are seniors and/or have disabilities. Check with the office where you receive your benefits and see if the fund is offered in your county and if you qualify. There usually is only one day a year that the application pool opens, and it fills quickly.

Other Services

Your county or state may offer special programs for low-income seniors. For example, in Illinois, if your income is low enough, not only can you qualify for a reduction on your property tax, but you can also qualify for savings on other basics, such as phone service. Those who are low-income and receiving services from their federal, state, or county government, such as food stamps and/or Medicaid, can also see if their state has a program that provides free phones and/or low-cost service. In Oregon, where my niece lives, any recipients are eligible to apply for Lifeline. Applicants can choose either to apply for discounts on their landline phone bills, or for programs that offer free, minimal-function phones and very low-cost service. Ask the office where you get your benefits whether your state has such a program and whether you qualify.

Some municipalities offer services to seniors, such as plowing snow for them or offering chore services. Once again, ask your local senior center. In my area, there is also a reduced fare transportation card available and transportation for just a dollar or two that will take you to go shopping.

Overall Support

Remember, it is ok to look for and ask for whatever help you need. Support is out there if you know where to look. Many communities have social services to provide information, and there are 24-hour support lines available for people to talk to if you experience various types of crises. There are specific crisis lines for people who need support around mental health issues, drug and alcohol issues, surviving violence, grieving, thoughts of self-harm. These issues can come up for anyone at any income level; the 24-hour crisis lines can be particularly helpful to people who can't afford to pay for and don't have insurance to cover counseling. Whatever you need, you are worth it.

CHAPTER 14

Make a "Just in Case" List

I don't consider it morbid to look ahead; I consider it practical. No matter how young or healthy you are, the unexpected could happen. I also consider it a kindness to those who would be left behind. When someone dies, or becomes seriously ill, there are so many things to think about. Why not plan ahead, and make it easier for your loved ones? On my computer, I have a file, titled, "Just in Case," that contains all the information that someone would need, if I should die.

I also made sure that I mailed or emailed copies of this file to my brother and my son, and I gave them the passcode for my computer. All the proactive planning in the world won't help, if no one can find it when they need it, or if they can find it, but can't unlock it. Speaking of unlocking, make sure they have keys for your house.

Here are some of the topics that I address in my "Just in Case" list, and that I recommend that you have available for your loved ones.

- People who need to be notified in case of death. Your current or former employer, for example, and particular friends and relatives.
- Companies, organizations, and government departments that need to be notified: Social Security needs to be notified; your medical and life insurance companies need to be notified; your

Alumni Association should be notified; and the schools attended.. Those are just some of the ones to think about. If you are part of a religious congregation, especially one that supports loved ones who are grieving, prays with them, or assists with services or burials, include them in your list. If you have a home health agency that sends caregivers, include them in your list.

- Your intention for how your body is respected after your passing should be documented, if that has not already been made clear to them. Do you want to be cremated or buried? Do you have a special request for any ceremonies involved? Did you prepay for anything?

- If you wish to be buried, you should buy a cemetery plot ahead of time, rather than taking the chance that a plot in the place you want to be buried might not be available at the time of your death. It took me a while to find a gravesite in the cemetery I wanted, that would also be close to the area where my relatives are buried. Also, I saved some money by checking Craigslist and buying from an individual, rather than the cemetery. Of course, I made sure it was coordinated with the cemetery and legally binding. You need to have that information available. Where is the plot, and where is the document that shows your ownership of it?

- If you are on social media, list which ones, and how loved ones can post a notice on them.

- If you want a memorial plaque engraved, or a scholarship endowed, provide some details.

- What are the financial institutions in which you have funds, savings deposit boxes, and/or investments? Where are they located, and what are your account numbers and passwords? What about life insurance policies? What companies are they with, what are their terms,and what are their policy numbers? Are there special accounts that you may have somewhere that don't come to mind immediately? Where are the checkbooks or other documents related to them?

- Do you have a pension or annuity? What is the contact information, and are there survivor benefits?
- In case you are incapacitated, what information can you provide on your health, long- term, and if you have it, short-term care policies?
- Do you have any special requests, regarding to whom you want to bequeath portions of your estate? Very often, what people do is say, "I have the following bequests, and the remainder goes to my heir." There might be specific items you have in mind for specific loved ones to inherit, or to be returned to them upon your passing. Perhaps you want to donate a certain amount of money to a charitable organization. All this may or may not have been included in your will when you wrote it.
- Make sure that there's more than one copy of the bequest list available, and that it goes to more than one person. My great aunt and I discussed what things she was going to leave for me and my brother, and she showed me where the list would be. She also told me that her relatives were not very nice. I did not want to seem pushy, so I did not ask for a copy of the list. Guess what? The list supposedly was never found, and no one in my family received anything. You don't want that to happen.
- Which papers should carry your death notice? Is there anything in particular you want included?
- If you have a safe deposit box, where is it, and where is the key?
- Where are important documents, such as your will, powers of attorney, and living will? Are there lawyers or other professionals you've been working with?
- Do you have IRAs or other investment accounts? What are they? Is there an investment advisor you work with?
- Who has the keys to your house? Which bills, such as mortgage, home equity loan, taxes, and utilities have to be paid to prevent foreclosure?

Where is the Information on your Gravesite?

Yes, it is a lot of work, and can be tedious or emotional, to gather all this information together; but imagine someone trying to do this when they are coping with grieving your loss. You don't want that to happen. You want to make everything easy for your loved ones, and you want to see that your intentions are fulfilled. So, put everything in writing, and see that it goes to more than one person – and only people you truly trust. You don't have to do it all in one day, but you really should compile, in one, known place, legibly and intelligibly, as much of this information as you can. A final, important point is to check your list and update it, as needed, every once in a while. You might find it helps you and your loved ones have a little more peace of mind.

CHAPTER 15

Financial Matters

Taxes

Don't ever stop filing your taxes. I have a friend who stopped filing, because his income was so low that he never owed any money. Now, he is in trouble with the government. If you need help, there are many tax services; and in fact, many social services for senior citizens will help you with your tax returns, if you have a simple return. Sometimes, if you live in a university town, there may be Accounting students looking for some practice, who will process returns for free. Your local AARP might partner up with some local accountants to provide a free senior tax return day, like they do at my niece's town library. If you are computer savvy, there are relatively inexpensive services that can help you figure out how to file online.

A recent development is a bit of good news. As of your 2020 taxes, there is a new form available, which is the 1040 – SR. SR refers to Senior, and this form is specifically designed to help senior citizens to file. Visually, the font is larger, and there are specific lines for streams of income that retired and older citizens might have, such as Social Security. You don't have to hunt for those. They will be made easy for you to find. Did you know that there is a different level of deductions, for senior citizens? This is something that I just found out. I assume that my tax preparer has been aware of that and using that, but it is new knowledge for me. As seniors, we actually are entitled to a higher level of deductions. Of course, the standardized deductions are only used if you are not itemizing. Standardized deductions have changed significantly in the last few years, and many people find that itemizing is no longer profitable. How I collaborate with my tax preparer is, I go through the work of gathering all my information for itemized deductions, and then they see which would save me more: itemizing, or the standardized deduction. If you use a tax preparer, they should do that, as well. I would say, though, that if the standard deduction is better for 2 years in a row, I wouldn't bother adding up receipts again. However, I would still keep them, as there could be an extraordinary expense late in the year that changes that balance.

If, for some reason, such as when my husband died during tax season, you have to get an extension on your taxes, you can do that pretty easily. I simply called my tax preparer and told him I needed to have an extension. If you are filing for yourself, getting an extension can also be fairly easy. You can call the IRS office for information on how to do that. When you get an extension, it gives you until October to file your taxes. However, the one thing I was not aware of, is that *you will pay interest and penalties on any money that you owe. You just won't be in any legal trouble.* In my case, my preparer said that since it was my first time asking for an extension, and I was unaware of that, that I might get by with only paying interest, and not penalties. Given the financial repercussions, filing for an extension is something you only want to do if you absolutely must.

One area of taxes of which many people don't take is the medical deduction. I remember, years ago, I asked a tax preparer about that, and he informed me that there was no point wasting my time keeping track of medical expenses, because they would not meet the criteria to be deducted. That is, the total of one's medical expenses had to exceed 7.5% of one's income, in order to be able to deduct any of them. The very first time that I began keeping track of my medical expenses, they did, indeed, exceed that 7.5%. The reason is that it is not just a matter of your doctors' bills, which, depending on your policy, if you have insurance, might not add up to very much; but *it also includes all your medical-related insurance premiums.* Those can add up to quite a bit of money, when you think about Medicare, Medicare supplements, private insurance, dental, and short- and long-term care insurance premiums. *It also includes your prescription co-pays.* For us, that was always thousands of dollars a year. Nursing home care can be a huge expense. Certain durable medical equipment (DME), such as wheelchairs, and sometimes even eyeglasses and hearing aids, are also deductible. Even smoking cessation help and guide dogs! Sadly, the threshold of expenditures whereby one qualifies for such a deduction has just been raised to 10% of adjusted gross income, putting a greater burden on those who need help, and making it hard to qualify. So, keep those medical receipts in case of the unexpected, but it might not be worth your time to bother adding them up, unless they are substantial (or unless your income is small)

If you are still working, you might have a health savings or flexible spending account that allows you to withdraw money for medical expenses, tax-free. If so, take advantage of it to the greatest extent you can. One of the good things about them is that the balance carries over from year to year if you don't use it all.

Life insurance is not deductible, but the payout is tax free. Please bear in mind that tax laws keep changing, and I recommend consulting with a professional. At least, though, this chapter gives you topics to ask about.

Funding Your Retirement

People are living longer and longer, so, you need to plan on having a significant amount of money in your retirement. Hopefully you have been thinking ahead about the situation.

Pensions

I am lucky in that I have a good pension, which is enough to live on. However, very few people are in this situation anymore. It is getting rare for companies or organizations to offer this kind of set pension. Actually, when I retired, I was offered a choice between a lump sum payment and a traditional pension payout. Fortunately, I did what seemed obvious to me and chose the traditional pension. I figured that since it was my primary income, and not extra money, I didn't want to take chances with investments and the fickleness of the stock market. The people I've talked to who took a lump sum were sorry, as they couldn't count on a definite income, and they worried every time the stock market went down. A relative of mine actually had to hold off on retiring for around a year and a half, when much of his retirement fund evaporated overnight in the bank collapse of 2008. That's an example of the importance of not relying on the investment markets.

Social Security

The majority of Americans are covered by Social Security. According to the National Academy of Social Insurance, nearly 1 in 5 Americans, more than 61 million people, collected some form of Social Security benefits (in June, 2017). According to the Center on Budget and Policy Priorities (8/14/19), approximately 97% of American elders aged 60-89 do receive or will receive Social Security. Some people have not paid into the system and are not eligible, but most people are eligible at some point in their 60s. The age of benefit onset traditionally was 65; but in recent years, policy has changed, so that onset can be variable up to 67 for full benefits. You can receive reduced benefits at 62. Go to the Social Security site to check your required age. That would be SSA.gov. In order to get Social Security, you must have credit for 40 quarters. The quarters are not determined solely based on the calendar. They are determined by how much money you make. In order for a period of time that you have worked to constitute an eligible quarter, you have to make at least a certain minimum amount of money. That amount changes each year. So, theoretically it could take you 20 years to equal 40 quarters, rather than the 10 years it would take if you have a full-time, fairly high-paying job. The amount of your benefit for Social Security depends on what you made. It is based on an average of your earnings, and it is adjusted, each year, for the cost of living.

Spouses

Your spouse can receive benefits, even if they have not put in 40 quarters, just based upon your earnings, once they reach Social Security age. Spousal benefits are typically 50% of the primary earner's benefit. They can choose to accept that spousal benefit, or opt to accept their own, earned benefit, if it would be more. These are all things you can check by calling Social Security. It is too complicated to cover in this book.

There are also Survivor Benefits available for everyone who is legally married. If the spouse was covered by Social Security, the surviving spouse will receive a $255 burial allowance. In addition, they would normally receive a portion of their spouse's payment. Depending on when they accept the Survivor Benefit, that benefit could range from 50% to 100% of the spouse's payments.

Pension Offset Provision

Watch out for a little-known provision, the Pension Offset Provision. If you are someone who receives a public pension, which does not have to be federal, you will be affected. For example, I retired from a community college, I paid into the pension system instead of Social Security, and I receive a state pension. So, it would be viewed as "double-dipping" to receive Social Security based on my husband's eligibility. For every dollar that one earns from the pension, that will offset one dollar you would have received from Social Security. In most cases, that will leave you with no Social Security payment, as either a spouse or a surviving spouse. This is important to know. I know someone who was planning on retiring with the combination of the small pension she knew she would receive plus Social Security and was shocked to find out too late that she would be affected by this provision and not have as much income as she planned on. Likewise, if you have quarters on your own for Social Security because of other employment, your social security payment will be reduced by the pension offset provision. However, if it's on your own, you will receive a small portion of it, unlike the spousal or survivor benefit. I am currently acquiring quarters through my acting work towards qualifying for social security.

When to Take It

Social Security is the main form of income for many seniors. It is not a lot to live on. A typical payment might be $1300 a month. It can be more or less than that, and it can be as much as $3000 a month, if you were a high-income earner. Of course, for most couples, you can add 50% to that amount. Even at a lower level, Social Security is an important source of income for many Americans.

Some people choose to delay taking Social Security benefits because, if you can afford to do so, you will receive a higher benefit amount and will come out ahead in the long run, if you live a fairly long life. While you can start taking it as young as 62, you will receive up to 30% less than if you wait until full retirement age (currently 66.5), and your benefits continue to increase 8% each year you wait after that until you're 70. An important tip: There is no advantage at all to waiting, once you have reached 70. Your benefits will not continue to increase, so you should definitely accept your benefits then, if you haven't already. Once again, contact someone at Social Security or a financial advisor to talk about those possibilities. The people at Social Security are actually pretty nice and helpful. Instead of calling the (800) number, you might want to go to your local office in person.

A Few Final Notes

If you are on Disability, it will automatically switch to Social Security when you are 65. You can earn some income while receiving payments, without affecting your benefits. Check on the limits. Be sure to arrange for direct deposit of your Social Security check. It does not necessarily arrive on the first of the month. Your payment date is based upon your birthday.

IRAs

Many companies encourage people to have an IRA, a 403B, or another retirement plan, either one that the employee totally self-funds, or one that the employee partially funds, with the employer making a matching contribution. If possible, make the most of any matching money, even if you are just a few years from retirement.

There are two main kinds of IRAs, traditional and Roth IRAs. Most people today choose the Roth IRA, rather than the traditional one. When you have a traditional IRA, whatever amount that you contribute to your IRA becomes an amount that you deduct from your taxes for the year in which you contribute it. Then, you do not pay taxes on it until you withdraw the money from it. By contrast, when you have a Roth IRA, you are taxed for the income that you contribute to the IRA in the calendar year in which you earned it; but then, when you withdraw it, you will not owe additional taxes on it. It's a gamble, either way to guess what your tax bracket will be when you do the withdrawal; but in either case, the money is accumulating interest, tax-free, for many years.

You should not put any money into an IRA that you think you will need to withdraw early. There are significant penalties for early withdrawals. You can begin taking money out of your IRA when you are 57 and a half. You must take money out of your traditional IRA when you reach 70 ½, though that age is scheduled to go to 72 soon. The percentage of your IRA that the government requires that you begin to accept, annually, from your IRA, once you reach a certain age, is called the "minimum required distribution" or MRD for short. Once you reach the specified age, if you fail to withdraw this minimum required distribution from your IRA, each and every year, you can face government penalties. You would think that all investment companies perform this annual deduction on your behalf automatically; but I found this was not necessarily the case. I was dealing with Paul's account, which was with Wells Fargo. I was very frustrated by it and moved the account to another company. Once you make the initial withdrawal, you should be able to set it up in such a way that it happens automatically each year, so that you don't have to think about it. If you want to continue contributing to your IRA after that point, you can still do that only if you are earning some income. In fact, what I did a couple of years was that I contributed to Paul's IRA the same amount that was taken out, so that it had no effect on the balance. We didn't need the money at the time, and there is the tax advantage to having money in there. You cannot contribute more than you actually earn, so one of the members of the household must have some earned income that year. Income from investments does not count. It must be actual paid work and I had some from acting. There is not a minimum required distribution for Roth IRAs.

There are many different ways that your IRA money can be invested. It can go into mutual funds, annuities, bonds, or many other forms. My financial advisor advises against variable annuities, because of their fees. Talk to an investment advisor that you trust, or a company that has a good reputation. Ask your friends. Check online for ratings.

Stocks, Commodities and Bonds

These investments can be part of an IRA portfolio, or separate. The advantage of having them separate is flexibility. You can buy or sell anytime, without being concerned about age or limits. The disadvantage is paying yearly taxes on profits. *Never invest anything in the stock market you can't afford to lose.* You must decide whether you are simply experimenting for extra money and fun, or whether stocks, commodities, and bonds are some things you're going to invest heavily in and study. Never invest heavily with one person or company. Think of Bernie Madoff. Don't put yourself in a position where you can't ride a market downturn. Even stocks that are "AAA – rated" can suddenly plummet, such as Fannie Mae/Freddie Mac in 2008.

You can, of course, save for retirement on your own; but you will be paying a significant amount in taxes. CD's lose money, by the time you pay taxes on them. No matter how you save, set up automatic monthly transfers into an account.

Material Objects

To avoid taxes, another venue that some people pursue is investing in material objects that they think will acquire value. This is risky. For example, baseball cards were a very hot collectible in the 1980s; but, for the most part, they are pretty worthless today. I fell into that trap. Fortunately, only for a few hundred dollars. Many antiques went down in value, once Ebay came along and people could buy them from all over the country. On the other hand, some very special collectibles that are quite rare do continue to increase in value; and you're not paying taxes on them, while that value is increasing. You just might have to pay taxes on them when you sell them. I would say that you should only invest in objects if either you're very knowledgeable about the subject, or the main reason you're buying them is because you enjoy them, and the possible increase in value is a secondary consideration.

Medical Savings Account

If you're still working, you want to contribute as much as possible to your medical savings account (MSA). If you are lucky, your employer may match your contributions. The money will then grow, tax-free, and it will be available to use for a wide array of medical expenses. It's inevitable that, at some point, you will need it. Talk to Human Resources.

If the place where you work offers retirement plans, then, by all means, take advantage of it, to the greatest extent that you can comfortably afford. If you're already retired, work with a financial planner. You'll be glad, afterwards, that you did. When you retire, you may have to convert your retirement account to an IRA. Talk to your financial advisor about that.

Financial Tips

Hopefully you have planned ahead, and you have enough money for your everyday needs. Sometimes, though, you have special expenses, such renovations, purchase of a vacation home, moving into assisted living, etc. So, what is the best way to come up with a chunk of money?

Using Your Real Estate for Cash

What is a reverse mortgage? If you are having a pressing need for money, you may consider a reverse mortgage. The way it works is you essentially sell your house to the bank, in return for being able to stay there the rest of your life for free. That sounds tempting, but there are better ways to raise money. The primary downside to a reverse mortgage is that nothing is left for your heirs. I admit that I haven't looked into reverse mortgages in detail, because they have a bad reputation. My nephew found it worked for him, but he is relatively young.

In my opinion, a better option is a home equity line of credit. This is a flexible option. If you own a home or condo, you can use your property as your asset to establish the line. You are given a set credit limit, which is a percentage of the value of your property. Unlike a conventional loan, where you borrow a specific amount and pay interest on the full amount, you take the money as you need it, and you are only charged interest on the amount you actually use. You don't need to re-apply when you need more money, as long as you don't exceed the maximum value of the line. You simply transfer the money, as you need it, into a linked checking account. The bank receives the interest, and if you do not pay, they can take your property. Of course, you should only consider this option if you think you can reliably make all the monthly payments, which often are relatively low. We used one for years to finance our home remodeling and other major purchases. Yes, ideally you have the cash, but we always figured that if worst came to worst, whatever remained would be paid off when we sell the house. Meanwhile, we would have years of enjoyment from the improvements.

Of course, the downside of this ease is the temptation to let the balance balloon up; so, be sure to set up automated payments that include paying not only the required interest payment but some principal, to reduce your balance. However, if you have a challenging month with unexpected bills, you can just pay the interest that month with no penalty. Actually, we finally paid ours off; but I kept it open, with a zero balance, in case of emergency. That doesn't cost me anything. These lines are not as attractive as they used to be, because you used to be able to deduct the interest from your taxes. Not only are fewer people itemizing, but now, you can only deduct the interest if it is used for a major home improvement. The interest charged is tied into the prime (official rate of interest), and it is variable, but it tends to be low. Do compare banks, as the percentage in relationship to prime is not the same percentage at all banks, and closing costs vary.

Credit Card Tips

One thing you do not want to do is carry a balance on credit cards. The interest rate is 4 or 5 times the interest on a home equity line of credit. Always pay off your credit cards in full each month, if in any way possible. If you need to make a large purchase that you cannot pay off immediately, you will be better off with a loan. You probably get balance transfer offers in the mail. Save them and see if they are needed. They can be a good deal or not. There are several factors you need to look at. The most obvious is the stated rate of interest, which is often zero – at first. So, how can they afford to do it? Not only do they have your money to use, but there is a balance transfer fee. This can be anywhere from 2 to

6 or more percent. The next factor is the length of time of the transfer. If, for example, the balance transfer rate is 4% and the time is only 10 months, your rate is really more like 5%. If it is 2 years, it is equivalent to only 2%. You then have to compare that to your home equity line, if you have one. It's always going to be a better deal than just carrying a balance, but there is another way the credit cards make money. Once your time has expired, you will get a huge jump in interest, and you might not notice. I have done many successful balance transfers.

What I do is wait until I get the first month's bill and see what the minimum payment is. I then set my bank account to pay that automatically, every month, for the specified length of time, and to notify me when the last payment is sent. I then pay off the remaining balance. There is one other problem you can encounter with balance transfers. That is if you plan to use that card for purchases, as well. Call the company, and ask how your payments will be distributed, and what you must do to avoid paying interest on purchases.

Generally now, since recent reforms, your purchases will be listed as a separate amount and if you pay that in full plus your regular minimum on your transfer you will not incur interest charges. However, I recently was charged interest by one card that applied my payment only to my transfer. I believe that is now illegal, but rather than bothering to contact the government I called and got my interest waived and stopped making purchases with that card. It is easier to use a separate card for purchases. Be aware that some card offers have perks that you receive only if you spend a certain amount within a specific, short time frame right after you are granted the account. This is especially true for credit cards linked to airline mileage and/or hotel points. For this reason, those might not be the best for transferring balances.

Be sure to find out if the points you acquire with your card expire. Some do and some don't. I recently closed a card that deleted points after 2 years without any warning. Most of mine do not. I do have one that does, but it states clearly on every bill when the points will expire. I will keep an eye on that and be sure to redeem them before that.

Do not apply for credit cards lightly. I have sometimes made the mistake of saying yes at a checkout counter when being offered a few dollars off my purchase. The problem is, that it will be reflected on your credit report and you may be turned down for a card that you really want. They are programmed to not allow anyone to add too many new cards in a short period of time.

Which Are Better, Credit Cards or Debit Cards?

Debit cards are often necessary for ATMs. If you have trouble with finances, you may want to use them as a form of self-discipline because the money is drawn from your checking account. However, it is not always the case that a debit card will prevent you from over-spending. Some purchases can take 24 hours or more to post, during which time you might withdraw cash. Always check your for "pending" transactions on your debit cards, to more accurately keep track of your remaining balances. You might find it helpful to keep an old-fashioned check book and record your use of your ATM/debit cards. Ask at your bank or credit union; many give those blank check books away. Also, keep in mind that debit cards typically require a p.i.n. for use. If you have trouble remembering a 4-digit code, it might be hard for you to use a debit card.

I prefer credit cards. First, I don't have to keep checking on my current bank balance. Furthermore, some of the cards offer great incentives for use. Some offer cash. This can be in the form of a steady percentage on all purchases, such as Citi Double Cash, which gives 2% back, so $20 for every thousand dollars you spend. Others offer different percentages for different categories, such as groceries or gas. Still others offer rotating 5% categories every quarter. These can be the most lucrative but require effort to keep track of what the current categories are. I keep a list on my computer.

Other cards offer points that can be used for purchases or travel. Some are tied into a specific company. Every large hotel chain and every major airline offers their own loyalty card. Typically, you get one point per dollar for all purchases and a larger number of points when you spend money on their product or company. You can then use your points for free nights, free flights, etc. The initial sign-up usually offers an incentive of many points -- large enough for a complete round trip or hotel night or two. Many have a yearly fee but waive it the first year. Other cards are not tied into a specific airline or hotel. Capital One, and some Citi Thank You cards, for example, let you acquire points and use them for any travel any time, with a point-to-dollar conversion. Between all these, I don't think I've paid for a flight in about 10 years.

Bank Accounts

Most bank accounts pay almost no interest. You can, however, get a better rate of return with online accounts, such as Discover Bank, or by getting a CD (certificate of deposit). If you get a CD, your money is tied up for a specified length of time; so, you must be sure that you won't need that money before then. Do compare rates.

Never pay fees for a checking account. Many banks have free checking, and a few even provide free checks. This is true all the more among credit unions, in which you become a member, rather than a customer. Ask if they have a special account for seniors. Many do.

Be sure to set up overdraft protection. You never want to bounce a check. It's very embarrassing and expensive, and it might hurt your credit rating. If you have overdraft protection, it's like a line of credit. Instead of your check bouncing, the money will be drawn from that line. You pay interest until you have paid it back, which you will want to do quickly.

Another factor to consider is whether there is a minimum which you must maintain in an account to keep it open. Almost all banks and credit unions have a free account without a minimum for seniors, but you have to ask for it. If your account is in the wrong category you can incur high fees for going below the minimum. It's true that the free accounts often do not pay any interest, but the amount of interest you could receive is very little and not worth the risk. If you have extra money, put it in a savings account. Always read the fine print! One other thing you should look out for is avoiding a dormant account. Be sure to make a transaction at least once a year or the account may go to the state. The bank is supposed to notify you but don't count on it.

Stocks and Bonds

It can be fun to play the stock market; but it is a form of gambling. You should never invest money you can't afford to lose. Mutual funds are not guaranteed, but they are considered safer than individual stocks, because your money is spread out among many companies, and the fund is professionally managed. The bond market may seem safer, but if you are using your money for more than a hobby. you should find a good financial advisor. You never know when there will be another coronavirus or other unexpected developments, so don't invest more than you can afford to lose.

Real Estate

This may seem like the safest of all investments, but people, including people close to me, have lost loads of money investing in real estate. Investigate thoroughly. Owning your residence is a kind of long term savings plan, but speculating in real estate otherwise is another matter. Being a landlord can be a huge hassle that sucks up a lot of your time and combined real estate investment options are risky.

CHAPTER 16

Insurance

Life Insurance

Life insurance is a very complicated, and often emotional, matter. You are going to want to work with an agent, if you haven't already done so. Even if you already have a life insurance policy in place, you might benefit from re-evaluating your situation and what you purchased years ago. Most definitely, if you've never purchased life insurance before, you're going to want to consider having it now.

One kind of insurance that I cannot understand why anyone would get is mortgage insurance.

As you pay off your mortgage, you're still paying your premiums; so, you're getting less value for your money. It seems to me that life insurance would take care of this matter. The only reason to have mortgage insurance would be if you are worried that you might lose your income and not be able to pay your mortgage. This is less of a concern if you are retired. If you are worried about your death, then buy life insurance.

There are many variations of life insurance; but the two most common kinds are called "whole life" insurance and "term" insurance. There are also variations such as "universal life", which has been developed since we bought Paul's whole life policy, and which is supposed to be an improvement. It allows you to change the value and payments. This would be something to ask your agent about.

Here is how whole life and term insurance compare. If you get whole life insurance, the way it works is that you pay higher premiums than what the term insurance premiums would be for your age; but, you are stockpiling reserves of money, to be used towards those premiums, as they increase with your age. That extra money that you stockpile can earn you interest, without accumulating any additional taxes. One question I know I had in my mind, that I had to call my company to ask about, was: If someone dies, does their estate get that reserve? *The answer is no.* Your policy statement may say that you have $10,000 in accumulated value -- but if you die, your estate only gets the face value (e.g., $100,000) of your policy. Your loved ones do not get your accumulated $10,000. It is just lost. As you get older, in order to keep your policy in force, you'll have to keep paying a higher amount; so, I don't know that "whole life" is really that good of a monetary value. Every few years, they may ask if you want to increase your payments. Because no one inherits the accumulated value, I *definitely* would *not* overpay more than you have to. However, the one big benefit of a "whole life" policy, is that it does guarantee that --as long as you keep it in force (meaning, you are in compliance with the terms and current on payments) -- you won't be dropped for health problems. For this reason, it is sometimes referred to as permanent insurance. From what I've read, term insurance is actually cheaper. However, I'm glad we got a whole life policy, because Paul became uninsurable at a certain point, and we wouldn't have had any life insurance if we hadn't started early on a whole life policy. As such, the only regret I would have is that what seemed like a fair amount of money in 1980 wasn't very much with inflation today. However, since you readers are older, that wouldn't be that much of a consideration. So, if you are healthy, you might want to consider at least a small policy, for peace of mind.

Term insurance is the least expensive kind of life insurance. It is issued for a specific term of time, and there is no guarantee that it can be renewed after that time. It does not accumulate reserves, and you may be required to have a health exam. They will send someone to your home, if this is the case. I had someone come out once. It just took a few minutes, and it didn't cost me anything.

If you buy term insurance, you want to have it be "level"(i.e., with a set yearly cost, which doesn't increase) term insurance, for a long period of time. Don't buy a 5-year policy; buy a 10- or 15-year policy, for example. It doesn't cost that much more, you don't have to worry whether you will be healthy enough to extend it at the end of the shorter term, and if you die before the end of that time, then your premiums will end, and your beneficiary will get the payout from it. Of course, you may feel that at a certain point in your life, you don't really need to have as much insurance, because your children will be on their own, and your mortgage will be paid off. However, you may want to leave the money to your children as a gift, or to see that your spouse is left in comfort. At the very least, you want to leave enough to pay for your funeral, which can be pretty costly. When my level term was up last year my premium more than tripled and I dropped it because I have made sure my son would have access to my bank accounts upon my death and so wouldn't really need it.

There are some policies that allow you to withdraw money before death for certain situations, such as grave illness; so, that is something to ask about. One other point: Never lie when getting any insurance, because it could prevent a payout. Also, be sure to name not only a primary, but also a secondary beneficiary. Nearly all policies understandably exclude suicide the first year or two.

You see and hear ads all the time for policies that say you will "just answer a few questions," or that you cannot be turned down. If you have significant health problems, you might have to get one of those policies. Those vary, as well. Some say things such as "All you have to do is answer a few simple questions. No exam necessary." In this case, a question might be something along the lines of, "Have you been hospitalized within the last two years?" If you have, you probably can't get that policy. If you have not had any major health problems in the last few years, then you can get one of those policies. However, these policies tend to be pretty expensive. It doesn't seem so bad when you look at the monthly cost; but, when you multiply it times 12, it's a fairly hefty expense. So, in most cases, regular term insurance will be less costly. However, there are policies that will accept you, even with some health problems. Shop around or ask an agent. AARP offers some policies, though they aren't cheap.

When you buy a policy, see if there is some way to set up automatic payments. Generally, the companies are happy to arrange that, to make sure that they receive their money. If you do this, check to see if there is a difference in cost between paying monthly, quarterly, or annually. Very often, if you break it down into monthly payments, you will be paying more on an annual basis than if you paid in a lump sum annually or quarterly.

Generally, they do not accept credit cards for recurring payments, but they will allow them to be withdrawn from your bank account. You don't ever want to forget about paying a premium and potentially lose all the money that you have put into a policy over the years. All our insurance policies have always been set up with automatic payments. It's just that much less to worry about. You might consider having an overdraft policy on your checking account, if you are concerned about not being able to make an automatic payment.

Buy your insurance while you're healthy. Currently, under the health insurance legislation instituted by the previous administration, you cannot be turned down by health insurance for pre-existing conditions. However, you may be limited to costly policies; and one never knows how the laws might change. Keep in mind that, once you have an active policy, the life insurance provider cannot cancel on the basis of your health problems. This is one reason why people buy whole life insurance. We bought our whole life policy right after we married. If I had tried to buy life insurance once Paul began to have major health problems, it would have been difficult or costly. Besides our whole life policy, I also had a policy that I carried over from work. In order to have the policy for Paul, I had to have a policy on myself that I didn't really need, since I had good, less expensive term insurance. But it was worth it to have that extra little bit of coverage on him, over the years.

Keep inflation in mind. Fifteen years down the road, what seems like a fair amount of money now might not effectively be that much. Unless you have a large estate already set aside (in which case, you might not need it), do buy your life insurance while you can.

Long-Term Care Insurance

Absolutely everyone should have long-term care (L.T.C.) insurance. The one exception would be if your income is so low you can't afford the premiums. In that case, you might be able to obtain some comparable coverage, if you qualify for your state's Medicaid, varying with the policies in your state's Medicaid.

What is L.T.C.?

Medicare is designed to take care of temporary conditions, whether illness or injury, and does an excellent job of that, overall. It is not designed to handle long-term stays in assisted living or nursing homes. Medicare will cover the first 100 days of care, including therapy. You might also be able to get your Part B to extend therapy for a while, if your therapist documents that "the patient is showing progress". However, Medicare will not pay room and board after the 100-day cap. So, at that time you will be asked if you are going on Medicaid or will be private pay. If you make too much for Medicaid, or if you don't qualify for it on other grounds, or if you don't want someone else controlling your assets, your only choice is then private pay. The average shared room in a nursing home is over $250 a day. That's over $7000 a month! If you want --and can find-- a private room, it will be even more. Your stay in such a facility can go on for years. Who can afford that? If you need a ventilator, the cost almost doubles!

Now, you may be thinking, "I don't want to end my life in a nursing home." But you might not have a choice. I told my husband I'd only put him in a nursing home if it were a temporary stay for rehabilitation. When he went in because he was recovering from West Nile Virus, we thought it was. He was making progress, but then he plateaued; and we were facing the prospect of his possibly being there for years. What can you do? If someone is unconscious, you might face the decision of whether/when to disconnect them from life support. When they are aware and conversing, you do the best you can for them while they are alive. As it turns out, Paul died suddenly from an unknown cause 5 months after arriving there, but his stay could have been for years. Since the U. S., unlike other countries, does not pay these expenses such stays often drive families into bankruptcy.

L.T.C. pays a set amount per day. That means it might not cover everything, but it makes everything much more affordable. In our case, it covered over 60% of the costs, and I could handle the rest, even if it went on for a long time. It was a great relief. I paid the bills and was then reimbursed by the company. It was a little work to set up the initial claim, but then the second month's payment came automatically.

When you are choosing a nursing home, it would be a good idea to check with your insurance carrier. to make sure it is on their list. I didn't think about that, and I was relieved when they said it was an approved facility, and that we did not have to move Paul. Just imagine the added trauma, risk, and expense, if you start out with your loved one at a facility, then find it's not in your network. Most facilities are accepted; but do check. Even if you think the stay is only going to be for a month or two, you never know.

Finding L.T.C..: Many companies that used to offer it have stopped doing so, because it was costing them so much. A couple of companies to check out are John Hancock and Mutual of Omaha. If you belong to a union or credit union, see if they have discounted rates. If you haven't heard of the company before, be sure to check their ratings online.

Pricing: Once you have been given and accepted a quote, it stays the same forever, unless there is a group increase, which actually has been happening more and more frequently the last few years. That is why you want to buy it relatively young. Not only can the unexpected, such as a stroke, happen at any age, but you will get a lower rate by buying younger. I bought mine when I was 49, figuring the rate would be higher at 50, and I'm glad I did. Furthermore, you can be turned down or charged a much higher rate if you have existing health problems, which becomes more likely as you age.

Buying L.T.C..:I suggest using an agent; but know what you want. Once you choose a company, you want to stay with them forever as your money pool grows. *I threw money out paying into an agent-recommended policy for 2 years before I realized it didn't have any home care coverage.* Sometimes there are financial incentives for agents to recommend a particular company, even if it is not the best for your personal interests. Ask your friends if they have someone to recommend. Unlike Medicare supplements, L.T.C. Policies vary widely in features, not just price. Be informed and ask a lot of questions. Here are some aspects to look at:

- How many years are covered? You want, at the very least 3, but more if possible.
- How much is the daily benefit? If the average cost is $250 a day that doesn't mean the policy has to cover all of it, but it has to cover enough that you feel confident handling the rest.
- Is there an inflation rider? What percent? Many policies automatically increase the daily coverage amount, so it keeps pace with inflation. This can be very important.
- How long is the waiting period before the benefits kick in? Once you are old enough for Medicare, you don't need it for the first 100 days, so why pay for that period? If you don't have Medicare, either talk to your insurance rep, or have some money in a bank account, just in case. We had a 20-day waiting period. Once we were both on Medicare I asked if I could change that to 100 days, but the company did not allow that change. However, when they had a rate increase, they offered various options to keep your costs down. That was one of the options offered, and when I made that change our rates actually went down rather than up.

- Is there a shared pool option? This may add to your cost, but it is worth it. If you have, for example, 3 years of coverage, and your spouse is covered, when your benefits have been depleted you can use their pool to double the length of your coverage. True, the spouse would lose some of their coverage, but better to use the money for a definite expense rather than keep it for a hypothetical one that might never happen. Most people do not live long enough to deplete both accounts. I had 2 questions answered recently. First, no, you cannot use the pool to increase daily coverage rather than extend the length of it. Yes, if the pool for one person is not depleted when they die, the balance is transferred to the pool of the other person. That was a nice surprise. Since my husband only used 2 months of his coverage, my coverage has essentially doubled in length.

I believe this is standard for all companies, but ask if your premium ceases when they begin paying a claim. The company actually refunded part of the annual payment they had received for Paul. I continue to pay my premium.

Here is a really important point: What is the coverage for home health care? Most people, given the choice, would prefer to remain at home while being treated. Depending on the illness or injury, that may be possible with skilled care nursing or skilled caregiving. There are a growing number of agencies that will send trained personnel to your home. Depending on the needs, this could be anywhere from a few hours a day to around the clock. My sister-in-law, who was injured in a fall, which could happen to anyone of any age at any time, has really benefited from her home health, and even become friends with her home health worker. L.T.C. policies vary greatly in this area. They may pay nothing for home care compared to what they would pay for a nursing home. Typically, they pay half as much. If you would rather be at home, be sure to ask about this. The one downside is that they will probably require that you use a certified agency and not just hire whomever you want, which, depending on the coverage may even be cheaper. Check with Senior and Disabled Services (SDS) in your state. In Oregon, my niece is an independent contractor with SDS, and she can be hired by anyone qualified by SDS for home health, including loved ones. If you get registered in a state that has this option, you can be paid to provide home health in your own home for your own spouse. Overall, it's probably worth going with a licensed company and getting some reimbursement from your L.T.C., unless you require live-in help. If you do, there are agencies that can place someone.

Realize that it is not always possible to treat someone at home, and don't feel guilty if that is not possible. I had to accept that it was not possible for Paul after the West Nile Virus added so many new health problems for him.

There are many variables that affect L.T.C. costs, but figure around $1,000 to $4,000 per person per year. That can be a challenge for some. The older you are when you get it the more you will pay. If you itemize your medical expenses it is deductible. Oregon recently became the first state to pay for long-term care. Let's hope that becomes a trend.

I considered putting this information in the section on illness, but decided it really belongs with the things you need to take care of when you are healthy. It is incredibly important. I've known too many people in dire straits because they didn't have this coverage.

CHAPTER 17

Important Documents and Enrollments

Here are some documents and other things you should make out while you are healthy.

Wills

Naturally, you want to have a will. You do not want your relatives to fight over your estate, and you do not want them to have to deal with probate court -- the court which decides who gets what. Even if you only have one heir, you still want to have a will to avoid probate court. Because even if who should get what is straightforward, probate court adds months to the process, which could mean that it's quite a while before your beneficiaries can sell or utilize your property. Also, what about smaller items such as jewelry?

You do not have to worry if you have joint ownership with your heir, such as if you have joint ownership of the house or car. If that is the case, then they will inherit it without any problems, and with no transition. However, what about when they die, as well? What about when they want to sell? You need to have contingent beneficiaries. You also do not need to worry, if you have something such as an insurance policy or an IRA with a death beneficiary. If that is specified, then they will not have to go to probate court.

Naturally, you're going to want to specify who gets your house and other property, and who gets the bulk of your possessions. However, you may want to make specific bequests to other people, such as bestowing a particular object to a particular person, or a specific amount or percent of money from the estate. You can have a significant list, specifying gifts, and then say the bulk of the remaining estate will go to the primary beneficiary. This list can either be an addendum to the will or be on the list I talk about in another chapter.

If you are raising a grandchild, you want to arrange for a guardian and make sure they have the money that is needed.

There are things most people might not think about. One is your pet(s). If your animal companion(s) are alive after you, who gets the pet? Is there going to be any money set aside to care for the pet? Some people have done crazy things. There is one cat that is a millionaire, which I personally think is illogical, because so many worthwhile groups could use the bulk of that money. On the other hand, you don't want to give someone a pet who has no money to care for them. If you have a pet, you know that there is a certain amount of expense involved. It's traumatic enough for a pet to lose their owner, without possibly being sent to a shelter. Ideally, someone they are familiar with will agree to take them, if needed, and you should leave them a little money for expenses.

Recently, a friend brought up to me a problem I had never thought about. She wants to leave a large part of the money that she made to her nieces. That wouldn't be a problem, but she is concerned that if she should die first, and if her husband should survive her and remarry, that his second wife could spend a lot of the money, and there might not be any estate left for the nieces. So, think ahead. What are the possibilities? You truly don't know which spouse will die first. Even if someone is in poor health or is older, that certainly increases the odds that they will go first; but people do sometimes experience sudden deaths from various causes. So, consider not only what will happen upon the first spouse's death but what will happen after the second spouse dies. In this friend's case, it seems as if a gift immediately upon her death would be in order.

Be sure that you make copies of your wills, and make sure that a couple of people in the family have the copies. Put the originals in a safe place.

Freewill.com is a possible option if you have a straightforward estate, and that site can also help you get started, thinking about what you want to say. Find an attorney for more complex options. Tip: Don't bother with legal sites that say the first month is free. I tried that and spent a significant amount of time filling out a form, only to find that when I printed it out most of it was blank. You might want to consider a general legal service that has a monthly fee.

A Note on Notaries

If you need a signature, and if you are able to travel, or if more than one signature is needed and all parties can travel, you can normally get notary service for free. Call the bank where you have an account, and ask if they have one available. Banks and credit unions normally do have notaries, and they normally do not charge their own account-holders, though they might have slight charges for others. Check whether your document requires an additional witness. If it does, bring a friend with you; don't count on finding an additional witness. I once tried asking people in the bank lobby, and I was shocked that no one would act as a witness to the signature.An employee finally agreed to do it.

Recently, I went to the bank where I usually get things notarized, and they told me they were between notaries. However, they told me I could go to the Township office, where Senior Services is located, and they would notarize for free. They did. So, this is yet another reason to get acquainted with whoever runs the Senior Services in your area.

Trusts

Trusts are a very complicated subject matter. If you want to have a trust, you have to make sure you have the right one. There are revocable trusts, irrevocable trusts, etc. You want to work with an expert. The point of creating one is to make it easier for your beneficiaries to inherit and to avoid probate and taxes. I spoke with a lawyer, and he told me that I did not need one, because our estate qualified for the Small Estate form. This applies if your estate is under $100,000. This sounds like a low number, but your home, plus any accounts, such as insurance policies and IRAs, that have specified beneficiaries, do not count in that figure. Also, to have to pay estate tax, the estate would need to be millions of dollars. If you do own multiple properties and investments, talk to a lawyer. Setting up a trust is expensive.

Deed Upon Death

The one valuable asset I have is my house. Obviously, if you count that, my estate is worth more than $100,000, and my heir would have to go through probate to get control. If you have joint ownership, such as with a spouse, they automatically take control with no problem. However, my son would have a problem because he is not a co-owner. A couple of experts told me that you should not add an adult child as a co-owner, even if you fully trust them, because if they have any financial problems at any point, your house would then be considered a seizable asset. Instead, the best thing to do is set up a document that gives them ownership of your property automatically upon your death. It cost me $350 to do that, which is much cheaper and simpler than a trust. I had a lawyer draw up a "Deed Upon Death," so that David would immediately own the house and be able to sell it.

I also filled out a form I downloaded from the Secretary of State that does the same thing for my car. If you buy a new property or car, you will want to do that again.

I contacted my bank and made sure that my son would have access to my checking account upon my death.

Medical Power of Attorney

No matter what your age or marital status, you should have one of these. If you are conscious when you go into a hospital they may have the forms available and help you complete them --but what if you are not conscious? I think it's well worth the cost of a notary to have one made out and have copies in locations handy to you and known to loved ones. If, for whatever reason, you are not capable of making your own medical decisions, who do you want to make them for you? This isn't just for "pull the plug," life-and-death decisions. When Paul was in the hospital and unconscious for a couple of weeks, I had to give permission for various procedures, just about every other day. I'm not sure what would have happened if the form hadn't been in the records. We filed at one hospital, when Paul went in for a procedure several years ago; and once it was in the electronic records, it could be sent from hospital to hospital. However, they did also ask to see and copy the original. Fortunately, I had filed it in the little metal, and hopefully fireproof, box, where I have my most important papers. The personnel often asked, "Are you the POA?" That is a common acronym (the person who has the power of attorney) with which it is important to be familiar. There are two types of POA. The first is medical. The second is financial. These might be the same person, or they might be different people.

Financial Power of Attorney

A financial power of attorney allows someone to make financial decisions for someone else, without their presence or signature. While Paul was hospitalized, I was offered a settlement of $300 for a timeshare foreclosure, and I lost the money, because when I went to a notary in the bank, they said that they had to have both signatures. I explained that my husband was in the hospital; but that didn't help. By the time

I found out there was a way around this. It was too late, and I lost the money. If I'd had a financial power of attorney, I wouldn't have lost that money. In order to get a financial power of attorney, you need to have a notary witness the signature of both parties. In addition, you need another witness to the signing. The important thing to know is that you don't have to go to a notary. *The notary can come to you.* When we sold our condo, the realtor arranged for a local notary to come to the hospital to get Paul's signature, as well as mine, since the condo was in both our names. I kept her contact information and called up to arrange for her to come and establish a financial power of attorney.

The tricky part is that such documents require an additional, impartial witness. You would think that in the hospital or nursing home, this would not be difficult to find, as there are so many people around. However, I found that the employees of the institution, at least the ones where Paul was hospitalized, were not allowed to do this. This makes no sense to me, as all they're doing is saying that they witnessed the signature; but that was the policy of the institution. So, if you do need a witness, I would suggest that you call the facility first and ask what their policy is, so you don't waste the notary's time and have to pay them for an unnecessary visit. Our notary was able to provide a witness for an additional fee. Of course, you could bring a friend.

I realized that, in addition to getting a power of attorney for Paul's affairs, it would make sense to have a power of attorney made out regarding myself. I then made out a power of attorney so that if anything should unexpectedly happen to me, my son would have that authority with no problem. For this document, I was able to go to the notary's house, and she charged even less. My cousin who lives nearby came as the impartial witness. One thing you need to specify is that this only applies if you are unable to make decisions yourself. If you don't trust the person completely, don't let them know about it except in your will.

These documents are very important. If you don't have such documents, and if something happens where you are not able to access the Internet, no one else will be able to access your bank accounts, credit cards etc., without a great deal of problems.

The one thing I did not realize is that this power expires when the person dies. There is an alternative known as a durable power of attorney. The durable power of attorney continues the permission after the person has died. If I'd known about that, I probably would have gone that route. So, this is something for you to investigate and consider. After all, there are a lot of financial matters that need to be taken care of after a person dies. I was able to do almost everything important, but it would have been easier if I'd had the durable power of attorney.

Living Will

A living will expresses your desires about what you want to happen in the case of a grave illness. You may be comfortable with simply a power of attorney. However, if you don't have someone to take that power of attorney, or if you're not certain that that person will follow through on your wishes, you may want to make out a living will. This might also be important if, let's say, something happens to you, and the other individual is hard to reach, because they are not there, because they are on a vacation, or for other reasons. The hospital needs to know how you feel about Life Support, and whether you want your life extended if there is little chance of recovery. Hospitals have gotten more reasonable about how they treat patients in those circumstances, and letting them go; but having a living will provides peace of mind.

Special Circumstances

If you have a domestic partner, to whom you are not legally married, you might want to consult a lawyer to see if your state gives you the same access to your partner in a hospital and the same legal rights as those whose partner is legally wed. This is especially true if your partner is of the same sex as you. There have been famous cases in which blood relatives have challenged non-married partners, especially same-sex partners, having rights to make decisions over the health of unconscious life partners. If your lifetime relationship is with someone of the same sex, establishing durable powers of attorney in both medical and financial realms is even more important. If you are raising kids with someone who is not biologically related to them, such as if you and a partner have adopted or foster kids, having a legal paper trail that establishes desired custody relationships after your death can be very important.

Medicare

Be sure to contact Medicare shortly before you turn 65, and enroll right away. You will hear a lot of ads for the 'Medicare Enrollment Period" every fall. That is the *only* time you can change coverage. However, it's important that you realize that, when you turn 65, you are not supposed to wait for that period. You can, and should, enroll whenever your birthday is. Medicare, especially the supplements, is very complicated; so, you will want to work with an agent who specializes in it. If you don't have a recommendation, Google agents in your area, and read the comments. I recommend getting an independent agent, rather than one who works for an insurance company. One important thing to keep in mind is that, if you've been on state Medicaid prior to enrolling in Medicare, once you *qualify* for Medicare, even if you are not yet enrolled in it, you stop having access to the full benefit package that comes with your state Medicaid (which might, for example, include dental benefits). The state Medicaid in which you remain enrolled now serves only to cover any copays for what Medicare covers, and no longer covers what Medicare does not. I will talk more about Medicare in Part II of this book.

Part Two: Surviving

Introduction to Part Two

In the first part of this book, I covered some of the opportunities presented to seniors. Let's face it, though; the older you get, the more you will realize that your conversations with your friends largely revolve around health or other problems.

In this section, I am going to briefly take a look at some of the medical and other problems that are common for older people. Once again, I'm not a doctor; but I'm glad to provide you with a chance to familiarize yourself with some medical terminology and what to expect if you get these conditions. This is helpful, not only for your own experiences; but also because, for example, if your friend should say they have a UTI or a DVT, you might wonder what those things are, but feel reluctant to ask. I'm not embarrassed to reveal what I don't know. My husband Paul, and sometimes other family members, experienced many health problems, so I've asked a lot of questions. In this part of the book are some of the things that I've learned through asking or from experience. If you do have any of these problems, this information can serve as a springboard to do personal research in more detail. You will also find some practical advice I want to share.

I'm also going to share the personal experiences I went through with my husband, Paul. He had so many of the conditions you might encounter, so much of what I will be covering will be based on personal experience. So in addition to providing helpful facts, this will also be a personal memoir.

CHAPTER 18

Avoiding Scams

It's sad that anyone would ever want to scam anyone, but scammers especially target senior citizens. By now you probably have learned to ignore emails that say you have won a contest you never entered, or in which someone begs you for emergency money when they are traveling. It is much easier to believe someone with a sincere-sounding voice, who talks to you on the phone and tries to sell you something. I recently received a call where the caller said "Hello, Grandma". Considering my grandson was one year old, that's quite something. Obviously, the idea is if they do it often enough, they'll find someone who believes them. My friend, who is a police officer, said they then say they need money. Others ask for ransom for someone who is OK. It's despicable. If money is involved, always ask for some private information, such as a contact as proof. If you suspect a scam, one possibility is you can say that you need to check how much you have and will have to call them back, and ask for a phone number. If they provide one, you can then see if it is someone related to you or not; and if it is a scam, you then have a number to give to the authorities.

My advice would be: Never buy anything over the phone that a stranger tries to sell you. The only time you should ever buy anything over the phone is if it is a company with which you have done business before, or a very well-known corporation. Of course someone could claim to be with one of those companies, so be cautious. Never buy back braces over the phone. Even if they are free, do not accept them. Those scams have cost Medicare millions of dollars. Never buy travel packages presented to you over the phone by companies with which you're not familiar. If for some reason you cannot complete the package as described, including the presentations, you will be hounded for years, not only by that company, but also by other companies to whom they have sold your information. I found this one out the hard way.

One of the most common scams is someone saying there is a problem with your computer. They claim to be from tech support. Don't fall for it. Just hang up. The most famous scam is the "pigeon drop". Someone on the street claims to have won or found some money and is going to share it with you,

but you have to give them some money for some reason.

Another bit of advice dealing with people over the phone is never say "yes". If, for example, they ask "Is Helen there?" Never say, "Yes." Just say, "This is Helen." The reason is that they can clip together a recording of your voice saying yes and attach it to a proposal for whatever they are trying to sell, and then play that recording back to you and convince you that you owe them money. If it is a robocall, it's better to ask, "Who is calling?" A bot won't be able to answer.

A common scam is utility companies calling and promising to save you money by switching providers. They may call or even have a table in a public place with gifts as an incentive to stop by.   Their introductory rate may not last and may wind up costing you a lot more money. It couldn't hurt to take a brochure and research them. Do not sign anything.

Others include verifying purchases you did not make, most commonly on Amazon or threatening legal actions by government agencies. These are always scams.

Two other types of scams for which to be vigilant are that some "charities" are not legit; and some legit charities take most of their fundraising and give it to administrators. If you're not already familiar with a group calling itself a charity, be sure to look them up online and see what percentage of the money goes to actual programming, and what is their overall rating. There was one organization that called me with breast cancer in their name, and I did not recognize the organization, so I told him to call back the next day. When I looked them up online, it turned out that only 10% of the revenues went to actual programming. When they called back, of course I did not donate. Be careful. An excellent way to check them out is to go to guidestar.org, which rates charities.

If you get an email that claims to be from a company with which you do business, and it tells you to click on a link or call a phone number to solve a problem, *do not click on the link. Look at the URL of the link. It probably will not even include the name of the company in it.* See what the full email address is by clicking on that address, if it isn't already visible, and you will almost always see an odd address that isn't from that company. If you think that you really do need to contact that company, which is always possible, go to their website and contact them directly.

If you have an elderly relative and are worried about their mental stability or think that they may be getting Alzheimer's or other forms of memory loss or cognitive decline, try to become a co-signatory to their bank or credit union accounts, and require a double signature on all checks, to prevent them from being scammed. There have been stories of people whose entire bank accounts were wiped out by scammers. If you can become someone's fiduciary representative, I would suggest changing the numbers on their bank accounts so they cannot give them out, and contacting their credit card companies and telling them that they have to have your approval before they make any purchases.

Another type of scam involves checks. Someone claims they need to pay you for a service or an item that they are purchasing. They then inform you that, for whatever reason, they need to send you a check for greater than the amount of the purchase. You are then to send them a check for the difference. The check they send you may seem completely legitimate. It may even be in the form of a money order. However, it is almost certainly a scam. Never accept payment for more than the amount of the purchase. You will find out later that the check or money order is not legitimate. This once happened to me, and I reported it to the police; but they said that because I had caught on to the situation and had not lost any money, it was not categorized as a crime. That's a shame. It is certainly an attempted crime, and whoever tried to do this to me probably successfully bamboozled someone else.

If you see an unfamiliar number on your caller ID, and they do not leave a message, do not bother calling back. Spoofers can put any number as the Caller ID number. I always assumed these were unused numbers, until they recently chose my number. Dozens of people started calling me back. If it were legitimate, the caller would leave a message. If you have anything other than a traditional landline, you can block the number, so they can never call with that number again. If you don't know how to do it, ask your carrier. You just go to "recent calls," and scroll down to "block this number". You can even buy a call blocker that plugs into your landline phone. I have one and derive great satisfaction from hitting the big red button during the call, rather like "The Gong Show." While it has not eliminated 100% of spam calls, it has dramatically reduced the number that get through. I bought it on-line, I believe through QVC.

If you are targeted for **scams via the US Postal Service**, you may report the fraudulent attempts. Here are the instructions on contacting the US Postal Inspection Service, from the post office's website: Call 1-877-876-2455. Visit www.uspis.gov to report suspected fraud online. To learn more about mail fraud or to report suspected fraud, visit the U.S. Postal Inspection Web site at www.uspis.gov.

If you are targeted by **scams via email**, here are instructions from the website of the Federal Trade Commission: Report Spam: Forward unwanted or deceptive messages to: your email provider. At the top of the message, state that you're complaining about being spammed. Some email services include buttons you can click to mark messages as junk mail or report spam.

If you are targeted by **scams via phone,** here are instructions from the website of the Federal Trade Commission: Report Phone Scams.

If you've lost money to a phone scam or have information about the company or scammer who called you, report it at ftc.gov/complaint.

If you didn't lose money and just want to report a call, you can use a streamlined reporting form at donotcall.gov.

Report the number that appears on your caller ID — even if you think it might be fake — and any number you're told to call back. The FTC analyzes complaint data and trends to identify illegal callers based on calling patterns. They also use additional information you report, like any names or numbers you're told to call back, to track down scammers.

They take the phone numbers you report and release them to the public each business day. This helps phone carriers and other partners that are working on call-blocking and call-labeling solutions. Your reports also help law enforcement identify the people behind illegal calls.

If you are ever uncertain about any company, go to your browser's search bar and put in the name of the company or organization along with the word "scam" and see what results you get.

If anyone asks or demands money you don't owe, even if they say they are with a government group, call the police.

CHAPTER 19

When to Stop Driving

There is no easy answer to this question. We have all heard horror stories on the news about an older person who obviously should not have been driving, and who steps on the accelerator instead of the brake and drives right into a store, or even worse, kills somebody. I think that is a great fear for a lot of older people. I cannot tell you a specific age when people should stop driving, because everybody is different. When I was young I remember thinking that no one over 80 should be driving, but I now know many people in their 80's who are as sharp as many people half their age. Several years ago I attended a college reunion in Champaign and met a woman who was 100 years old. She lived independently and had driven herself to the meeting. While it's true that the traffic in Champaign isn't what it is in Chicago, I was still amazed. The best part was that she seemed perfectly capable of doing what she did.

This particular woman was far from typical. Many states require that if you're over a particular age, such as 80, when your license gets renewed you must take a road test. Some even require the tests more frequently. Personally, I think that's a great idea. Taking a written test really wouldn't tell anyone much of anything. So that is one way some people wind up ending their driving, because they don't feel up to the test or fail it and their license does not get renewed.

Causes

Why is it that older people are more likely to have accidents? When you are older your sight or hearing might be diminished, or your reflexes might be slower. Also you might not react to emergency situations, such as if the car in front of you pulled into traffic in front of you, as quickly as you should. Also, the older you get the more likely that you might have a medical condition or be on medications that could affect your driving ability. As your corneas thicken with age, you might have trouble seeing and reading road signs or obstacles at night.

Signs

Some signs that you might consider giving up driving would be first, if you have more than one fender bender, small accident, or near miss in a six-month period. Another might be if you find yourself getting honked at a lot. Another would be if your passengers or your family express concern about whether you should still be driving. Finally, if you yourself feel nervous about driving when you get in the car, then maybe it is time to stop.

Solutions

In some cases it may not be necessary to completely give up driving. Depending on what the problem is, limiting driving to daytime or short distances or not using expressways may take care of the problem. This can also be a good way to gradually get used to the idea of not driving. If memory, sense of direction, or the ability to read street signs is beginning to be a problem, get in the habit of using directional apps or a GPS all the time, even if you are sure you know the way. Be sure to program it so it gives spoken instructions and you don't have to look at it.

Of course, it isn't just a matter of you and how you feel, it can be a matter of how do you convince someone else you care about that they need to stop driving? It isn't easy because driving gets very tied up with ego. It hurts your ego and your sense of independence to have to give up driving. I know it was difficult for Paul. The day he realized he could no longer predict his seizures, he gave up driving. It's funny, but the hardest part for him was selling his car. I think that made it much more final than just cutting back on his driving. He kept his license in case he just moved the car or something, but was one of those who knew he shouldn't take the road test; and so when his license was up for renewal, he switched to a state ID.

As I pointed out to him at the time, you could take as many taxis as you want, whenever you want, and it still would not equal the cost of maintaining a car. And of course today, there are Lyft and Uber whenever you want to get somewhere. I have a cousin who has a regular driver she calls when needed. Your local senior service provider may offer special transportation for you. If you are handicapped then there's definitely going to be a service that will provide transportation for you at little or no cost.

Taking the Keys Away

In terms of telling other people to stop driving, sometimes it can create quite a bit of antagonism, and you may have to be forceful. After my dad retired, largely because of health problems, my parents spent every winter in California. My generous brother and sister-in-law provided a condo and a car for them to keep there, so they could simply fly out and not make the long drive from Chicago. After several years, the whole family became concerned about my father's ability to continue driving but didn't know what to do about it. They convinced him to limit his driving to short, daytime trips by pointing out that even if he didn't care about himself, he might hurt someone else. One winter, my parents arrived in California, and the car was gone. That was the end of my father's driving. By the time he got back to Chicago, after not driving for several months, he no longer had confidence that he could do it and gave his car to me. Most people are not in that position of being able to take away someone's transportation, so it may take quite a bit of persuasion. If you want to get advice about this, I suggest going to the AARP website, where they have information on this topic. They talk about how to best manage the discussion and how to find specialists that will help you evaluate the ability to drive.

CHAPTER 20

How to Pay for a Medical Problem: Medicare and Insurance

Medicare

Selecting the Medicare plan that works best for you can be an overwhelming task. If you don't want to deal with it yourself you can either find an insurance agent that someone recommends or you can google and contact the SHIP (State Health Insurance Assistance Program) for your state and an impartial volunteer will help you.

I have known people who have lost their houses because of medical expenses, so it is crucial that you know how you are going to cover what could be millions of dollars of medical bills. If for some reason you have bills that are not covered by insurance medical providers so have payment plans and even a fund to reduce bills if you ask. Hopefully, you will not find yourself in that position.

Let's assume that you have qualified for and enrolled in basic Medicare. You have, hopefully, also chosen a supplemental policy to pay the other 20% percent Medicare does not pay. Here is a look at some things that you need to expect, and some tips.

Most medical providers accept Medicare, but not all. Before going to a new doctor or medical facility, it is important to call and verify that they do accept it. Be sure, of course, to bring your insurance card with you. You're going to want to keep that in your wallet all the time, anyway. After all, what if something should happen, and you suddenly have to go to the hospital? Be sure to always also have with you your photo ID and information on your supplemental. For some reason, they always seem to ask for that, as well.

Your supplemental should be linked to your basic plan. You should not have to contact them directly, because Medicare will automatically bill them after they have paid their part. You will get an EOB (explanation of benefits) from Medicare, and you will find that they have not covered the entire amount. Don't worry, because they have billed your supplemental for the remainder. So, the only statement that you really have to be concerned about is the one from your supplemental, which typically will leave you with a zero balance.

Medicare Part A is free, once you and/or your spouse have earned your forty quarters and enrolled. However, Medicare part B is not free. You must have part B. Part A only covers hospitalization. Part B covers doctors, whether it be in their office or in the hospital. The cost for part B is typically around $150 - $200 a month. If you receive a Social Security check, this payment will be automatically deducted from your Social Security check once you are enrolled. If you do not receive Social Security, as, for example, I don't, you will receive a direct bill. You have the option of having it automatically deducted from your checking account or paying it by credit card. If you know you will reliably pay it, you can do either one. If you are worried that you might forget to pay the bill, then go with the checking account. I personally pay by credit card every quarter and get the credit card points. I pay the bill the day it arrives, even though you have the option of waiting a couple of weeks. You never want to be without your medical coverage. Of course, you will also be paying for your supplemental policies if you do not have a Medicare Advantage plan. That is your regular supplement and your

Part D prescription supplement. So Medicare Bills can add up to quite a lot. However, having adequate coverage is a necessity.

For most things, Medicare is extremely easy to use. Once you have given your information to your doctor's office, you're all set. If you have an HMO, you will have to pay a copay every time you go to the doctor, and you can only use your benefits at an office that is in your assigned network. If you go with a PPO, you just walk out without paying any bills. The most important difference between an HMO and a PPO is that the HMO limits you to network providers, dictating which doctors you can see, while a PPO allows you to see any doctor you want. So why do people use an HMO? HMOs cover some things that PPOs don't.

Medicare Advantage plans, or Medicare Part C, many of which are PPOs, will often cover things such as dental insurance, prescription, over the counter medications, vision, and gym memberships, and a growing number cover hearing aids. I recently switched to an Advantage Plan. Here is an important tip: I was assured that if I am unhappy about the change anytime in the first year I can switch back to a traditional supplement. That encouraged me to give it a try. I made sure that all my doctors are in their network. If I should go to one that is not, I just have a co-pay of $35 or so, but I do not have any monthly premium for the plan, just Medicare part B. So I save money every month. If you have frequent doctors visits or hospital stays you may not save much and some people prefer knowing they won't have any hospital bills. The one thing I didn't like is that Advantage plans push you to go to a major pharmacy chain. However, I can continue to go to my local pharmacist (yes we still have one in town) if I am willing to pay $15 for a month's supply of my main drug,instead of getting it for free, and I am. I had asked my insurance agent a few years ago about switching to an Advantage plan and he was negative about it, so I didn't. When I told him last year that I was switching and thanked him for past help, he told me that the reason he had dismissed them is that he wasn't licensed in IL to sell them. So, as nice as your agent may be, look out for yourself and get varied input in making these important decisions. Keep in mind that sometimes the "advice" people give you is self-serving, more for their benefit than your own.

One feature of my Advantage plan that I do often take advantage of is Silver Sneakers. I get a free membership. There are in-person classes, but what I use as a supplement to my Park District class is the online feature. There are multiple classes offered every day you can participate in from home. Each class lists the level of difficulty to help you select. I sometimes attend a full class or sometimes just do 15 minutes of one. In addition to live classes they have recordings you can access at your convenience.

I am going to talk about some of the things you'll have to deal with if you are paying for these things on your own and not going through a Medicare Advantage plan. If you have, or are considering switching to, an Advantage plan, talk to your insurance agent, or to someone who has a Medicare Advantage plan. Be sure to ask what your maximum out of pocket is.

The newest feature of Medicare is telemedicine. Sometimes it is difficult to go out to see a doctor. Perhaps you have mobility issues, don't have transportation, feel too ill or have a chronic issue that probably doesn't require an office visit. During the Covid-19 pandemic, people first widely needed to avoid medical offices to avoid contaminating others or becoming contaminated and many medical practices expanded telemedicine. With telemedicine, Medicare will cover the fees for consultation by Skype or similar services, so your doctor can not only talk to you, but see you, while you remain at home, not spreading contagion. Not only are physicians covered, but also nurse practitioners, psychologists, nutrition professionals, and other health care professionals, such as licensed social workers. Ask your health care offices whether this is a service they offer. Ask your insurer whether this is a service they cover.

What happens if you're hospitalized? Medicare may limit the amount of time that you stay in the hospital. But then again, so may some insurance companies. We never had any problem with hospital coverage. After complications from heart surgery, Paul was in the hospital for three months and we never had a bill! In recent years they have penalized hospitals for patients who return too soon for treatment for the same problem. Paul wasn't really there for 3 months straight. He was twice sent home before he was fully well and just wound up back in the emergency room within a couple of days. These new measures are designed to prevent something like that from happening.

One very important piece of information to know, that I had to ask about, is the hundred-day question. Medicare only covers the first hundred days of treatment for a medical problem. I know that sounds like a lot, but if you have a serious illness or wind up in a nursing home, it's often going to go well beyond 100 days.

One very important thing to know is that, when you change to a different level of facility, your 100-day clock starts over. So, Paul, for example, was in a traditional hospital for West Nile Virus, then a long-term care hospital, and then a nursing home. I was concerned that when he arrived at the nursing home, his 100 days would almost be used up. However, I found out that because this was a new level of care, the countdown of 100 days started over. I was not responsible for payments for the first 100 days. Transferring to another facility of the same kind, however, will not restart the count. One good thing was that, when Paul got an infection and was in the hospital for a few days, those days were subtracted from the count. So, if you have a situation like that, make sure they have subtracted those days. After 100 days, I went to private pay, and our long-term care insurance kicked in. Keep careful records, because I had to show the long-term care insurance company that Paul had been there on Medicare for 100 days, before they would begin their coverage. In the section on nursing homes, I also talk about how Medicare Part B can give you an extension on your physical therapy, beyond the 100 days. Just bear in mind that there will be a few days where you do not have coverage, when you enter a new phase of therapy.

Some false information that someone told me was that the 100 days would start over in a new calendar year. The only way the 100 days will start over would be if you were actually discharged for a certain period of time.

Dental Insurance

Unfortunately, original Medicare does not have any coverage for normal dental procedures, vision, or hearing except in cases of surgery. This is unfortunate because your dental health and infections that can occur within your mouth can affect your entire body. Also studies have shown that being deprived of full hearing can diminish brain power.

If you should need a dental procedure due to an accident or other unusual circumstances, it would be worth asking if it is covered. So, should you purchase dental insurance? Some people feel that the cost of dental insurance is more than what you would pay in services. Or you may feel that your mouth is so full of crowns, etc., that there isn't much more to do with your mouth. Unfortunately, an unpleasant surprise that I had recently was to find out the crowns do not last forever, need to be replaced, and are very expensive. I personally recommend you at least consider purchasing a policy. Typically, depending on the level of coverage you choose, you will pay $35 to $65 per month. Even if you only break even, you will not have had to spend all the money at once.

Delta Dental is the most widely accepted dental insurance that there is, and it offers discounts on services, in addition to covering a certain percentage of the service provided. Humana offers a dental discount policy that is very inexpensive and sounds really good, but my dentist is not one of the 26,000 dentists that accept it.

However if you're going to purchase dental insurance, I recommend looking for a policy that also includes vision and hearing. Hearing aids, especially, can be very expensive, even with the new reduction of cost. Two companies that you might want to investigate are Medico and United Commercial Travelers of America. Both of them provide vision and hearing coverage, which can save you a lot of money. Be sure to check with your dentist before you purchase, to see if they accept that insurance. UCT does not require acceptance by the dentist or prior approval of procedures. This is an example of the type of dental insurance available in which, instead of giving your insurance to your dentist, you just pay and then submit the bill to the company and get directly reimbursed. It's worth exploring which option is best for you. You could go somewhere, such as Aspen Dental, that offers a free new patient exam and x-rays and provides you with an outline of a treatment plan, an overview of their recommendations. That will give you a sense of what level of dental insurance might be of most utility to you.

Every company and every policy is different, so compare carefully. One thing you have to keep in mind is that almost all policies do not cover major procedures the first year. They will cover part of exams and cleanings but not, for example, crowns. If you switch companies, you might want to consider paying both for a year, but be sure to cancel the first one at the end of the year. That is a mistake I have to admit making. Another mistake I made was not submitting a bill to my re-imbursement insurance within the time limits, so be careful about that if you choose a policy where the dentist does not bill them.

CHAPTER 21

Prescriptions

I tend to be a bit *pharmaphobic,* a word I think I just made up; but one has to use judgment about taking medications. Some medications are necessary. Others are not. How much, if any, you take is up to your judgment. All medications have side effects, so you have to determine if the benefits outweigh the risks. This comparison is called a "balancing test".

Antibiotics are a serious danger to society. Over-utilization of antibiotics has created "superbugs," -- bacteria that are antibiotic-resistant. Every year, thousands of people die from these bugs, and there is almost nothing doctors can do to help. The biggest culprit in this situation is the practice of giving animals antibiotics preventively. Antibiotics should never be used for prevention of diseases; only for the cure of them. Fortunately, many companies that sell meat are reacting to consumer pressure and shopping preferences and beginning to stop the practice. Another problem is that so many products in our society now say "antibacterial". I personally never buy products, such as soaps, that say they are antibacterial. Simple soap will take care of most situations. I also do not use those hand sanitizers that many people use frequently. There are exceptions; such as when I was on a cruise and they said that there were cases of Norovirus. Actually, I didn't have a choice, because they insisted that every traveler used hand sanitizers before entering the dining room, which, under the circumstances, made sense. Also, some-times, sanitizing wipes are appropriate, in certain situations, such as if you're uncomfortable with using the handle of a shopping cart, which tends to be highly germy.

Personally, I am not too concerned about these things. I do wash my hands -- always -- in the bathroom, or after touching raw meats or other dangerous products. Recent studies have shown that hand sanitizers are not any better than soap. They may also kill good germs. For some people, with sensitive skin, abrasive detergents, and hand sanitizers with too high of a percentage of alcohol (such as 90%, rather than the recommended 60%), can actually induce contact dermatitis, drying out people's skin to the point that it cracks or has an allergic reaction. It is best to see what works comfortably for you. What's important is to understand appropriate hand-washing technique, including scrubbing between fingers, under nails, at wrists, and for at least 20 seconds. If you do use hand sanitizer, you might find that brands that include aloe vera are gentler on your skin, or you might consider using a moisturizer afterwards.

The COVID-19 pandemic has made the use of sanitizers and wipes more commonly necessary. If you are in a situation where you can use soap and water on your hands, you're better off doing so. However, if you are out and, for example, you have just come out of a public building, you may want to use hand sanitizer.

Some people have gone overboard with hand washing. In the height of the pandemic I kept hearing on TV that you need to wash your hands every 20 minutes, and some people do so. This is appropriate if you are in a situation where you are in touch with many germs and potential contamination, but it's totally unnecessary if you are in your house and you or your family are the only ones there.

Another note of caution: Never leave hand sanitizer in a car, nor in any situation where it would be close to a source of heat. It is primarily alcohol and is very flammable.

I was rather shocked, one time, when I called my doctor about a problem, I believe a sore throat, and over the phone, he asked if I would like him to prescribe an antibiotic. I declined that offer and instead went in for an examination. It turned out that I did not have strep and did not need an antibiotic. Antibiotics are only to be used if necessary. They do nothing to fight any illnesses that are caused by a virus.

However, if you do receive an antibiotic prescription, it is essential that you take it for the full prescribed time. In most cases, you will start to feel better after 24 to 72 hours; but if you stop taking the prescription too soon, you will leave the strongest germs alive to multiply.

When it comes to other medications, you have to use your judgment as to how essential that drug is. All drugs, without exception, have some side effects. So, if for example, the drug is for pain, you have to assess your tolerance of pain. It's different for everyone. Recently, I had some dental work done, and the dentist said I would want to take Advil when I got home. Instead of taking the Advil right away, I waited to see if I really needed it. I did not. I first became aware of this problem many years ago when I was single and I had some impacted wisdom teeth re-moved. The oral surgeon prescribed Tylenol #3. I stayed at my parent's house for a couple of days so they could take care of me. Before making the almost hour-long drive home, I decided it would be best not to take any medication. I felt fairly good, got home and took the Tylenol #3, and I immediately began feeling sick again. I then realized it was the medication, itself, that was making me feel lousy. Since then, I have been more careful about my use of prescription and over-the-counter medications.

Unfortunately, some drugs are essential. For example, if you are on anti-seizure medication, you want to be sure to take it all the time, be-cause the seizures, themselves, are dangerous. Not only can they cause falls and car crashes, but they can also destroy brain cells. Sometimes, after a seizure, Paul would lose a memory, and that would bother him. Fortunately, these were minor things, such as a movie he had seen. Paul had a few prescriptions he absolutely had to take, such as his anti-seizure medication and his Parkinson's medications. He would not have been able to function without them. While they were of great benefit, the downside was that they tended to make him sleepy. Doctors often prescribe with a single-minded focus, without bearing in mind all the other prescriptions that someone is on, and they tend to over-prescribe. When Paul was given a mild opiate for his back pain, he found that, in combination with his other drugs, it made him so sleepy that it just wasn't worth it. After a few days, he simply stopped taking the drug and decided he'd rather deal with the pain then do nothing but sit around sleeping. These are the kinds of judgments that you have to make for yourself, when you do that "balancing test".

When I am given a new drug or even start taking something like an herbal supplement, my general policy is to take half of the prescribed amount. If it is a totally new drug, I will take one dose and wait another day before taking the second dose, to make sure that I don't have any side effects. Paul used to do this, as well. In many cases, the half-dose is sufficient to do what the pill needs to do. Very often, doctors do not take into account the cumulative effect of multiple drugs, such as those that Paul was taking. Once you already have one drug in your system that causes dizziness or fatigue, and you add another drug, the effect that those cause together may be intolerable. You always want to ask your pharmacist to check for contraindications, when you add a new prescription medication, over-the-counter medication, or supplement. This is especially important when you have more than one prescriber or more than one pharmacy. My brother said that they sometimes saw patients who were taking double doses of a medicine without realizing it, because one pharmacy filled it under the brand name and another under the generic name.

Sometimes, you may feel that a drug just doesn't agree with you. You're probably right. When I started menopause, my gynecologist prescribed a hormone replacement pill. I was coping and not really complaining. I didn't feel it was necessary, but she prescribed it, so I tried it. I immediately put on several pounds, and frankly, mostly for that reason, I stopped taking the pill after a few weeks. It made me uncomfortable and unhappy and was not really necessary. Shortly after that, studies came out that showed that hormone replacement pills are unhealthy. I'm glad I went with my instincts.

If you listen to TV commercials, you know that every drug does have side effects. One of the questions that you have to ask yourself is how rare are the side effects. For several years I was taking a pill to strengthen my bones. I began to hear information that it actually can destroy your bones and wasn't sure what to do. I then met someone whose jaw actually dissolved from her taking it. That made it very real and certainly made up my mind. When I spoke with my doctor, he said, "Oh, it's fine as long as you haven't been on it for more than three years. Oh, you've been on it for five years." If I hadn't said something, he would have kept me on the drug, and who knows what the effects would have been. Don't be afraid to question your physicians about prescriptions.

In all cases, with medications, you have to weigh the advantages and disadvantages of taking them.

One of the problems and dangers of taking multiple medications is keeping track of what you have taken and when. There are many simple, inexpensive aids for this, available at any drugstore. There are pillboxes where you can lay out an entire week's pills. Yes, they take some time to fill, but you would be spending that much time during the week. You're just doing it all at once. You must have a system. Paul marked the top of every bottle as to how many times per day he would take it. He knew that a.m. meant at breakfast and night meant bedtime etc. As he was taking them, he would set them to one side of the counter. This was a good system, though not perfect, and occasionally he would be uncertain if he had taken something. I encouraged him to buy one of those week-long pill layouts but he did not do that. Fortunately, he never had a serious problem from that, but it could happen.

A Prescription Question Checklist

However, here is a checklist of some questions you are going to want to ask about prescriptions. Be sure to bring a list of your current drugs with you, even if you think the doctor has one. Be sure to include not only prescriptions, but any over-the-counter drugs or supplements you take on a regular basis.

New Prescriptions

What is the purpose of the medication?

What are the side effects, both likely and rare? Which side effects, or potential adverse/allergic reactions, at what level would indicate (A) that I should call you to evaluate whether I should stay on the medicine; (B) that I should immediately stop taking the medicine; (C) that I should go to the emergency room?

What is the best way to take it? With or without food? Times of day?

Has the doctor checked the list of all other medications being taken? Are there possibilities of interaction or duplication?

Can the prescription, if it is a long-term one, be written for 90 days rather than 30? That saves effort and money.

What are the consequences of not taking this prescription? If I were to have to stop taking it, for any reason, does it require a taper-down (gradually taking a little less of it at a time, rather than being safe to suddenly quit it)?

How long until the medicine begins to take effect? How long before I will be able to notice the benefit?

Old Prescriptions

If you have been taking prescriptions for a while, once a year or so it is good to review them with your pharmacist and physician.

Based upon your current conditions, is this prescription still necessary, and is the dosage still the most appropriate one?

Are there new drugs that are considered better for the condition?

Is there a recommended limit as to for how long this drug should be taken? See my story earlier in this chapter.

Are there interaction possibilities, based upon other drugs, herbs, or supplements that may have been added since the drug was prescribed?

Never take drugs without asking all these questions.

CHAPTER 22

Mobility Issues

As people age, they are more likely to have mobility problems; in other words, problems walking. A recent study just of middle-income seniors estimated that 60% of them will eventually have mobility limitations. These problems may be temporary or chronic.

Temporary mobility issues may be caused by either injury or recovery from surgery. In either case, you will be under the care of a physician and have guidance on how to handle the problems associated with this new stress. Be sure to follow all the instructions of your doctors and therapists thoroughly, and do not try to push yourself to do more than is safe. Not healing fully from one surgery has often caused people, including ones I've known, to wind up having another surgery. This is especially true for any part of the legs, such as knees.

More insidious are chronic conditions that cause mobility problems. These can creep up on you gradually, and some people stubbornly refuse to acknowledge how serious the problem is. Falls can cause long-term disabilities and even death. Some conditions that can cause mobility problems include Parkinson's, arthritis, heart problems, joint problems, and reactions to drugs.

If you have chronic problems you may want to consider modifications to your house. There were some things we did that helped significantly. The easiest step was to change out some of the chairs.

One of Paul's most difficult problems was getting up from a chair and pivoting in another direction. This was helped greatly by using swivel chairs both inside and outside the house.

We also installed a small railing next to the chair he usually sat in on the porch, so he could hold on as he stood and as he took the step up to get in the door.

The second-easiest and least-expensive aid is to add grab bars in critical places, such as at corners of rooms where you may be turning, and in bathrooms. There are companies that specialize in this type of renovation process, and it may be covered under Medicare (check your plan's Durable Goods provisions), but you can also have a handyman install them. Do not waste your money and time or risk your health with grab bars that use suction cups. Grab bars need to be screwed into the wall, or they could actually make a fall worse, if they disconnect under your weight. Yes, when you go to sell your house and remove them, that will leave holes; but those holes can be filled in. Grab bars in showers are helpful for everyone and should be left in place.

He found that, once he could hold on with both hands, he was able to navigate the stairs without any help. I originally thought all changes would be removed, whenever the house goes on the market; but while I did remove the center rail, I kept the round hold rail that was installed with it and added one on the other side. So far, I have also left the little railing we added to the right of the door as you look at it. I sometimes put a beverage on it when I'm in the chair next to it.

People who have trouble walking, or especially going up stairs, will usually also have problems getting up out of chairs, particularly soft ones. Fortunately, there is a wonderful aid to help with this problem. It is known as a lift chair. I have seen lift chairs advertised for $1200, but we purchased one at a local furniture store for about $400, which is about what you would pay for an ordinary recliner.

The lift chair does recline, too; but the difference is it also goes forward to raise

up and lift you up, so that you are in a standing position when you leave it. It uses a remote control and a power cord, which is plugged into the wall. It moves very slowly, so that you are not thrown out of the chair. Sometimes, Paul found that slowness to be frustrating, but it is an important safety feature.

Before we bought it, sometimes when I had plans when Paul was having a bad day, I would worry about leaving. Paul would say "Don't worry I'll just sit in the recliner and watch TV while you're gone." I would then say "What if you have to get up to go to the bathroom or something?" Once we had the lift chair and his rollator (a type of walker) nearby, I didn't have that worry.

Here are a couple pictures of the lift chair and its reclining position and its standing position.

You can see how easy it would be to get out of it. You can also see how it blends in naturally with our regular recliner. Depending on the nature of your mobility impairments, you might be able to get a physician's order for a lift chair, to get it covered as Durable Medical Equipment on your Medicare. It's well worth the attempt.

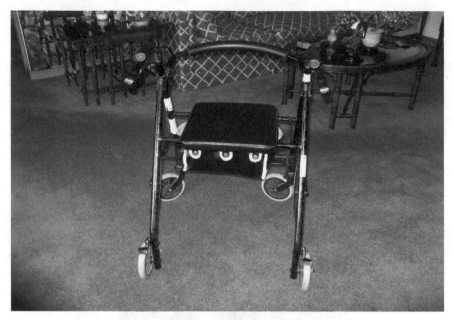

This is a rollator. There are various models and sizes. Paul's had a flip up seat and no storage compartment. There are brakes in the handles.

Mobility Devices

As Paul's mobility problems progressed, he started by first holding onto furniture when he walked, then using a cane, and then pushing the rollator.   Eventually, for longer walks he sat and used a motorized mobility scooter. Getting someone to use these aids may require ingenuity and persistence. It was a relief to get Paul to use aids, as he kept falling and broke an antique table and a spinning wheel. We would sometimes be late for engagements, because he fell down on the way to the car and it took a few to several minutes to get him up. By luck and lack of osteoporosis, he did not suffer anything more than bruises. He refused to use a walker because he thought it made him look old. I went to the township lending closet and signed out a rollator, figuring I could return it if he refused to use it. I told him to just try it for a day -- and it never went back. He later called it a "lifesaver". I'm going to talk a little bit about mobility equipment and the options available for them.

There are various kinds of canes, A basic cane is simply a wood or metal object that helps support you. However, there are variations. There is a tripod cane that may be prescribed for you, but this is basically only for navigating stairs. It is not convenient for walking. Some commercial canes have a slightly wider base, so that they will stand when you let go of them and you do not have to reach down to pick them up. This can be not only convenient, but also a safety feature, as bending over to pick one up can throw you off balance. Some of them also have a small handle under the main handle, so that you can use two hands to help pull yourself up. A favorite of ours was a folding cane. One of the good things about a folding cane is that if you go to performances, such as movies, plays, or concerts, you don't have to worry about your cane sticking out into the aisle and tripping someone. You simply fold it up and put it on your lap. Even when Paul was using a mobility scooter, he would take the folding cane along on the floor of the scooter, so that when he transferred to a seat at the theater, he would have that to help him get into his seat and then put it on his lap. The usher or I would put the scooter in a safe place.

If a cane is not enough, you may want to use a walker. I'm sure you have seen people with metal walkers, and those come in two kinds. I do not recommend the simplest and least expensive, which is the kind which does not have wheels. That necessitates slightly picking up the walker, every time you want to move forward. These are sometimes used for therapy, but they are really not practical to use at home. The standard walker does have wheels on the back two legs, and/or its front legs, and I have seen people put tennis balls on the other two legs to make the whole thing easier to use. Walkers will be paid for by Medicare as DME (Durable Medical Equipment), and they do fold up and are lightweight, so they are easy to put in a car.

Most people today prefer a rollator. Paul would not use a walker but got used to the rollator. A rollator is less noticeable, because they are generally cushioned with black vinyl rather than being plain aluminum, and they look a little more elegant. They also have a great advantage.

They have a seat. So if you are in a situation where you have to stand for longer than expected, or you need to take a break during a walk, you never have to worry about having somewhere to sit. You simply set the brakes on the rollator, which is of course very important, and sit down. For this reason it is important that you test out a rollator before buying it and get one that is appropriate for your height and weight. Rollators do come in various sizes, even though they are adjustable and have different weight limits. I was advised to subtract 50 pounds from their weight limit to be safe. So, for example if you weigh 200 pounds look for one that has a 250 pound weight limit, to be safe. You don't want to have it collapse while you're sitting on it. The same advice goes for wheelchairs.

Rollators do fold up and go in the car, even though they may be a little awkward to get in there. You will have to experiment and see if it fits in best in the trunk, the backseat, vertically, etcetera. Here is a tip for you: I was worried about carrying the rollator down the stairs and the possibility of my tripping on it or falling. I came up with a solution. We bought a second rollator, which we kept in the car all the time. So we had one in the house, which was the heavier one, and depending on how Paul was feeling that day, we would either just leave it in the house, and he'd walk across the porch to the stairs; or if necessary, he would roll out to the stairway, and I would bring it back into the house. Then I would have a car pulled up in front already and get out the car rollator, which I would put at the bottom of the steps. Of course, I'd make sure that the brakes on the rollator were set. So, I never had to worry about injuring myself, carrying a rollator down the stairs. It was well-worth the hundred dollars or so that I spent on the second rollator. Rollators are something that you can buy used. There isn't much to break down on them or go wrong. There are stores that sell used medical equipment, and that is where we got our second one. Check with your senior services to see if they have walkers and rollators available, or check ads and online. Sometimes the ones in catalogs are pretty overpriced. Be sure to comparison shop.

I just saw an ad for a rollator that looks like a big improvement, compared to traditional ones. I was very impressed with everything they said in the ad about how traditional walkers and rollators can cause back problems, while theirs is ergonomically preferable. So, if you're looking for one, I would check this one out. It's called Perfect Walker II. Call 1 (888) 233-1968. I do not have any personal experience with it, but everything they say makes sense.

For longer distances, it might not be possible for a person with any rollator to walk that far, and you may want to consider a mobility scooter. These can be a wonderful convenience. We used ours frequently. We kept it in the car trunk, and if we happened to pass a park on a nice day, we could just get it out and have a walk around the park. We also found that it was useful as a substitute for renting a wheelchair, at places such as museums and zoos. Most often these public places will have wheelchairs available, but they will be manual and require that somebody push them. This gets very tiring, and if there are hills, it can be difficult pushing them up, and very scary going down with them. If you have your own scooter, you don't have that problem.

There are three kinds of mobility scooters. The first is a permanent one, which is not meant to go inside a car. These can be used for people who are simply navigating around the house or in a complex around their neighborhood. They can also go into a van with a lift, as they are too heavy for a person to lift. They are the most expensive, but they are also the most comfortable and have the longest range. The combination of the scooter and the lift will be at least a few thousand dollars.

There are two kinds of portable mobility scooters. The first kind breaks apart and reassembles. The advantage of this kind of scooter is that no part is too heavy for one person to lift. The disadvantage is that it can take a few to several minutes to reassemble them. Our first one was this kind, and Paul said he didn't want to travel with it because he didn't want to cause a delay with a taxi or bus while we assembled it. We preferred a folding scooter. With a folding scooter, you press the button, and the scooter folds up flat, so that it can go in a car trunk. People often marveled about how our scooter was like a Transformer. I would press the button, and it would open up. The disadvantage is that even a lightweight one, such as the one we had, weighed 42 pounds. While I was able to lift it out of the trunk and lower it, even if not easily, I was not able to lift it to put it back inside. I was dependent on someone coming by and offering to help. Rarely was this a problem. Sometimes people did not offer, and I would simply approach someone who looked like they were able to lift 42 pounds and ask. I never had a problem finding someone to help me. One time we got our scooter into a parking garage, and after the performance, we were the last ones there, and I managed to get the scooter inside by tilting it. After that, I kept a step unit in the trunk, to be able to hoist it less distance by hoisting twice, each half-way. Overall, our use of the scooter went very well. People are generally very nice and very helpful. It cost about $2200, which is more than the cost of the type of scooter that breaks apart. There were some less expensive, smaller ones, but Paul was 6'3" and weighed over 200 pounds. If it's for a petite person, you could buy a smaller one for less.

Finally, if a person really cannot walk safely at all, you might need to resort to a wheelchair. There are various kinds of wheelchairs.

When you check catalogs, you might see a type of wheelchair referred to as a transport chair. A transport chair is lightweight and folds up and is, as the name implies, intended to transport people for a short distance, and not for general daily use. In other words, you're getting them to and from a vehicle. A transport chair must be pushed by someone else. The person sitting in the chair cannot wheel themselves.

A traditional manual wheelchair has large wheels, so that they can either be pushed from behind, or the person in the chair can grab the wheels and propel themselves forward. Traditional wheelchairs are fairly heavy and require a van and a mechanical lift to get the wheelchair inside the van. Unfortunately, Medicare does not pay for mobility scooters and does not seem to think that people need to get out of the house and go to a doctor or have recreation. So, if you want a mobility scooter or anything very portable, you will have to pay for it yourself. That is one failing of Medicare.

On a positive note, though, not only will Medicare pay for a manual wheelchair; they will, if it is certified medically necessary, pay for a motorized wheelchair. If you have a motorized wheelchair, no one needs to push you. You can use a little joystick to navigate for yourself. The difference between a wheelchair and a scooter is that a motorized wheelchair is quite compact, while a scooter has a control column with a steering wheel in front of you and takes up more space. The disadvantage of the mechanized wheelchair is that it is heavy, and just like the manual wheelchair, you will need a mechanical lift to get it inside a van.

There are some elaborate variations on motorized wheelchairs that do things such as climb stairs, change height, etc. You can contact Medicare to see if these can be deemed a medical necessity and be covered. Any money you do have to spend on medical equipment is tax deductible, if you itemize.

If you have to use a wheelchair, it is a problem to get it upstairs. Many weigh well over 50 pounds. Traditionally, people have built ramps for this purpose; but ramps have disadvantages. Because the incline has to be gradual to be safe, ramps can take up and eliminate an entire yard, and they might have to be removed before putting a house on the market.

Another possibility is installing an outdoor elevator or chair lift. I was actually looking into this possibility right before Paul died, and I found out that it costs about $8000. Not cheap, but I would think it might be tax-deductible; and if you have home health coverage, it might be paid for with what you don't pay for a nursing home. If the person could be cared for at home (Paul was not at that point yet), it would be worth it to them. Some special options are available within Medicare, Medicaid, and Veterans' Benefits to assist with funding modifications to the homes of patients in need of mobility assistance. Those with physicians' orders requiring a ramp, for example, could submit the costs of the ramp under coverage for Durable Medical Equipment. Find an excellent summary of that information here: https://www.payingforseniorcare.com/financial-assistance/wheelchair-ramps-medicare.

Airports

When you travel, airports can be a big issue. Walking around an airport can require the ability to walk for a mile or more. This isn't an issue if you are a full-time user of a wheelchair you bring with you, but it is if you just have some mobility issues and use a cane or walker. If you are traveling, don't let that deter you. When you make a reservation with the airline, you can request a wheelchair at either end of your flight. There is no charge for this service, but you should tip whoever wheels you around at least five dollars. They will even take you to pick up your luggage and help you with it, stop while you purchase a food item, etc. The more time they spend with you, the larger the tip should be. Do use this service if you genuinely think that you would not be able to walk for the potential mile-long walk in the airport. Never cheat and use this service simply because you want to get priority boarding or are too lazy to make a walk you can make. People have misused this service, and that means that people who genuinely need it have a much longer wait for a wheelchair and attendant. Once Paul purchased a mobility scooter, we preferred to take our own with us. This avoided waiting for someone to show up with the wheelchair, and we felt we had more control over what we did in the airport. You can ride your own scooter or wheelchair all the way down the ramp to the plane itself, where they will take it from you and tag it. It will then be delivered to you as you get off the plane. You will want to bring a cane along for walking through the plane itself. I suggest that, somewhere on the scooter, you have some indication of your name, as there could be similar-looking ones. Be sure to always take the key to the scooter with you on the plane, and never leave the key in the scooter when you check it. This is not so much for concerns about theft as it is about the key getting lost. We always had a duplicate key with us just in case, but you still don't want to lose the key, as they are fairly expensive to replace.

Paul enjoying Florida from his mobility scooter.

Tips on Dealing with Mobility Scooter Batteries

One of the big challenges we faced when Paul got his new mobility scooter was how do we charge it? With the old scooter, which was much more lightweight, we could take it out of the car and plug it in. With this one, which weighed 42 pounds, and was not meant to be taken apart, it was more of a challenge.

After taking it in and out of the car one or two times, I realized we had to do something different. We got an extension cord and connected it to the outlet in the garage and charged the scooter in the trunk of the car.

One thing I had to be careful about was that, if I had the trunk open and I forgot about that and opened the garage door, the door would hit the edge of the lift gate. So I had to keep the trunk closed while charging. I was concerned about putting pressure on the cord, so I would place a cushion, such as a blanket, over the cord after connecting the charger to it, and then close the trunk. This worked out fine, as the way our car was placed, I had to walk around the back of the car to get to the driver's door and would see the cord. If it had been a different situation, I can only imagine what would happen if someone were to pull out of the garage with their scooter still plugged in. Another concern is that, even though your scooter may have a full charge when you put it away, the charge depletes over a period of time. It is important to charge your scooter the day before you plan to use it. Since these devices are intended to be used for special situations and not everyday use, this is something about which it would be easy to forget; so, I recommend putting a note on your calendar to remind you, about each occasion for which you will know you will want to use it.

When we were traveling, he would ride the scooter to the unit, no matter what. We would then just plug the unit into the wall in the room where we were staying.

Another possible solution is to remove the battery to charge it. I spent a little over $100 to purchase a special charger that works with the battery directly. I was afraid that when we traveled, we might come across a situation where there would be steps or other impediments, and we would not be able to get the scooter inside to charge it. Since we looked for places where Paul didn't have to climb steps, anyway, I don't think this ever happened; and it was difficult to remove the battery, so that was a waste of money. On the other hand, it did provide some peace of mind to know that we had that. Of course, when you travel, just as you want to be extremely sure that you bring your phone charger, you want to be sure to pack your scooter charger. I would write myself a prominent note to make sure that I remembered it. You can buy a second battery, if you think you will be using the scooter past its range; but as long as we started out with a full charge, it was never a problem. Be sure to charge your battery fully before leaving, and pack the charger in your carry on, just in case.

One difficulty that we came across, which might possibly be limited to the particular model that we bought, and I have no way of knowing that, is a problem if you hit a bump. When, once or twice, our battery ran out and we were on the perimeter of a park, I simply got the car and pulled up and got the cane out that we always kept in the car. Paul would walk to the car, and I put the scooter inside, and it was not a serious situation. The one time it became something of a crisis was when we were in Florida and in the center of a very large park, with a fully charged battery, and Paul hit a bump. We found out the hard way that a safety feature of the scooter was that, when you hit a bump, it would stop operating. We tried turning it off and turning it back on, the universal reset; but even when we waited a few minutes and turned it back on, that did nothing. Fortunately, I was able to go back to the ranger building of the park, and they had a vehicle, so they could come and get Paul and the scooter and bring us all to our car. Another fortunate thing, as luck would have it: When I called the company from which we had bought the scooter, they told me that their main headquarters was only a few miles from where we were staying. Because we had purchased their scooter and knew it was under warranty, the technician came out to meet me at the car near where we were staying. Paul waited inside, and the technician inspected the scooter and informed me about the safety feature, and that the way to solve the problem was to remove the battery and put it back in. However, I was unable to do that. The technician examined it and found that there was a piece interfering with battery removal. He was able to saw that down and make the removal easier for us. From that point on, I carried a screwdriver with me in the car, just in case I ever had to remove the battery, which, indeed, did happen one other time. So that's a tip for you: If you have a scooter that is not intended to be taken apart, but the battery can be removed, bring a screwdriver or other pry tool with you in your car, just in case.

Out and About with Mobility Issues

There are many places where people who are not normally wheelchair-bound are still going to have problems with mobility, if they are not agile.

Museums, zoos, and parks can require extensive amounts of walking. Nearly all of these places have wheelchairs available for visitors. Occasionally, they may be free; but usually, there is a rental fee. They tend to be manual and not motorized, so you must have someone with you to push you. Do not go alone. Normally, there are enough available that it isn't a problem; but you might want to arrive early in the day, just in case, or call and see if you can reserve one.

Other outings for which it is worth considering mobility issues are plays and concerts. In such cases, it is not so much a matter of obtaining a mobility device, as what to do with the one that you have. When you purchase a ticket for a play or a concert, be sure to talk to the box office and explain your mobility issue. If the representative is experienced, they will ask you the appropriate questions; but they might be inexperienced and not think to ask; so, it becomes your responsibility. You need to find out how many steps are involved in getting to the area in which you are seated. If you arrive in a wheelchair **or** scooter, you have to decide whether you will want to stay in your device, or will you want to -- or be required by the size of the rows of the venue to -- transfer to a regular seat. I know that Paul would arrive in a mobility scooter but then transfer to a regular seat, which he found to be more comfortable for an extended period of time. That means that he needed to have an aisle seat with no steps to get to it. There isn't a problem with the device during the concert, because the ushers are nearly always trained to take them and put them in a specific place. Or your companion can put it in the designated place. Then you can remove the key. And a trained usher will ask if you're going to want to use your device during the intermission. If they don't ask, you may want to raise that issue. Many theaters have a space for wheelchairs and a companion seat next to it reserved for that purpose, for those who are not transferring.

Many movie theater chains also now have designated rows for mobility-impaired moviegoers, with enough space between seats to allow those who prefer to remain on their walker, in their wheelchair, or on their scooter, and for those who prefer to have assistance with a transfer. Many of those same movie theater chains allow you to purchase your tickets in advance and require seat selection in advance. This gives you the safety of knowing you will have a seat in the correct row, if attending with a mobility device.

Some larger venues have one person who specializes in dealing with accessibility issues. Generally, they will go out of their way to help you. I am a subscriber to Broadway in Chicago, with a regular seat in the back of the balcony. I go with a friend or by myself. I have found ticket exchanges to sometimes be difficult. A couple of times, though, they had a show Paul wanted to see. It turns out one of the staff specializes in dealing with disabilities. I called and explained that I needed to buy a ticket for a main floor seat my husband could get to with his scooter and I wanted to sit next to him. I asked if I could just pay the difference in cost for myself to upgrade to a main floor seat. To my surprise, she offered to move me for free so I could be with him. When I called a year or two later for the next show he wanted, they had it all on the computer.

I once took a friend, who is in her 90's, to a concert at the huge United Center, where the Bulls play. She had experienced a recent injury, and we were both worried about how much she could walk. As I pulled into the handicap lot, the attendant asked if we'd like a wheel-chair. I said that would be great. I expected I would be pushing, but an attendant met us at the car, wheeled my friend, and stayed with us the whole way to our seats. As soon as the concert was over, he was there with the chair and even stopped at a private handicap bathroom.

In general, having to use a device such as a scooter or wheelchair should not keep you from going wherever you'd like. However, you do need to check ahead of time, because there are some buildings that are older that have not been brought up to ADA standards. Make sure you call and ask if the building is handicap accessible. Even one step can be a problem, if you are unable to stand up for a minute and get off of your mobility device or if it is too heavy to lift up over the step. You need to know if there is a particular entrance you need to go to. The other question to ask is if the bathroom is accessible. We have had a couple of unpleasant surprises in that regard. In some cases it was difficult to get to the bathroom and in others it was a challenge to manipulate the space with a mobility device. One concert venue we used to go to did not have a bathroom on the first floor and did not have an elevator. The orchestra that used to perform there did move to another place that did have a bathroom on the first floor, but that did not have a handicap stall. Very surprising and disappointing. If possible, have someone perform a scouting mission before going to a new place.

One final tip: I've learned it's worth it to pay (and tip) for valet parking, when you are dealing with mobility problems. At first, I used to drop Paul off and pick him up if we went to a performance, medical visit, or whatever. It was a hassle. It was such a relief to start using valets. Often, it doesn't cost much more than self-park, and you are able to stay together and provide any needed help. The valets are also experienced and willing to help with getting your equipment into the car.

Disability

I used to think that "disability" meant being a paraplegic. In actuality, *any* condition that keeps you from working can qualify you for disability benefits. For example, my husband first qualified because he had a seizure disorder, and the medications he was on made it difficult for him to learn new tasks. Never, ever lie about disability. You can go to jail for that. But on the other hand, if you do have a problem, don't hesitate to inquire about disability. Start by contacting Social Security. Go to your local office or their website. Do not contact a lawyer, unless you have tried and failed on your own. If you are turned down once, apply a second time. If you are still turned down, and if you feel you really have a legitimate case, that would be the time to contact whomever specializes in this area. Be sure to get clear information about fees, and whether they differ based on whether they do or do not succeed.

An important note: Be sure to save the official letter of determination of disability in a safe place, and/or scan it into your computer. You may be asked for it, years later. I wasn't careful about that and had to contact a doctor to fill out forms.

Your disability payment is essentially an early social security payment, and it will automatically convert to Social Security when you hit the qualifying age. Here's a nice surprise: At one point, I remember my cousin, a social worker, saying to Paul, "You've been on Disability for almost 2 years now, haven't you? That means you'll be on Medicare soon." And indeed, shortly thereafter, he received notification that he was Medicare eligible, even though he was only in his 50's.

Handicap Parking

This is not automatic with Disability, and not every condition that keeps you from working affects your walking. When you apply for handicap parking, you will be given a permit with an expiration date. After a couple of years, if your condition continues to be affirmed by a doctor's statement, you will be given a permanent permit. You can get a handicap license or hanging placard. I recommend a placard, because when you travel and rent a car, you can take it with you. In many states, if you park in handicap parking, you don't have to feed the meters. Be sure to find out when you travel. That used to be true in Illinois, but the company that purchased the Chicago meters started charging the City for lost revenue, so the law was changed. However, if a doctor certifies that your disability makes it difficult for you to feed a meter, you can get a different kind of placard that does allow you to park for free. You have another choice to make, in regards to the type of placard. It can be tied in to the driver's license of the handicapped person, or to that of their driver. Originally, Paul was still doing local driving, and I had the permit in Paul's name, in case he went somewhere without me. A few years ago I had it switched to my license, because I realized that Paul's license was going to expire, and if he were asked to take a behind-the-wheel test, he would decline and lose his license and therefore his permit.

A few more words about handicap parking. I have never used our placard to park in a handicap space when Paul wasn't with me. It just isn't right. Also never park on the space with the yellow stripes. That is intended to allow space for unloading wheelchairs, etc. If someone is in that space, a van with a lift or ramp can't lower or extend it. Finally, if someone has a placard but doesn't look handicapped -- to you, from the outside, do not assume they are misusing their placard. They may have a heart condition or other hidden disability. Don't be too quick to judge. I always had our placard displayed. One time I pulled up to the grocery store door, close to the motorized carts Paul used, and then parked in a handicap space, so Paul could quickly get to it when done. A woman came up to me in the store and yelled at me for parking in the handicap section and walked away before I could explain why. If, however, you do see a car without a handicap sign in a handicap space, it is legitimate to tell management.

Discounts

There are some discounts and perks that come with an official handicap designation. Illinois offers a discount on property taxes; I assume some other states might, as well. Hospitals, and sometimes other places, offer free, or at least reduced-price valet parking. Governmental services of various kinds are sometimes reduced. It's another case of "it can't hurt to ask."

CHAPTER 23

Sensory Problems

When we were children, we learned that the five senses are sight, hearing, taste, touch and smell. There can be some diminishment of all of these with age, but a significant diminishment is probably an indication of a problem.

Taste

One of the ones that is less likely to change is taste. If you have a sudden loss of taste, this may be a symptom of COVID-19; so get tested right away. However, some people find that they gradually have less taste with age. The problem is that they may lose some of their appetite. While we hear a lot about the prevalence of overweight status and obesity being a significant problem in our country, being underweight can also be problematic. If you should, for example, become ill, you may lose some weight, and you would need reserves to not become frail. If you, or someone you know, is losing interest in food, you may have to think about creative ways to stimulate appetite, such as adding new dishes to your menu, or eating treats or whatever. If someone does not get sufficient nutrition, they may need a supplement, such as Ensure.

Smell

Smell does not usually diminish very much with age, So if you do have a loss of sense of smell, it is something to discuss with your doctor. During the COVID-19 pandemic loss of smell has become identified as a symptom of the disease. It could also be a sign of oncoming Parkinson's, though that would probably have happened a while ago. It could indicate a sinus infection or a blockage in your nasal passages from a tumor. In any event, any change in your health should be discussed with your doctor.

Hearing

Pretty much everyone loses some hearing as they age. I know I have noticed that occasionally, when I am at an event such as a play, I may miss a word or two and wonder why people are laughing. When we were young, we may have gone to rock concerts and discotheques, or worked around loud machinery; and continual or continuous exposure to loud sounds has long-term hearing consequences. It is sometimes difficult to determine at what point the hearing loss is no longer acceptable. If you find yourself asking people to repeat what they said frequently, or if someone makes a comment to you that they think you may have a hearing loss, see an audiologist. Last year, I told someone that she had hearing loss, and she insisted that I just mumble. It took awhile for me to get up the nerve to say something, and I tried to do it nicely; but since she lives alone and doesn't go out much, I figured someone should say something. Her loss was quite evident: She was doing things such as leaning towards the person speaking, and I wish she had taken my suggestion to get an exam. Not only are these exams covered by Medicare, but even if you don't have Medicare, most places that sell hearing aids are happy to give you a free hearing exam, because of the possibility that you might want to purchase one.

A wonderful recent development is that prescriptions are no longer required for hearing aids for anyone over 18 who has a moderate loss of hearing. This is expected to lower costs by half. Anyone who has a sudden or severe loss should still see a doctor.

If you do have a hearing loss that requires a hearing aid, it is important to get one, not only for socialization and enjoyment of such things as music, but also because hearing loss can affect brain function. This was something that really surprised me when I learned it. *See my section on Medicare coverage for information about hearing aids.*

There are health problems that can be associated with hearing loss, in addition to a gradual diminution of ability. One of my cousins noticed, when he was speaking with someone on the phone, that he heard more in one ear than the other. Fortunately, he told his doctor about it. It turned out that he had an acoustic neuroma. An acoustic neuroma is a tumor on the nerves that lead from the ear to the brain. He had surgery to remove it, and as a result, he lost his hearing in one ear and he has an uneven smile; but he is very happy to be alive. Had he not spoken with his doctor, that might not have been the case.

Paul completely lost the hearing in one ear, very suddenly. We found out later he had suffered a stroke in his ear, which is something that neither of us had ever heard of. We knew exactly when it happened, because not only did he make a remark about things sounding odd, but he lost some of his balance. Your balance is centered in your ears. We happened to be on our way to the Auditorium Theater, which is a building built in the 1800s where the floors are now crooked; so at the time, I thought that was throwing him off balance. But when Paul continued to be off-balance when we left, we decided he should see a doctor the next day, and that's when we found out what happened. When he went to get hearing aid, the audiologist tested him and said that he had absolutely no hearing in that ear. Since he already had lost about 30% of the hearing in his left ear, that left him without very much hearing. Of course he got a hearing aid, and we went through the whole problem of losing several hearing aids before we got one that had a Bluetooth connection. With the hearing aid, Paul could hear sufficiently, but he could never regain full tonal range. While we continued to go to classical music concerts, he no longer played CDs. That was a loss for him.

One very easy way to help someone with hearing loss is to use closed captioning on TV. Paul found that with the hearing loss, he had trouble understanding anyone with an accent, and we started using it for that. We got spoiled, as most actors today are encouraged to sound natural and not enunciate the way theater actors used to, so usually we had it on to look at when needed. If you don't know how to turn it on, contact whoever provides your remote control.

Another problem that Paul had, even before he lost his hearing, is one which is not uncommon, called tinnitus. I've heard that word pronounced with the accent on the first syllable and sometimes on the second syllable, so I guess you could use either one. Tinnitus is a constant sound in your ear. It can be from an unknown cause, but in Paul's case he knew it happened when he was in the Army and a thoughtless soldier shot a gun very close to his head and then laughed. He was plagued by tinnitus the rest of his life. Tinnitus is incurable. There were early experiments where people operated and cut the nerve to the ear, but it did not help, because the problem consists of damage to the brain itself. Tinnitus may manifest in such ways as popping or hissing noises.

If you have tinnitus, it can be a minor problem; but if it is a major problem, you might want to investigate a couple of things. One thing that Paul used, which is a simple and inexpensive aid, is a sound machine. They can be purchased from catalogs. You can choose from sounds it creates, such as ocean waves, "white noise", etc. He would turn this on when he was trying to go to sleep, and the sounds would help block the tinnitus and help him go to sleep.

He also, for a while, had a special hearing aid-like device, called a masker, that actually produced a sound that was individually pitched to match the sound of what he was hearing. This is something else you can ask an audiologist about. It did help, and I don't recall why he stopped using it. Most likely, when he lost the complete hearing in one ear and had reduced hearing in the other ear, he did not want to have anything interfering with the little bit of sound that he had.

Touch

Another problem Paul suffered from was peripheral neuropathy. Peripheral neuropathy is the deterioration of the nerves that go from the brain to your spine and extremities. It results, at first, in tingling, and then numbness. Eventually, it is difficult to feel anything in your feet and/or hands. This is dangerous, because you can injure yourself and not even realize it. It is most common in people who have diabetes.

One of the other causes is chemical exposure. I believe that Paul developed peripheral neuropathy because he owned a one-hour photo shop for six years, using developing chemicals without proper ventilation. We really didn't think about it at the time. It wasn't until the shop had been closed for a few years that he began to develop several illnesses. Even then, when I expressed my beliefs, he said that the danger was only for black-and-white photo chemicals, which he rarely used; but I still believe that was a cause.

However, another factor that we learned is that relatives of people who have diabetes also have a higher chance of developing peripheral neuropathy, even if they themselves are not diabetic. Paul's older sister did have diabetes for many years. So there may have been a genetic predisposition, as well as the chemical exposure. When Paul walked in his later years, his toes didn't touch the ground; which, of course, did not help his balance. He also got an infected toenail that had to be removed.

I also just read that anti-seizure drugs can increase the odds of peripheral neuropathy. And of course, this is something that Paul took and could not do without. So he had three times the odds of developing peripheral neuropathy, compared to the average person. However, 3 million people are estimated to suffer from this condition. In addition to the numbness, neuropathy can also cause actual pain. This pain is most commonly treated with a drug called Lyrica (Pregabalin). Lyrica does have some bad side effects, if used for a long period of time, but there isn't much choice about it. This condition cannot be cured. It can only be treated symptomatically, and that is usually with Lyrica.

We did hear about a clinic that does electronic nerve stimulation as a treatment, and Paul did go there and have the treatment several times. However, he did not feel that it really made a difference. From what I've read, it does for some people. If you think you might have peripheral neuropathy, of course consult with the doctor, and be extra careful about avoiding accidents by installing handrails, walking carefully, etc.

Vision

As we age, most people's vision diminishes somewhat. It is unusual for someone to not have glasses or contact lenses by the time they become a senior. I am fortunate that I only use reading glasses, which I often just buy at Dollar Tree. Because of that deterioration, you might not notice if your vision gradually deteriorates in a way that is not normal. For that reason, it is very important to visit your eye doctor every year for an exam.

First of all, your prescription may need to be adjusted. Also, as you age, your tear ducts often don't work as well, and you may develop dry eyes, which can make them feel irritated. I had a problem for a while with tears coming out of my eyes, even though I wasn't crying. My eye doctor said that that was, ironically, because my eyes were dry. My tear ducts were over-compensating. There are a number of over-the-counter eye drops that help. I keep a bottle on my nightstand, and I use it every morning, as soon as I wake up. The problem may be partly age and partly "fry eye". This means you've been sitting in front of a computer screen too much. I've read a couple of times recently about the 20-20-20 rule. That is, for every 20 minutes you're on the computer, you need to look at something 20 feet away for 20 seconds. You could set a timer to remind yourself.

Paul had what the doctor termed "tired eyes". He was such an avid reader all his life that his eyes were worn out, and he had to limit the time he read. It was also complicated by Parkinson's. One of those un-expected side effects we encountered and didn't understand for a long time. His eyes, like his hands, had trouble staying steady.

Do not be concerned if you occasionally see wavy lines in front of your eyes for a few minutes. This is known as a visual migraine, and can be an allergic reaction. I have had them a few times. Just see if you can sit down, relax and close your eyes for a few minutes. If the problem doesn't resolve in 10 minutes or so or happens frequently, talk to a doctor. You may also occasionally see floaters, which often happen because you have rubbed your eyes and irritated them.

There are, however, several serious eye disorders that your doctor can catch that can be corrected.

Cataracts

The first and most common of these, is cataracts. It seems to me that everyone I know has cataract surgery eventually. It is completely routine at this point. I remember when my dad had cataract surgery, and it took several days to recover. Nowadays, with cataract surgery, you may even be able to go back to work the next day. If you don't know what cataracts are, the lens in your eye becomes cloudy and interferes with your vision. You may find that you need a lot of light to read. A certain amount of increase in need for light in order to read is normal with aging eyes, as your corneas thicken. However, if this is particularly significant, it may be an indication of cataracts, which are not letting in enough light to your eye. Another symptom is that headlights and other lights at night seem to have a halo around them.

Your eye doctor can definitely diagnose cataracts fairly easily. If you do have cataract surgery you will, of course, only replace one lens at a time, so that you can see out the other eye. It is a pretty painless out-patient procedure done in a hospital. You must have someone pick you up and drive you home. You will stay indoors for the rest of the day, and the next day, you'll go to visit your eye doctor. They recommend having someone drive you to that visit; but my eye doctor was just a few miles away, and I drove myself with sunglasses on and had no problem. Probably the biggest annoyance of cataract surgery is that you have to follow a very specific regimen of eye drops, in a very specific way, for a period of time. Be sure to do exactly as your doctor tells you to do. He or she will also schedule various follow-up visits.

The surgery involves removing the damaged natural lenses in your eye with an artificial one. The standard replacement lenses are covered by Medicare. You can pay to have the more deluxe adjustable lenses, but I don't consider it a big deal to occasionally pull out a pair of reading glasses. However, if you have worn glasses or contacts for years, which I have not, this surgery is not to be confused with the somewhat riskier Lasik surgery that corrects vision, and you may still need glasses.

After you have finished your second surgery, a few months later, be sure to take advantage of the one free pair of glasses that Medicare will ever give you, even if it is only just for reading glasses. I found that it was easier to drive at night, and I could read the supertitles at the opera from the balcony without glasses, after my surgeries were complete.

While the replacement lenses last forever, you may develop certain problems after the surgery. I actually was told by my doctor a year or two afterwards that I had to have a laser procedure because of a build up of materials behind one lens. This procedure, however, is simply done in the office and just takes a few minutes.

Glaucoma

There are other eye problems that sometimes develop and are more threatening. One of them is glaucoma. Glaucoma, which is caused by a buildup of pressure in the eye, can cause a loss of peripheral vision, and if left entirely untreated, sometimes lead to blindness. Today, most people have doctors who catch the problem early on, and if caught early on, it can be treated simply with eye drops and follow up visits. If not caught early on, or if the drops do not work, surgery may be needed. There are two simple tests that check for glaucoma These tests are generally done as part of an annual eye exam. Testing you does not mean they think you have it. It is a good idea for everyone to be checked every year.

Macular Degeneration

Another serious problem is macular degeneration. It is a common problem. It is estimated that almost 11 million people in the United States have some form of it. My brother's mother-in-law went blind from it in her 80s, and Paul's mother had some vision loss from it. The cause of macular degeneration is not entirely known, though heredity and smoking can increase risk for it. The macula, itself, is the region of keenest vision, when intact; it is near the center of the retina. Macular degeneration can happen fairly quickly. Someone can suddenly notice their vision being impaired. Typically they will see a dark spot in the middle of their vision in an eye. If this happens to you, be sure to get to your doctor immediately, before the problem spreads. It can cause total loss of vision in the eye.

Significant Vision Loss

Losing a significant part of your vision is particularly difficult for seniors. If a young person loses their vision, they may learn braille or get a seeing-eye dog. You are not likely to do that when you are older. If you become totally blind, you may need to go to an assisted living facility. However, most people only lose partial vision and can continue to function, though with difficulty. No one with significantly impaired vision should drive.

As part of the societal trend towards helping the disabled and the growing number of older people with problems in society, there are several new developments in the last few years to help you.

Some theaters offer descriptive audio during performances. You would ask customer relations for a set of earphones, and as the play progresses, you would hear a description of the visual events on stage. Of course, you would want to check with your theater to see if they offer this. It's generally only going to be for larger, better-funded productions. Some shows on TV offer this, as well. Check the closed-caption options to see what's available for a particular show. I know I accidentally turned that feature on while watching Hamilton.

Reading can become difficult, but there are things to help you. Some magazines and newspapers offer large print versions. We once ordered the large-print New York Times and were disappointed to find that logically, if you stop to think about it, it did not have everything in it. It was easier to read, but not complete. You can check with your favorite magazine or newspaper to see if they offer a large-print version. Some libraries may also have large-print versions that are not available to the public.

Holding a magnifying glass while you read, because you can't get glasses that are strong enough, can be difficult. Paul tried a couple of magnifying glasses on stands that were offered through catalogs and had difficulty using them. If you do order one to try, I would suggest that you check the return policy and keep the packaging materials until you see whether it works for you.

While I was researching various kinds of magnifying devices for Paul, he once mused, Wouldn't it be great if there was some way to project the page onto the TV? I said I really doubted that there was such a thing, but I would research it. In fact, there is such a device! There are devices I found online for institutions, which are extremely expensive, but I also found Carson ezReader. It was wonderful. The way this device worked was that you plugged it into your TV. Rather than using our regular TV set, we actually bought a very small, inexpensive desktop TV for less than $100 for this purpose, so we could leave it on a table that had enough room for a book. The ezReader only cost about $60. You plug a cable into your television set, and then use their mouse. You pass the mouse over the page of the book, magazine, or newspaper you are reading, and it is projected onto the television set. You can also adjust the magnification. This extended Paul's ability to read for a couple of years at the end of his life, which was a real blessing. We did have some technical problems, but the people at the company were very helpful.

CHAPTER 24

Bones and Joints

Joints

It is extremely common for people, as they age, to wear out some part of their body. I think everybody knows someone who has had either hip replacement or knee replacement surgery. Some people have a tendency to need multiple replacements. One of my best friends seems to have had just about every joint you could think of replaced or at least fixed: knees, shoulders, etc. The surgery has gotten to be more routine, as doctors have done hundreds of them. I've also seen advertisements for procedures that they say can be used instead of knee replacement surgery. I have no idea how good they are. This is one area where, fortunately, Paul and I never had any first-hand experience. I do know that it is essential that you do not try to speed things along by not listening to your doctors. For example, I have known people who have had operations on their knees or feet and put pressure on them too soon and wound up with additional surgeries.

The Back

A common place for people to have problems, and this is one where Paul did have problems, is the back. It seems that after a certain number of years, a large percentage of the population develops back problems, with a great range of seriousness. For some people, it may mean simply taking over-the-counter pain relievers or going to a chiropractor for relief. Chiropractors are now covered by Medicare, which is a change from past practice. Pain patches and wraps that heat up can be very helpful. They really do heat up quite a bit. Because of this, however, you have to be careful to avoid burns. It is safest not to wear one to bed, because you may exert pressure on one spot without moving for a long time and may not notice as it is starting to burn. Wrap-around back braces also provide support and relief for many. However, never buy them from telephone solicitors. They call and say they know about your back problem. They don't. They just figure that there is a good chance that whomever they call will have one.

Back surgery can be extremely difficult and involve months of recovery. If you have a serious back problem, be sure to get more than one opinion about what to do about it. In Paul's case, we liked and trusted his back doctor, so he did have surgery to put spacers in his back, but it was a complete waste of time. When he told the doctor that it hadn't really provided relief, he recommended seeing another doctor. That doctor said that no one does the procedure anymore because they found that it just does not help. Fortunately, at least, Paul did not have any complications from the procedure, but I sometimes wondered if it had made things worse. We saw three different back doctors about his increasing pain and bend, and essentially, we were told that he had an arthritic back and that there's really nothing to do about it except take medication for the pain. One of the doctors referred us to a pain specialist ,who gave him a prescription medicine which was an opioid, just as all the publicity came out about how dangerous opioids are. Art told me that as far as opioids go, it was one of the safest; but even so, Paul stopped taking it. It made him feel too lethargic.

One thing we did to help Paul's back problem was that we switched from a sedan to a small SUV. Getting in and out of a car is surprisingly difficult with a bad back. It is much easier to get into an SUV, because it is higher and you don't have to bend as much to get in. I didn't want to have problems parallel parking with a big car, but the Kia Sportage we bought was actually shorter than our Malibu. It just looked bigger because it has a higher roof line. So next time you are car shopping, keep that in mind. If you are concerned about city parking, ask what the length of the car is.

Besides arthritis, there are other back problems. One term you might hear is stenosis. Stenosis is a narrowing and compression of the spinal cord. Another is scoliosis, which some people are born with, but others develop it as they get older. I was told last year that I have a little bit of it. It is a curvature of the spine and can range from almost imperceptible to a severe curvature that presses on organs and causes other health problems. Also, today many people have what is called, "text neck". As it is, many of us develop poor posture as we age, but text neck can develop even in the young. It is a hunched neck caused by habitually looking down at your phone. So try to hold your phone at eye level when you are looking at the screen.

Osteoporosis

Another common problem, and one of the few that I have, is osteoporosis. Osteoporosis is a thinning of the bones. As an intermediary development, you may be told that you have osteopenia. Osteopenia often is a precursor to osteoporosis. While there are some causes that can affect this process, such as poor nutrition, it is largely a genetic disease and cannot be avoided. It is most common in older, thin, white women, but it can affect anyone. My mother had very bad osteoporosis, and I inherited it from her and have some broken bones. However, it isn't anything that I feel, nor anything that affects anything I do. The only reason I know that I have it is because I've had a bone scan. A bone scan is a simple, non-invasive, non-painful test. So if your doctor recommends that you have one, by all means get it. It is covered by Medicare when prescribed, and there's really very little to it. It's completely outpatient, and it's just a scan. If you do have osteoporosis, there's a serious question about what you should do about it. One thing that everyone will agree about is exercise. Weight-bearing exercise is supposed to help osteoporosis. It is easier for it to help certain parts of the body than others. For example, I exercise regularly, and that helps my arms and my legs but doesn't particularly help my hips. The great thing about exercise is that even if it doesn't help your osteoporosis that much, it's good for your entire body and your overall health, so you have nothing to lose. When my primary care doctor of decades retired I went for a final exam. Everything was good, so the only advice he said he could give me was "Don't fall". Easier said than done, but I am more careful than I used to be.

Taking medication for osteoporosis is a much bigger question. One of the major medicines for osteoporosis is bisphosphonate. I actually took it for quite a while until I started hearing about its side effects. Strangely, it can actually dissolve some of your bones. We all know how you hear drug ads and their side effects on TV, and they mention things that are very rare. In this case, however, I actually met someone whose jaw had been dissolved by taking that drug and had to have their jaw rebuilt. Later on I came across another person, secondhand, who had the same problem. When I heard about that, of course I spoke with my doctor. He assured me that it is all right as long as you are not on it for very long. Then when he looked at my records, he found that I'd been on it for five years. I stopped taking that immediately! Years later when my new doctor wanted to prescribe it I told her about the person with the dissolved jaw. She said that almost always only happens if the person is being treated for cancer. I recalled that she was and I accepted the prescription for a weekly pill. There are also treatments that are injections done on an annual or semiannual basis, rather than as a weekly pill. If you are considering taking any of those, I would do some serious investigation as to the side effects.

For a very long time, I heard recommendations from people that if you have osteoporosis, you should be taking very high levels of calcium every single day. I've always been reluctant to take high doses of anything, so I never did that, and later on, I was glad that I didn't, when I heard that doing that can cause kidney stones. I drink milk and consume some dairy products. I take some occasional calcium supplements, and vitamin D which is also supposed to help, and am more careful walking.

If you do have osteoporosis, you want to do something about it to try to help, because even though it is a silent disease and it might not bother you on a day-to-day basis, it increases the chance that you will break a bone when you have an accident. I have broken a humerus (upper arm), a toe, and a cheekbone. Fortunately, only the humerus had a serious break. The other two were just small fractures. The biggest danger is breaking a hip or damaging your spine in a fall. So if you have osteoporosis, be a little extra careful about falls. I would suggest that you do not ride a bike and that you do not run on a sidewalk, because of the danger of tripping if one of the sidewalk squares is a little bit raised. That's how I fractured the cheekbone. When you run instead of walking, not only do you have less time to react to whatever happens, but also you tend to put your center of gravity forward instead of centering it directly over your body, which is hazardous. Avoid walking on ice; if you have to, make sure you have deep ridges on your boots or buy cleats to slip over them. This winter I started carrying a cane tucked under my arm or a fold up cane that I could put down for support when crossing corners that had been plowed under.

Frozen Joints

This is an area where, unfortunately, I *do* have experience. This could be a problem for anyone, but it is most commonly a problem when you are older and less active. After I broke my arm in two, when I was only 40 years old, I experienced a complication. That complication was a frozen shoulder. I had never heard of this condition before that happened to me. Because of my yet-undiagnosed osteoporosis, my arm didn't heal the way it was supposed to. It is standard for broken bones to heal after about 6 weeks. Normally, after that time, the cast is removed. However, in my case, my arm did not heal after 6 weeks. This was probably due to my osteoporosis, combined with the fact that the arm has a very heavy bone to support, and the break was quite far up in the arm. The only things that were holding my arm in place were the rod that had been inserted into the center of it and the cast on the outside. The bone itself was not healed. My cast stayed on for a couple more weeks, but the break still had not healed. It is amazing to me that my doctor still did not recognize that I might have osteoporosis and scan me for that.

Anyway, the cast stayed on for an additional two or three weeks, and at that point, he said it may never heal. I was then very wary, and while my cast has been removed, I continued to keep my arm in a sling for a couple more weeks. After 2 1/2 months of not moving my arm and shoulder, I was fortunate to go into the staff lounge at the school where I worked one day and encounter someone who taught in the medical field. She said that I was holding my arm funny and that I should see a doctor about it. I did go to see a different doctor, and he told me that I had a 100% frozen shoulder. He explained that the joint had lost its ability to move -- and that if it were not fixed *immediately* I would have a *lifelong* disability. I was actually more upset about this than I was about breaking my arm. When I broke my arm, I thought it was really a horrible thing to happen, but I knew that it was a temporary condition and assumed it would be healed after a certain period of time. The talk of having a lifelong disability upset me quite a bit. He said the only way to avoid that would be to work with physical therapy; and if that did not work, to have surgery.

I went back to my original doctor and asked him why he had not recommended physical therapy. He said that because physical therapists are rough, they could re-break my barely healed arm. I then asked for suggestions, and he suggested that I do some exercises at home at my own pace. Of course, this is something he should have suggested without any requests. I should have written a letter of complaint about that doctor to the hospital administration, but I was less aggressive then than I am today and didn't. The exercises were very simple. The main one was that I dangled a scarf down my back and held each end with a different hand, and then I slightly pulled and gradually increased the range of motion as it felt comfortable. This should not involve pain. If it does, then you're going too fast. Eventually, this worked! I regained my full range of motion and have kept it because I have continuously been in an exercise class.

When I had to leave my exercise class because of the pandemic, I substituted climbing stairs as a basic exercise. I realized, however, that doing that did not address every joint in my body. It only addressed the lower half of my body. Even carrying weights, as I did, did not address the full range of motion of my shoulders. So before I began climbing stairs each morning, I would simply rotate each of my arms and legs in every possible direction and do a few squats. This only took about five minutes, and it made me feel comfortable that I was keeping my joints from stiffening up. I strongly suggest that if you are not in a general exercise class that addresses all parts of your body, that you do this every morning. After all, it only takes about five minutes. Of course, if you want to get true cardiovascular benefit from it, you will need to do it for a longer period of time; but if it's just maintaining a range of motions, it only takes a few minutes each day and can save you a lot of grief in the future. If you cannot do the complete full range of motion, aim for a gradual increase each day.

The other thing that I do is, each morning I stand with my heels, back, and head against the wall and my arms to the wall, with my palms on the wall, and I gradually raise the arms toward my head. Once again, this does **not** take a lot of time. I just do it perhaps two times. Just raise your arms as far as they will go, keeping them against the wall, and lower them down again. If you get to the point where you gradually increase the range of motion so you can raise your arms all the way up, this is very good for posture. Nothing makes you look older unnecessarily more than slumping. I have to constantly remind myself about that.

CHAPTER 25

Digestive Problems

Everyone has indigestion occasionally, and sometimes that can be taken care of by an occasional antacid tablet; but for some people, it does become a chronic problem.

The most common digestive problem associated with aging is constipation. As you age, your system tends to slow down, so constipation can become a frequent occurrence. I recommend against using prescription laxatives or over-using laxatives in general. Laxatives should only be used in extreme situations. The best thing to do is to drink more water and increase the fiber in your diet. You can choose how you want to do that, if it means eating more fruit or adding bran to your cereal or consuming other high-fiber foods. If this does not work for you, then you can add a fiber supplement to juice in the morning, using something like Metamucil or a generic fiber supplement. The oldest remedy in the world, prunes and prune juice, are really effective. A tip: Try warming the juice in the microwave. I personally also find that coffee helps me. However, it is most effective if I only drink it every other day, rather than every day. Anything you use every day loses its effectiveness as the body becomes used to it.

While you should not worry if you don't defecate for a day or even two, extended constipation can become dangerous. Paul once spent a couple of days in the hospital because his Parkinson's caused his digestive system to slow down and become blocked, which resulted in nausea and discomfort and when diagnosed, was considered a health threat.

Do not worry too much if you see a little blood come out with your stool. It is probably hemorrhoids or a cut along the track. If you have anything like colon cancer, it will actually become black, not red. Of course, hemorrhoids, which can result from the pressure and irritation of pushing too much from constipation, should be treated, but are usually not serious.

Ulcers and Reflux

We've all heard of ulcers. People used to think that they were only caused by stress. Now we know that a bacterial infection can also cause ulcers, and this type of ulcer can be treated. If you suspect you have one, talk to your doctor. Stress can exacerbate it, so treatment might include finding ways to change your life to reduce stress, as well as taking medication.

One common problem to look out for is acid reflux. I think we've all experienced it at some point. You eat something that doesn't agree with you, and in the middle of the night you burp up some stomach acid, and it tastes terrible. Immediately drink some water, take an antacid, and put some pillows behind your head instead of lying flat. You might benefit from also sipping seltzer water or eating plain crackers to mitigate the acid. If these symptoms are happening frequently, this is a condition that must be treated by your doctor. Acid reflux isn't just annoying; it's actually dangerous. The acid can burn your larynx and throat and cause permanent damage. If you have it on a repeated basis, be sure to talk to your doctor. There are actually two different types of reflux and your doctor will assess which you are experiencing. If you have any Nexium, a common treatment for reflux, in the house, throw it out now. It is no longer approved by the FDA.

IBS

IBS stands for irritable bowel syndrome. People with irritable bowel syndrome frequently have stomach pains and diarrhea. If you suspect that you might have it, I suggest keeping a diary of what foods you eat and marking those things that potentially might cause problems. Look for patterns. When Paul developed IBS his doctor told him that he thought it was because he was a nervous kind of person and that his nervousness was irritating his stomach. That can happen; however, we went for a second opinion and saw a holistic Doctor, who did a food allergy test on Paul. The results were quite eye-opening. There were several foods to which he was allergic, and they were not the most typical ones you might expect. Once he stopped eating those foods or reduced his consumption of them, because after all some foods are harder to give up than others, his digestion greatly improved. It's easy to give up radishes or even iceberg lettuce, but not so easy to give up wheat, for example. It was also sad that he had to give up chocolate. However, after a long period of time without it, he did a bit of an experiment and found that if he ate a small amount, he could digest it well enough. He learned to find what his threshold amount was and how much he could eat before it caused an upset stomach. As long as your allergy only results in indigestion and not something more serious, you can do a test like that yourself and experiment with changing your food.

A couple of foods that commonly cause problems are lactose, which is in dairy products, and gluten, which is in bread and many other wheat-based foods. In Paul's case, he was told that he was allergic to dairy, not just lactose. However, many people who have trouble digesting regular milk can digest Lactaid milk, which has the lactose removed. If that still doesn't work for you, there are so many alternatives available today that it's easy to substitute. You can get rice milk, coconut milk, almond milk, etc. You can even buy ice creams that are made with these instead of dairy. Many people ask for milk substitutes at coffee shops now. As far as bread goes, if you have trouble digesting it and it's just a mild digestive problem such as bloating, which happens to me, you can decide if it's worth it or not to you. I, for example, rarely buy bread to eat at home, but if I'm in a restaurant and they have really good bread, I'll deal with a little bit of bloating and discomfort for the pleasure of eating the bread. Some people however, actually have celiac disease, and it is a more serious problem. For any digestive problems talk to your doctor.

Colorectal Cancer

There are many c's associated with this that you should understand. Those are cancer, colon cancer, colorectal cancer, colonoscopy, colectomy, and colostomy.

The Colon

The colon is the large intestine. It is one of the most common places to get cancer. If caught early it is completely survivable. However, when caught late it is a significant cause of cancer deaths.

The term, colorectal, is basically synonymous, but it includes the rectum, below the intestines.

Colonoscopy

So how do you catch it early? You have a colonoscopy. A colonoscopy is an outpatient procedure done in a hospital, where a cable with a camera is inserted through your anus and into your intestines, so a doctor can look at them. Everyone should have a baseline colonoscopy when they are 45 years old. This is a recent change from the longstanding 50, because many younger people are getting colorectal cancer and not taking it seriously because of their age. Recently there was the tragic case of actor Chadwick Boseman, who found out he had Stage 3 Colon Cancer when he was only 39 and died at 43. So please tell your family to start their colonoscopies early. They should then follow the doctor's recommendations. If you do not have a family history of colon cancer and no problems are found in your exam, you'll probably only have to undergo a colonoscopy every five years or so. However, if your doctor says to have one more often, you should do it, because it can save your life. Having a colonoscopy is a big pain. Everyone hates it. It isn't the procedure itself that everyone hates, since you are sedated and probably don't even remember it. It is the preparation. You have to totally clear out your intestines before the procedure. You've probably had one by now, but just in case you haven't, keep in mind when you schedule your procedure that you must mark off on your calendar not only that day but the day before. All you're going to be doing the day before is basically running to the bathroom.

When you have your colonoscopy, it is possible that they may find polyps. Polyps are small growths, rather mushroom-like, protruding from the intestinal walls. They are easy to remove during the procedure. They do not normally require a separate procedure. In most cases, you'll simply wake up and be told that they removed some polyps. The polyps will then be sent for testing, to see if they are benign or malignant. If they are benign and small, it really isn't anything to worry about, but it will probably mean you will be back in less than 5 years.

If you do have malignant polyps or recurring polyps, your doctor may suggest removing a section of your colon. My father had polyps removed twice, and then a section of his colon, and then finally had a colectomy.

Colectomy and Colostomy

A colectomy is a complete removal of the colon. It is fairly rare. In most cases, they simply remove a section of the colon. If you do you have a colectomy, some people have a colostomy. A colostomy is an exterior bag for solid excretion, which has to be emptied manually. Sometimes people are given a colostomy bag as a temporary measure, but some people have one permanently. In my father's case, he did not have a colostomy. They simply stretched the small intestine. I don't know why that option isn't used more commonly.

Unfortunately, there is a history of colon cancer among many of the men on my father's side. Also, his own father died from stomach cancer at the age of 28, so the whole digestive system is a bit suspect. However, there's nothing like that on my mother's side, and everyone who got colorectal cancer got it in their 50s, So while it is a concern and it does result in my having colonoscopies on a regular basis, I am not that worried at this point. Also, my genetic testing through 23 and Me, something you might want to consider, says I do not have the genes that make cancer more likely. It could, of course, still happen.

Another thing to discuss with your doctor is that there are certain foods that are more likely to cause or prevent colon cancer. So try to eat a healthy diet. Colon cancer sometimes does not have symptoms until too late, but if your stool is black and tar-like be sure to tell your doctor. If you see red blood, it is because of a problem lower down, such as polyps. Possibly not as serious, but not to be ignored.

CHAPTER 26

Cardiovascular Problems

Heart Disease, Heart Attack, Heart Arrhythmias

Heart disease is the leading cause of death in the country -- or was, until the pandemic, but many people live with a variety of heart problems.

Heart attacks are, of course, something that everyone knows about. While they may cause immediate loss of consciousness, or even lead to the immediate death by cardiac arrest, they can be mild or slow-rolling. If you have any suspicion that you may have had a heart attack or might be experiencing one, be sure to call 911 (or your local emergency medical service number), or have someone drive you to an emergency room immediately. Do not drive yourself. Classic signs include chest pressure and shooting pain going down your left arm, but my brother had it on his right side, so don't rule out other symptoms. Sometimes women have the misconception that only men get heart attacks, but of course that isn't true. Women are more likely to have pain in the jaw or other symptoms that are perhaps not considered as "typical". This is just a lingering effect of the initial research on heart attacks having been done on males and defining what a heart attack looks like based on its presentation in males. If you don't feel right, be sure to get immediate medical help. Better to be told it's just indigestion than to take a chance of getting help too late. Many people recover from heart attacks. They are almost always sent to cardiac rehabilitation afterwards, which is a kind of monitored exercise class. Medicare pays for that for a while, but many people, such as my brother, continue on their own for years to stay healthy.

One type of problem that some people develop is **heart arrhythmia**. This means that the heart is not beating at a regular rate. It could be skipping beats, adding extra beats, changing rhythm quickly or frequently, or start beating too quickly or too slowly. Such arrhythmias can result from high fever or just a problem with the heart. They can cause shortness of breath and lack of energy because the heart can't pump well. An arrhythmia can be detected with a stethoscope and confirmed with an EKG, which only takes a few minutes right in the doctor's office. Certain types of arrhythmias are typically treated with drugs. If it is a continuing and serious problem, as it can be, then the cardiologist may have to resort to a cardioversion. Among the conditions for which cardioversion is considered are atrial fibrillation (sometimes called a-fib) and atrial flutter. This procedure can be done as an outpatient or in-patient procedure. The process of a cardioversion is that they shock your heart and put it into a regular rhythm. It is similar to what you see in TV shows when someone's heart has stopped, they apply paddles to the chest and they call out "Clear!" It sounds scarier than it is. When the doctor called, while Paul was in intensive care, and proposed it, I was very worried; but my brother, Art, himself a physician, spoke with him and gave the okay. There are dangers associated with cardioversion, because it can create an embolism (blood clot), which could be fatal. So it is important that you and your doctor discuss the use of blood thinners before and after the procedure. In Paul's case, he had already been on blood thinners for quite awhile, which was an advantage. Sometimes a cardioversion is only effective for a short period and sometimes for years. Paul, had four cardioversions, and the first and fourth lasted for a long periods of time and were worth the risk. As his cardiologist predicted, he knew the moment they failed. That's how effective they are.

I asked why Paul couldn't have a pacemaker to regulate his heart. Pacemakers cannot be used for arrhythmia when the arrhythmia is a rapid heartbeat, as pacemakers are only used to stimulate the heart, not to slow it down. Pacemakers are only used if the heartbeat is too slow, not too fast. I asked that question because pacemakers are not normally a particularly dangerous operation, because they are placed above the heart and not inside the heart. The batteries have to be replaced periodically, but it is a very long period of time between changes, and you may never need it.

Since that time, I've run into someone who has an implanted defibrillator. The purpose of this would be to shock the heart back into rhythm if you have arrhythmia. This must be a newer development, or I'm sure that our cardiologist would have recommended it for Paul. So if you are told that you have an arrhythmia, this would be something to inquire about, if medication doesn't seem to take care of the problem.

Congestive Heart Failure

Congestive heart failure needs to be treated immediately or it can be fatal. It happens when the heart isn't working efficiently enough to clear fluids from the body. It can be caused by arrhythmia. One early indication is swelling of the legs. A test to see if your legs are really swollen is to press your thumb in for a moment and see if a mark is left there for a few seconds. That is a bad sign, as is difficulty breathing or climbing stairs. If fluid retention is caught before a crisis, you will be put on some form of diuretic, such as Lasix pills. If it gets to the crisis point, you may have to get it intravenously; and if that doesn't suffice, you may need a cardioversion or fluids drained from your heart area and lungs. As with a heart attack, it is best to call 911 if you cannot easily walk to the car. I managed to get Paul to the car when he had it, but I probably shouldn't have tried. When we got to the Emergency Room, they said his heart efficiency was so low he was on the brink of collapse. Once he was released we knew what to look for and could call the cardiologist if we saw a problem developing. **He did have it again, but we knew what to look for and caught it earlier, before it was so serious.** If you ever think your legs and feet look swollen be sure to consult your doctor.

Heart Valve Repair or Replacement

In 2011 Paul began to have problems climbing the stairs to the second-floor bedroom. He would get out of breath and have to stop halfway up the stairs for a break. We consulted a doctor, and when listening with a stethoscope, he determined that Paul had a leaky valve that was not working right. The cardiologist told him to have heart valve replacement surgery. This is a surgery that is not that rare. There are options as to the kind of valve that you have, and the most common kind is a pig valve. It seems a little odd to think of a part of an animal being inside your body, but that is what is usually recommended. As it turns out, when they looked at Paul's heart during the surgery, they decided that he only needed to have the valve *repaired,* rather than replaced. I guess this is something they don't really know until they actually look at it. Some valves, depending on their location, require open-heart surgery, and others do not. Paul had the kind that requires open-heart surgery. It sounds very scary; but if you should need it, it's actually not as hard to recover from as you would expect. Open-heart surgery involves cutting open and pushing away the ribs to get to the heart. It is surprising how quickly he healed from that. He had a sizable scar, but the chest really healed up quite quickly, so do not be dismayed if you have to have that procedure. The doctors are quite adept at it. In Paul's particular case, he did develop a complication, but it is an extremely rare one. I will talk about that in the last part of the book.

Coronary Bypass Surgery

This is also not an uncommon procedure. It is a way of diverting the blood flow around a blocked artery. People can have one artery that is bypassed or they could have up to all four, which would be called quadruple bypass surgery and would be the most serious. It tends to be a very successful procedure.

Heart Stents

A stent can be placed as a tiny wire mesh tube that can be placed within an artery and left there permanently to help keep the artery open if there is a blockage. It reduces the chance of a heart attack.

Blood Pressure

I'm sure you've noticed that one of the first things they do when you go to visit a doctor is take your blood pressure. Usually they will immediately tell you the results. If they do not, be sure to ask and keep track of that number, so after a while you know if there are any significant changes. Blood pressure is an important indication of your health. Although low blood pressure can make someone faint or feel faint, and it can have some medical causes, what people are usually concerned about the most is high blood pressure (hypertension). High blood pressure is very common and has gotten to be more of a problem as obesity has increased in the United States. Obesity is certainly not the only cause, but it is a common one.

Discuss your blood pressure with your doctor. If it turns out that you have high blood pressure, the doctor will almost certainly recommend putting you on medication for it. I would think twice about that. If you have very high blood pressure, you definitely want to get on medication right away, because high blood pressure can cause a stroke. However, if your hypertension is only borderline and you just have a somewhat elevated reading, ask your doctor for recommendations of ways to lower it without medication, such as changes in your diet or lifestyle habits and decreasing stress. Then see if it decreases over a month or two.

Years ago I used to have low blood pressure. Nurses would take my blood pressure, which was typically 90/60, and say that it was great and

and when I would ask if it was too low, they would say "Oh, you can't have too low blood pressure" or something along those lines. That is absolutely incorrect. Low blood pressure can also be quite a significant problem for some people, People who are thin sometimes have low blood pressure naturally. It can also be caused by medications that you are taking. The advantage of low blood pressure is that it isn't going to cause a stroke, but it could cause you to feel weak or faint. Some of the medications that Paul was on caused low blood pressure, and sometimes he would fall down because of it; he was lucky not to have a serious injury from that.

Other than medications, among the most common recommendations of physicians for patients with hypertension is to decrease the amount of salt in your diet. In fact, they often recommend that for everyone. The best way to do this is to simply avoid overly processed foods, because most processed foods do contain a lot of salt. Start reading labels on food, if you are not already doing so, and look at not just the calorie count, but also the sodium count. You may be surprised at how much sodium there is in a lot of foods. Adding salt when you cook is less of a problem, but there are many salt substitutes available in the grocery store, so your food does not have to be bland if you are really watching salt intake. When Paul was falling down because of low blood pressure resulting from his medications, I was actually told by one doctor to increase the amount of salt in his diet.

You can monitor your blood pressure at home with simple devices that you can buy at a drugstore, but I recommend that you only do this if you feel ill. You do not want to take your blood pressure every day and become obsessed with small changes in it.

CHAPTER 27

Respiratory Problems

If you have chronic respiratory problems, such as asthma or bronchitis, you've probably had them for quite a while and have learned how to deal with them. If you are a smoker, you almost certainly have chronic lung problems.

The major respiratory problem that becomes more common as you age is pneumonia. Pneumonia can be fatal if someone is already weakened or it takes hold for too long. Presently, in the pandemic, pneumonia is a very scary and potentially fatal complication of COVID-19. When occurring for reasons other than COVID-19, there is the potential that pneumonia could be a less serious illness. Paul had pneumonia four times, leading to interventions ranging from intensive care to an outpatient treatment. The first time was the most serious, because we didn't recognize what it was and didn't know he was going to have a repeating problem with it. It led to several days in intensive care and his first cardioversion. It was less serious as we learned to recognize the wheezing and whistling sounds that he would make when he had it and get quick treatment for it. You can listen for these sounds without a stethoscope, just by putting your ear to someone's chest, though a stethoscope would probably be helpful.

If you suspect that you might possibly have pneumonia, be sure to see your doctor immediately. If it's to the point that you are having trouble breathing or walking, or you think you could pass out, be sure to call 911. Do not try to walk to a car, and certainly do not try to drive. When I drove Paul to urgent care one time I was told I should have called an ambulance instead.

Pneumonia can develop in one lung, or more seriously in both lungs (bilaterally). It can be treated with antibiotics (if due to bacterial infection), bringing the fever down, and suctioning of the fluid that builds up in the lungs.

Another thing that older people sometimes have to deal with is temporary or even lifetime use of oxygen. There are a variety of heart and pulmonary conditions that can lead to insufficient oxygen. I remember a number of years ago a woman who worked at the same college I did would drag a canister of oxygen on wheels around behind her wherever she went. Nowadays carrying oxygen with you is much simpler. They have devised oxygen devices that are lightweight and portable, and there are even some that pull their oxygen from the air. So having oxygen going into your nose for a long period of time is not pleasant, but it is something people do learn to live with and continue to be active.

Being Put on a Ventilator

The COVID-19 pandemic made everyone significantly more aware of the issue of respiration (breathing) and how critical it is. There were so many stories of people who were put on a ventilator for weeks or even months. A ventilator can either be used to completely take over a patient's breathing, or it can be used simply to aid their breathing if their breathing is not sufficient.

Hopefully, you and your loved one will never be placed on a ventilator, but I can give you an idea of what is involved in case that ever happens, because Paul was on a ventilator twice.

There are two ways a person can be attached to a ventilator. Those are through the mouth or through the throat. Occasionally on medical shows you will see that someone's airway is blocked and they have to immediately punch a hole in their throat and do what is called a tracheotomy. However, normally what they will do in the hospital is put a tube through someone's mouth down their throat, rather than cutting a hole in their throat. The hole in the throat is usually for emergencies in the field, or if their airway is blocked above that point. When you put a tube down the throat that is called intubating. Obviously it is extremely uncomfortable for the patient if they are conscious. However, in most cases when this happens the patient isn't conscious. Paul was not conscious when they intubated him either time. If you were to become conscious and have a tube down your throat, you can imagine how uncomfortable it would feel. The removal is also uncomfortable, but people are happy to have the tube removed and will deal with the discomfort of the removal.

Paul first was intubated when he was in intensive care with his first and worst case of pneumonia. It was just for a few days. The second time was when he got West Nile Virus. He was breathing on his own, but not that well. He began with a tube down his throat; then after a few days, when it became clear that this would be a long recovery, they performed a tracheotomy. It is considered to be better that you have a tracheotomy, if a person is going to be on a ventilator for more than a few days. The tube down the throat can damage the airway. With the tracheotomy, there is no damage to the mouth or upper part of the throat. Also, if you are unconscious you might not be able to clear your own airway by coughing or clearing your throat. That was one of the scarier calls I received, when they called me for permission to perform a tracheotomy. Of course I checked with Dr. Art and got his approval. At the time, the doctors told me that a tracheotomy is completely reversible: When it is no longer needed, it is removed, and the hole heals up completely. That was reassuring. However, while Paul did get off of a ventilator pretty quickly once he was conscious, his tracheotomy collar (trach collar, for short) was never removed. The collar is a plastic circle that goes around the neck and has an opening in the front with a hole that the ventilator tube goes into. The collar holds it in place. When you are not attached to a ventilator, a cap is placed over the hole in front.

The doctors kept postponing the removal of the collar. There were a couple of reasons why they were hesitant. For the first couple of weeks, they wanted to be sure he would not need to go back on a ventilator. They kept telling me that it would be so much worse if they had to reopen the hole in the trachea instead of just removing a cap. Occasionally the respiratory staff at the nursing home did put him on a ventilator at night to supplement his breathing, just because they did that with a lot of patients. This was not necessary while he was awake, and I didn't think it was necessary at all. I didn't want him to get dependent on it and asked them not to do that. The other reason that the physicians were reluctant to remove the trach collar is because the presence of the trach collar makes it easier to clear phlegm. Paul did have a tendency to get a lot of phlegm, and it was much easier to simply open the front of the trach collar and put a suction device into his throat that way, rather than putting a suction device all the way through the mouth and down the throat as they otherwise would have to have done. The Catch-22 aspect of this is that the trach collar, itself, creates irritation, which makes phlegm more likely.

One of the challenges of having a trach collar is that when Paul first regained consciousness, he could not speak, because he was not getting any air sent to his larynx. The only way we could communicate was to ask him yes or no questions and have him shake or nod his head. This became very frustrating for both of us, and he would start silently mouthing words. Once in a while, I could figure out what they were. Then someone told me about a communications board. I searched stores and online for one and did finally buy one. It turned out that they had one at the nurses' station. No one had ever told me that, nor suggested that I use it. What is a communications board? It is a board that has various common questions and letters of the alphabet so the patient can point to them if they are capable, or if not, it helped me think of questions that I could ask him starting with common phrases such as I need, I want, etc. If the patient is capable of writing or using a computer, that would be easier, but Paul hadn't been able to do that for over a year because of his Parkinson's. Some of the clients my niece supported were largely paralyzed or unable to control their bodies other than their heads or eyes, and they successfully used a communications board to indicate by their gaze what they wanted or needed. As such, communications boards can also be helpful options when you are assisting a loved one in recovering from a stroke, and they are newly adjusting to not being able to use spoken words.

The speech therapist came in and was able to give him what's called a "speaking valve," for a limited period of time, which increased a bit on each visit. The speaking valve replaced the regular valve that was on his trach collar and allowed air to go to his larynx so he could speak. This was for a short period of time because it took a certain amount of oxygen, and he had to rebuild his strength to be able to both breathe and speak. His throat was also hoarse from the procedures and due to the fact that he was not drinking liquids. It was a bit of a challenge to begin speaking again. While Paul's brain did not lose any of his speech knowledge, his body had to learn how to get those laryngeal muscles going again and to allocate his breath between oxygenation and phonation (speaking). Basically what I'm saying is that speaking takes a lot of breath, and the body has to gradually relearn how to put a certain portion of the breath into speaking while still maintaining enough breathing to function. The muscles used in speaking also atrophy with lack of usage.

Eventually, after weeks with speech therapists, he did fully regain his speech, and we were able to have good conversations in a very normal way. We were surprised to find that, despite the brain infection he had gone through, he had only lost tiny bits of his memory. We could still discuss history, current events, etc. However, the trach collar was an impediment because it did mean that he had to be suctioned several times a day, which was one of things that contributed to preventing him from going home.

A tip in case you are in a situation like this is that I requested and received a second speaking valve, which I kept in a drawer in Paul's room. A couple of times the cap he had fell off and rolled somewhere. All the air was then going out without going to the larynx, and Paul was unable to speak to me. And if the call button was not nearby, as was often the case, Paul was helpless to call for assistance. I would then grab the spare cap from the drawer and put it on. Be sure to ask for that.

I was told that some people do retain a trach collar all their lives and can live a normal life with one. As long as you're not connected to a respirator, you can move around completely freely with a trach collar on around your throat. It could always be disguised with a high collar or a scarf. People with a trach collar do not necessarily have to be in a nursing home if that is the only reason for them to be there.

Having a trach collar had a couple of disadvantages. A big one was that most nursing homes will not take someone with a trach collar. They will only accept them if they have a respiratory staff. That gave us a limited choice of nursing homes. The social worker did give us a list of respiratory facilities to choose from.

However if you are in a position where you're being asked if someone should have a tracheotomy, there really aren't very many choices.

If they need it, they need it. However, you can take comfort in knowing that there's a possibility it may eventually be removed; and that even if it is not removed, that they will regain their ability to speak and can really live a normal life with it.

CHAPTER 28

Vascular, or Circulatory Problems

Vascular refers to the veins and arteries, also known as the circulatory system.

Some people, as they get older, have what they refer to as poor circulation. The result of this is feeling cold, especially in the limbs. In and of itself it is not a dangerous condition, it's just annoying. Some people however, do get peripheral artery disease, or PAD, in which case there's very little circulation to the limbs, and that can become dangerous. That is what happens to some diabetics, who wind up having limbs amputated. There are ways to test for this, so if you feel numbness in your limbs, have your doctor check. It could be due to circulation problems, or it could be due to a nerve problem, such as neuropathy.

Aneurysms

You may have heard of someone dying from a brain aneurysm, but do not know exactly what it is. An aneurysm is a protrusion of a blood vessel. It swells on the side of the blood vessel like a berry hanging from the blood vessel. Aneurysms in and of themselves generally do not cause problems and are often only detected because the brain is being scanned for some other reason. The problem is if it bursts, which certainly can happen. An aneurysm bursting can cause instantaneous death. Some people do survive aneurysms bursting, so if you should get a sudden intense headache be sure to call 911 and get to the hospital immediately. While age increases the risk, it can happen to otherwise healthy people at any age.

There is another type of aneurysm besides brain aneurysms. That is, an abdominal aneurysm. These can sometimes be felt in an exam. These can cause problems even if they don't burst. They can interfere with digestion. I had never heard of this until Paul's sister, Barbara, developed one. It made it very difficult for her to eat. She would often get nauseated when she ate and therefore lost her appetite and didn't eat enough. I think this is something that contributed to her death. If you are diagnosed with an abdominal aneurysm, you will want to discuss with your doctor if it would be safe to operate to remove it.

While the cause of aneurysms is unknown, your risk increases greatly if you are a smoker or heavy drinker. Barbara was a heavy smoker. She didn't think she had to worry about lung cancer because no one in her family had ever gotten cancer, but there are many other ways for smoking to kill you.

Varicose Veins and DVTs

The most common vein problem that people encounter is varicose veins. You need to know the difference between spider veins and varicose veins. Spider veins are little purplish-bluish lines along your calves or other parts of your legs. You see ads on TV frequently for vein clinics, because having spider veins is a very common problem. Spider veins are not dangerous, but they are unattractive. Insurance does not cover their removal because it is considered to be cosmetic surgery; that is, that you're doing it for the appearance, rather than for health reasons.

Treatment for varicose veins, on the other hand, is covered by Medicare and most insurance policies, because these actually do create a health hazard. Varicose veins actually bulge out. They are raised, so it is not the same as spider veins, though of course you may get both. If you have just the beginnings of varicose veins, try wearing support stockings. This may help. Varicose veins are considered a medical issue for a few reasons. First of all, they can create a tired, heavy, or even painful feeling in the legs. Secondly, they can lead to decreased circulation in the limbs, which creates problems. Third, they can lead to blood clots.

DVTs

DVT means deep vein thrombosis. DVTs are blood clots in the circulatory system and not just a bruise mark on the skin, which can travel through your circulatory system and go to your heart and cause a heart attack and kill you. Anyone can get them. I will never forget attending the funeral of a 13-year-old girl who had been in a play with me. She was in gym class, got hit by a ball, got a bruise, and the blood clot from the bruise killed her. No one could have foreseen or done anything about that, but you don't want to increase your risk factors. The other controllable risk factor for DVTs is lack of activity. If you are on a plane, at a long meeting, or even just sitting watching TV or on a computer for hours at a time, be sure to stand up and move your legs every half hour or so. A friend's husband almost died when he got a clot from a business meeting, so it can happen. When my Apple Watch chirps and says "Time to stand", I do so if at all possible.

If you do have really noticeable varicose veins, you want to see a doctor about them and see if a procedure is warranted. Years ago Paul had varicose veins removed with what was the standard of the day, which was known as vein stripping. That is an actual surgical procedure where the veins are removed. That is not done very often today. Today, the veins are killed, if possible, by either a laser procedure or by injections. I too, developed varicose veins, though not as severely as Paul. I had an injection procedure. I asked my doctor why he didn't use lasers, and he said because he had used lasers in the past and found that they were not as effective. You might want to get a second opinion about something like that, but this doctor was recommended by my primary care doctor, and I trust his judgment.

The way the procedure worked was that it was done on an out-patient basis. Probably the most painful part of the procedure was simply putting needles into my legs in several places to inject a local anesthetic, so that I did not feel the procedure itself. The procedure then essentially killed the bad veins through burning them at extremely high temperatures. I didn't really feel anything. The leg is then wrapped with bandages, and you have to wear prescription support stockings for a little while. You can actually resume normal activities the next day.

Something to consider: I held off having my procedure until autumn, because I didn't want to have to wear prescription stockings when it was hot out, and especially not when wearing shorts or a skirt.

Your doctor will have you go to a hospital for an ultrasound examination several days after the procedure, to make sure that you have not developed a DVT. In my case, I did indeed develop a DVT, which is the exception, not the norm. What I had to do was to inject myself in the abdomen with an anticoagulant for 10 days. That was really a pain in more ways than one. If you ever have to do injections, make sure you get very careful instructions about how and where to do it. The nurse at the doctor's office just showed me really fast, thinking the pharmacist would tell me how to do it. For some reason he did not. The first time I did the injection, it was very painful, because I wasn't doing it in quite the right place. I wound up going on YouTube to find out exactly how I should be doing it. It was then unpleasant, but only somewhat painful. Don't make the same mistake I did. Be insistent about instructions.

Carotid Arteries

Another place where there can be problems is in the carotid arteries. The carotid arteries are the ones that are in your neck and go directly to your brain. Sometimes those arteries can get clogged with plaque. There are special exams for this, and I have gotten ads in the mail for them, though I've never yet had such a test. You might want to ask your physician about that. My father had so much plaque in his carotid arteries, that by the time they discovered that, it was too late to do a procedure to remove it. It was too risky that a piece of plaque would break off and cause an immediate stroke. As a result, he lost a lot of the circulation to his brain, which affected his memory. He did not have Alzheimer's, because he always knew what was going on and who we were, but it bothered him that if he hadn't seen someone for a while, he would not be able to remember their name. As a result, he became fairly quiet his last few years.

Strokes

My father died of a stroke, which might or might not have been related to the plaque. Strokes are something for everyone to watch out for. A stroke results from your brain getting reduced blood flow, usually due to a blood clot of some kind. It does not have to travel to the brain. It could originate in the brain. There is a mnemonic for classic signs for a stroke, which is abbreviated as FAST: F – face drooping (possibly just a lip); A- arm weakness; S- speech difficulty; T – time to call 911.

A stroke can kill someone instantly. Yet, it is also something that in many cases people can recover from. A couple of common effects of strokes are difficulty in movement, usually on one side more than the other. Some people have to relearn how to walk. But also, depending upon in which part of the brain the stroke takes place, it can affect things besides movement. One loss that occurs sometimes is aphasia. Aphasia is a very frustrating speech difficulty, where a person knows the word that they want to say, but they are unable to translate the impulse to use a word into actual speech. Or sometimes they can almost recall a word, but not quite. This can be improved with speech therapy and time to heal. I do also want to mention that if anyone should be unconscious, always watch what you say around them, because they may be able to hear you even though they cannot speak.

There are many other possible results of strokes. We found out long after the event that Paul had experienced two small strokes in the part of the brain that deals with language, not movement. and so they were not recognized as strokes. What they resulted in was confusion and memory problems. rather than outward physical problems. The first one was misdiagnosed as a panic attack. In his case, he kept asking the same question over and over, such as, "What day is it?" So if anyone you are with suddenly seems very confused or behaves in a very odd way, make sure they get immediate medical attention. In Paul's case, it wasn't until it happened a second time that I got him to a neurologist, and that he got the right diagnosis and treatment.

There is also a condition known as a TIAs: transient ischemic attacks. A TIA is also known as a mini-stroke. The mini-stroke can mimic many of the same effects as a stroke, but it only lasts for a few minutes, and it doesn't necessarily have the same permanent consequences. However, a person can have a series of mini-strokes, and they are considered a warning sign. About a third of the people who experience one have a stroke within a year. So careful testing is essential.

Essentially if anyone is acting oddly, you always want to get them to a doctor. Stroke, heart attacks and many other conditions can cause unusual behavior and need to be treated immediately.

Blood Thinners

If you have any of the conditions above, there's a good chance that you'll be placed on blood thinners. There is more than one kind of blood thinner. Stronger kinds of blood thinners require that you get regular tests to make sure that your blood isn't thinned out too much. If you are on Coumadin (warfarin), you will regularly get tested for something called INR/Prothrombin time. Having your blood too thin can be dangerous, because even a little cut can result in excessive bleeding. You've probably seen ads for Eliquis, which is a milder kind of blood thinner. That is what Paul was on. When I mentioned that he was on a blood thinner, some of my friends on Facebook were giving me advice about how you can't eat certain foods, etc. But that is not true for the kind of blood thinner he was on. Plavix is the most common name of the stronger kind of blood thinner. if you are placed on Plavix, I would ask if it would be possible to be on Eliquis instead. Of course, everyone's medical case is different. If you are on any kind of blood thinner, you have to be extra careful and possibly adjust the dosage if you find yourself bleeding. This is a particularly common problem for men if they use a straight razor. If you are a man on a blood thinner, I would suggest switching to an electric shaver.

If you are on any kind of blood thinner, you need to be certain to tell all of your health care providers, even ones you might not necessarily think would need to know. Your eye doctor, for example, needs to know about your blood pressure and related things, when considering your risk for glaucoma. Your dentist and even your dental hygienist need to know, because sometimes, people who are on blood thinners have to have their doctors sign physician's orders indicating whether or not they are safe to receive dental procedures that could cause oral bleeding, especially extractions and even deep cleanings. For some dental procedures, your doctor might be required to provide your INR/Prothrombin time results to your dentist, and your doctor might instruct you to hold (refrain from taking) your blood thinner for between 1 and 5 days before the dental procedure, and/or, might prescribe taking an antibiotic anywhere between a day or two before and an hour before your procedure.

Statins

If your doctor tells you that your cholesterol count is high, she or he will want you to take a statin. Statins are drugs that lower the Cholesterol in your body. About 17 million Americans take them! You can also affect your count through changes in your diet. Many food chains have eliminated trans fats, which tend to raise your count and clog your arteries. Olive oil is often recommended for both cooking and eating. However, the fact is, no matter how healthy your diet, your genes are a big factor that you can't control and a reason you may have to use prescription drugs. I still remember shortly after we were married, Paul and I had blood tests. I was frustrated when I found that he, who had a bologna sandwich daily for lunch, had a much lower count than I with my salads. That's when I realized it is a combination of diet and genes.

These are things to discuss with your doctor. My doctor and I had gone back-and-forth over the years because he wanted me to take Simvastatin seven days a week, but I only took it four times a week. It generally does not have any significant side effects, but I always believe that every drug has some side effects, whether known yet or not.   And in more recent years I've heard that it may affect your memory. That is why I did not take it every night. Last year, I actually went down to three days a week, but my cholesterol count went up, so I agreed to go back to four. My current doctor cut the dose in half, so I agreed to take it every night. My doctors feel that the common use of statins is the main reason they have seen a lower rate of heart attacks and strokes over the years. It is true that high cholesterol does make it more likely that you will have health problems and is something that should be controlled.

If you take statins you need to have yearly blood tests, not just to check cholesterol levels, but also be sure to ask about your liver levels. Statins work by reducing certain liver enzymes, and do have the potential to damage the liver.

CHAPTER 29

Urinary Problems

This was one of Paul's major problem areas. Even as a child, he spent weeks in a hospital with nephritis, a kidney infection. It gave him a life-long dislike of hospitals. It is not unusual that he had prostate problems later in life. What was a serious problem came later on when he got a catheter.

Most urinary problems can happen to anyone, but there are some that vary with the type of urinary system you have, based on your biological sex.

Women

We all have been to a performance where the intermission had to be extended because of the long line at the women's bathroom. Older buildings were all designed by men. My friend Kate and I were the two women who helped design the theater section of the arts center at Moraine Valley. The first request we made was for extra bathrooms for women. Part of the problem is women's clothing, but part is that many pregnant and older women need to urinate frequently. You might want to consider limiting liquids before and during the performance.

Women, as they age, are likely to have occasional problems with what is called "stress incontinence". What happens is that when they laugh or sneeze, they may release a little unintentional trickle. This is very common. It does not necessarily indicate a health problem. It may be helped by doing a Kegel exercise where you stop and start your stream when you are urinating. I remember I learned that from Ann Landers. You can look online for more exercises. This helps the muscles. About the only other thing you can do about the situation is carry an extra pair of panties in the trunk of your car and in your flight bag, or if the problem is frequent, wear a pantyliner, or one of the new, discreet incontinence pads that look just like a menstrual pad, and can be placed, individually wrapped, in your purse or pocket. It does not mean that you have to go to the use of adult diapers. If you have a serious, continuing problem, then you would need to see your doctor to find out what the cause is. There is an operation that is sometimes done if you have a prolapsed bladder, which means it is no longer held in place. I know someone who had this surgery. It isn't a quick or easy recovery, but she felt it was well worth it. If you do you have to use adult diapers, then make sure that you get the pull-up kind and not the kind with tabs. The last thing you need is to worry about whether those tabs are going to stay in place. The exception is for those who leave home by themselves who are in wheelchairs or scooters. Many who have difficulty standing find it easier to use the adult diapers with tabs than to have to put both legs through the holes of the pull-up variety.

Men

Most men hate to go to a urologist and have a prostate exam, but it is essential. Older men very often have a problem with an enlarged prostate. This causes frequent urination and may mean getting up several times during the night, which can be very hazardous for those at risk of falling. If you have this problem, make sure that you have a night light on, and consider wearing grip socks like they have in hospitals to bed to make it less likely that you will fall down. We found that you can order them online quite cheaply. Of course you will want to see your urologist. Your urologist may suggest a procedure to reduce the prostate gland.

It is essential to have an enlarged prostate treated. Not only is the frequent urination and possible leakage embarrassing and inconvenient, but your urine may not be released fully, and this can lead to urinary tract infections. So it is not only a matter of convenience; it is a matter of health.

There are drugs that can help, in some cases. But if they are not the option your doctor thinks will help in your case, there are various surgical ways to treat an enlarged prostate, including with lasers and heat. These are generally done on an outpatient basis, and in fact may even just be done in your doctor's office. Of course, you will discuss the options with your urologist. If you have had these treatments more than once, the doctor will probably suggest actually removing the prostate. This is a pretty common operation, but it often leads to erectile dysfunction.

Of course today, there are erectile dysfunction medications that are widely available, such as Viagra. However, these are not as great as they sound. You certainly have heard the line about "If you should have an erection lasting more than...."If that happens it can be painful and serious. In addition, they can cause other serious side effects, such as loss of hearing. I would really think twice before taking any of these medications. There are many other ways that a couple can be intimate.

Prostate Cancer

Prostate cancer, unfortunately, is not rare. I have known people who have had it. That is one of the reasons you want to go for a regular urological exam. I have also heard of people developing prostate cancer and being told by the doctors that it is a slow-growing cancer and that it was best to just not treat it at all. I have known people who have died or been widowed by prostate cancer. If you were told this by your doctor, I would get a second opinion. Of course, If you are in your 90's and it's going to take 10 years for prostate cancer to kill you, you probably don't want to go through the rigors of treatment. However, if you're in your 60s or 70s, and otherwise in solid health, treatment would definitely be worth investigating.

General Urinary Problems

When you urinate, you may notice that the color is sometimes different. Usually the only change is that it is darker or lighter. If it is darker, that could indicate that you were not drinking enough water, or that you've had salty foods that make you retain water. Very simply, just drink more water and consider cutting back on salty foods. Another possibility is that your urine contains a concentration of vitamins, if you have been taking a lot of supplements.

However, sometimes urine can be an odd color. I wouldn't be too concerned about that unless it lasts for more than a few days. Changes in color can be because you started taking a new medication, even if it's over-the-counter. For example, a number of various kinds of vitamin products have artificial coloring in them that transfers to the urine. It can be disconcerting to notice that your urine looks rather blue, but it's really nothing to worry about. It can also be affected by what you eat or drink. One time, I became very concerned because my urine looked red and I assumed that it meant that I had blood in it. When I called my doctor brother about this the first thing he asked, in his calm manner, was, "Did you eat any beets last night?" Indeed, I had eaten at a Middle Eastern restaurant where I enjoyed the pickled red turnips very much.

There are times, however, where changes can be meaningful. If, for example, you should see a trickle of blood in the urine, rather than just a little bit of a pinkish color, and you are past menopause, I would be concerned about that. There are also other colors that can indicate problems. Very dark or cloudy urine can indicate problems, but once again I wouldn't worry about it if it is something that just happens for a day or two. If something goes on for several days I would definitely talk to your doctor about it. You can also google information and just put in something like "cloudy urine". Of course, you will often get worst case scenarios.

The one situation where you would need to seek immediate care would be if you could not urinate at all for several hours.

UTIs

UTI stands for urinary tract infection. These are pretty common and can range in seriousness from just an annoyance to being life-threatening. Some indications of a urinary tract infection would be frequent urination and discomfort or burning upon urination. This should be treated before it turns into something more serious. A serious urinary tract infection could potentially result in fever, dizziness and confusion. If it should get into the bloodstream, it becomes a condition known as sepsis. Sepsis is very dangerous, and if not treated, it can kill someone. Paul had sepsis more than once. Fortunately, it is something that can be treated if it is caught early enough, but it does result in hospitalization. So, if you should at all suspect that you have a urinary tract infection, be sure to contact your doctor right away. He or she will have you give a urine sample either at the office, at a hospital, or at home. However, if it is at home, you cannot simply collect your sample in an ordinary container. You need to get a special sterile container for the sample, and follow specific directions. It may take a couple of days to get results, and your doctor might have you start an antibiotic, just in case. If you have ever had any kind of negative reaction to an antibiotic, you want to always be sure anyone who might prescribe anything to you knows about it. Some antibiotics with different names are similar enough that if you are allergic or had bad side effects to antibiotic A, they not only need to not prescribe you that one, but also not prescribe you antibiotic B that is in the same family as A.

Bladder Cancer

Bladder cancer is one of the more survivable forms of cancer, because it is possible to remove a part of the organ rather than the entire organ. My father had bladder cancer twice, and both times they were able to cut out just a part of the bladder. He did not need to have a bag or anything. Of course, if not knocked out early on, it could result in death, but it is usually treatable.

Catheters

It is very common for people to be catheterized when they are in the hospital. If you are unconscious, you do not have a way to get up to go to the bathroom. Even if you are conscious, it may be decided that it's too difficult for you to use a bedpan or go to the bathroom, and so you are catheterized. Catheterization involves putting a tube into the urethra, which then goes out into a plastic bag. An advantage to your doctors and nurses is it is then very easy for them to monitor your urinary output. They can look at the color of the urine to see if it is normal, as well as looking at the volume. The repository for the urine has measuring increments.

When you are discharged from the hospital, they will often insist that you go to the bathroom first before you leave. This can be true for even short hospital stays. They want to make sure that your kidneys and bladder are functioning normally. Sometimes if a hospital stay is very long or you have underlying conditions, the bladder may have trouble restarting its function. The kidneys could be fine, but the bladder isn't. The kidneys do the filtering of the urine from the blood. However, the bladder is the organ that controls the release of the urine. Like a muscle, if not used for quite a while it can atrophy. This effect can also be magnified if you have Parkinson's or certain other medical problems. In this case the bladder may never regain its function. This happened to Paul.

If the bladder does not regain its function, then you will have to retain a catheter when you leave the hospital. If you see a urologist there are exercises they can try to get the bladder to restart. However, that doesn't always work. Having a catheter between your legs is of course not something anyone wants to live with, so you will be offered a couple of options.

One of those options is to catheterize yourself manually a few times a day. You would then not have anything permanent inserted. This is not something Paul wanted to attempt. It would have been next to impossible with his shaky hands.

Another alternative is a suprapubic catheter. Supra means above, so above the pubic area. This involves minor surgery to insert the catheter directly into the bladder. A tube then comes out from the bladder near your navel and hangs alongside the body to go to a bag. This is, of course, not a pleasant option, but it may be the better option for many people. Any permanent catheter is sometimes referred to as a Foley.

One advantage of having a suprapubic catheter is that you do not have to worry about getting up during the night to go to the bathroom. Indeed, you don't have to worry when you are at performances or any-where else. You simply have to make sure that you empty the bag when it gets close to being full. Of course, there are other reasons to go to the bathroom.

Neither one of us had any idea how to deal with many of the prob-lems associated with having a catheter. Once I knew how complicated it is, I actually considered writing a booklet and selling it to doctors' offices to give out to patients. I had to learn so much through trial and error. Because you have this book, you will have the advantage of my experiences.

There are various kinds of bags that you will be using if you have a suprapubic catheter at home. In a nursing home, they might not give you those options. The large bags that you see in hospitals are the night bags. You want to make sure that you have a larger bag at night so that it does not fill up while you are sleeping. These plastic bags have a hook that can be hung on a bed railing or dangled on the floor, but of course you do want to make sure that you do not step on them.

During the day there are much more discrete day bags. These are worn on the leg underneath pants. If the pants are a little bit on the loose side and not knit pants, the bags should not be visible. They even make very small bags that are designed to be worn with longish shorts or dresses. These do not have as much of a capacity, of course, and they have to be emptied more often, but they are discreet as long as you wear cargo- type shorts and not short-shorts. So you can lead an active, normal life with a catheter. The only thing that would be a problem would be swimming. I am not sure that the mini catheter that goes in underneath shorts would work with a swimsuit. Perhaps in male swim trunks it might be possible. We never investigated that because Paul didn't go swimming because he was conscious of his varicose veins, which had come back.

Changing Bags

You have to allow several minutes every morning and every evening for changing the bags. Be sure to do this procedure in the bathroom in case some urine drips on the floor. The leg bag is the day bag, and then there is the larger night bag that you have to prepare at night. Every time, before you remove a bag, you have to empty it into the toilet. When you have it off, place it in the sink while you are getting the new one set. Then empty it again if there is anything in it and then rinse it thoroughly in the sink. Your doctor may recommend that instead of just using plain water you use a combination of water and vinegar or something else to make sure it is clean. Talk to them about that. Make sure that the bag is completely cleaned out and clear, and then leave the valve open for it to drain. Then hang it in the shower stall so if anyone comes over they don't have to see it, and allow it to dry before changing again for the next time. You absolutely must do this, morning and evening, every day.

The Types of Valves

Day bags vary in a couple of ways. One of them is the type of valve opening. Whenever Paul would go home from the hospital they would give him one that had a *twist* valve. We learned from experience that I should bring one of his bags with me when he was going to be discharged. The twist valves tend to come open and leak. Plus, if you have difficulty using your hands, twist valves may be hard to manipulate. We much preferred the *tap* valve, where you simply raised and lowered the clamp. So if you do order bags, be sure to be specific about the type.

Straps

You also need straps to hold the bag to your leg, and those vary as well. The ones that they would give my husband at the hospital would be plastic and would start to become uncomfortable and binding. The bags we ordered came with cloth straps that buttoned. After a while I knew how many buttons to cut off for the top of the bag and how many for the bottom. While they were better than the plastic ones, you can't have them too tight, or they will be irritating; nor too loose, which will allow the bag to move around.   Also, above the bag we placed a leg band with a Velcro closure. On top of that there was a small Velcro tab to hold the tube. If any of this is confusing, check Youtube.

Anchors

One thing we found out about pretty late along was that you can order adhesive patches that are used to anchor the catheter tube. They are placed on the front of the thigh where the tube divides and will stay on for a few to several days, even with showers. The advantage is that you can then skip the leg band, which if too tight can cut off circulation.

Purchasing Equipment

When my sister-in-law had a suprapubic catheter, I would pay her aide to drive to a place several miles away and purchase a set of bags. I must not have done very much investigating, because the fact is that you can order over the phone and set up an account for your regular monthly order. It will be delivered to your house, and Medicare will pay for all of it. It shouldn't cost you anything unless there's something special that you want. It's a little bit of trouble to set up the account, but really not bad, and once it is set up you just go online or call up and say that you want your usual order and they send it out. It's that easy, For the initial order you will have to have them contact your urologist. You may want to order more than one size of bag the first time to see what works best for you. We used a company called McKesson, but there are probably others out there. They even sent monthly reminders and had good phone service. Occasionally there was a problem with an order, but if I called and said that we were out of supplies they would send it Express.

An Important Tip

Having a bag on your leg normally means that every time you go to the bathroom, you have to pull down your pants to have access to the drain. However, we learned to order an extension tube for the catheter. The bag then hung close to the ankle, and all that was needed to empty it was to pull up the pants leg a bit. The foot could be balanced on the rim of the toilet bowl and the valve opened. Paul would sit on a stool and do this. The alternative is to sit on a chair and empty into a small pitcher, which is then emptied into the toilet and rinsed. We ordered the larger extension tube and I would measure the amount that needed to be cut off, using my hand as a guide, cut it, and insert it as far as possible to attach it to the regular tube on the bag.

The Dangers of Suprapubic Catheters

There are two major dangers involved with suprapubic catheters. Of course no one has a catheter unless they really have to have it. So you need to learn to watch out for these dangers and deal with them.

Blockage

The first danger is that the tube can become blocked from blood clots. There are various causes for the blood clots, such as the catheter not being quite properly placed and scraping the bladder. Whatever the cause, you will notice that not much is coming out of the tube when you empty it. It is essential that this blockage be cleared or the urine can back up into the bladder, which is dangerous. We went to emergency rooms a few times because Paul's became blocked. If we were at home during regular doctor's office hours, he would go to the doctor, but sometimes we were traveling or it was the weekend and we had to go to an emergency room. Here is an important warning: Most urgent care centers, and even some emergency centers do not have a urologist on staff and will not deal with catheter problems, so be sure to call ahead. Of course it's a big pain because you wind up waiting for a couple of hours before you are seen. One time, fortunately, I watched a nurse as she cleared the tube and watched how she used a syringe filled with water to do so. I then asked the urologist to get me syringes, and I was able to successfully clear the blockage a few times at home. This was a great relief. I suggest that you talk to your urologist about how to do that. The day before Paul died, I told the head nurse three times that I noticed his bag was empty and she assured me she would check for a blockage. By chance I found out the blockage wasn't cleared until the next morning and I always wondered if it contributed to his death. I even considered an autopsy, but besides not knowing how to get one I decided I did not want to spend months in court.

UTIs with Catheters

Having a suprapubic catheter increases your chances of getting a urinary tract infection. There are various signs of having one that you can look for. I talked about some of these earlier in the chapter on urology, such as fever, dizziness, and confusion. Another sign that you may have one would be if you see that there is an odd color to your urine, or that you have an unusual number of clots. While the clots may be from the tube being misplaced, it may also be triggered by an infection.

If you suspect a urinary tract infection you need to get a sample taken at your doctor's office or wherever very promptly. If you take the sample at home or even a family physician's office you need to make sure that it comes from the catheter tube itself and not from the bag, and it must go into a sterile container. Even when we went to our family practitioner he did not know that until I told him. Paul was hospitalized several times for urinary tract infections, and in fact, when he got West Nile, that was what they assumed it was when he was first admitted because of his history. Remember: Urinary tract infections can be very serious, and if not treated, can even be fatal.

Monthly Visits

If you have a suprapubic catheter it is essential that you go to your urologist and have the tube changed once a month. This was never too much of a problem for us except when traveling. Then we had to research where we could find a urologist near where we were visiting at the time that it needed to be changed. They would have to have information from the home urologist about the correct tube to use. The biggest difficulties were when Paul was being transferred from one hospital to another, and then in the nursing home, trying to keep track of the fact that it had been a month. Do not count on any medical facility to keep track of that for you. You will have to do that yourself and tell them when it is time to make that change. I learned that the hard way. One of the facilities said they would change the tube before the transfer -- but they didn't. You have to keep track and stay on top of the situation.

A More Unusual Problem

In addition to changing bags twice a day, your doctor will probably want you to keep a bandage around the area on the abdomen right by where the tube comes out. Have them show you how to cut the gauze bandage and tape it in place. One time I noticed that there was an odd smell when I was near Paul but I had no idea what it was. I thought it might be a dental problem. When he started feeling ill, we were traveling, so we went to an emergency room. It turned out that the problem was not a urinary tract infection. Rather, it was a fungal infection in the area where the tube came out of the skin near the naval. The nurse told me, without my even saying anything, "That's what that odd smell is you've been noticing." So I knew for the future what to be aware of. Treating this required a special fungicide, but it did work on an outpatient basis. He did get a second fungal infection, but we were able to apply the leftover medicine and treat it very quickly so that it never required a doctor's visit. The fungicide that was prescribed was incredibly expensive. Fortunately, the pharmacist suggested an alternative, and we got it approved.

Be Prepared

You need to be proactive when dealing with catheters. First, think ahead about ordering your supplies. The bags only last just so long, and when you place your order, there may be a lag of a week or so until it arrives.

Also, occasionally there can be an accident, such as a leg brushing against a valve or a bag developing a small leak. Obviously, this is a problem, especially when you travel. I suggest carrying an extra bag and an extra pair of pants with you. One time Paul got a leak while we were in an airport and about to board a plane. After I got over my initial minute of panic, I was just lucky that I was able to find someone who worked there who had duct tape. That taught me to be better prepared after that.

CHAPTER 30

Cancer

There isn't any way that I can completely cover such a broad topic, but here is a little information. Few words are more feared than cancer. The name "carcinoma," to describe a tumor, was the Greek term coined by Hippocrates about 2400 years ago. He had a patient with a tumor that reminded him of the shape of a crab, and carcinoma, which is still used today to describe cancer tumors, derived from the Greek word for crab. In Latin, the word for crab was "cancer," and when Hippocrates' works were translated into Latin, "carcinoma" became "cancer". That is why there is an astrological sign with the same name. The constellation appeared to be a crab.

Causes

This history tells us that while there are environmental causes for cancer, there are also genetic ones. In fact, there is one gene that makes it almost certain that a woman will get breast cancer. Some women, including Angelina Jolie, have had mastectomies (breast removal) before they ever had any signs of cancer, just based on the presence of this gene in their blood tests.

However, our modern environment is full of carcinogens, which are pollutants or other chemicals that can cause or make it more likely for you to get cancer. Watch the PBS documentary, "The Great Invisible," about the oil tanker crisis involving the "Deepwater Horizon," or the Mark Ruffalo movie, "Dark Waters," as examples of extreme cases of environmental toxicity. I suggest reading up on this topic. There are difficult things you can do to help, such as giving up smoking or moving to a less polluted area, but there are simple things you can do ,such as avoiding heating and storing your food in plastic, and reading labels and trying to limit chemicals in your food. I just read a surprising article that being sedentary significantly increases your chances of getting cancer. So do some of your activities standing instead of sitting.

Kinds of Cancer

The most common kinds of cancer are skin, breast, lung, prostate and colorectal. However, you can get cancer in any part of your body. I've known people who got cancer on the spine, on the appendix, and even the male breast. What is cancer? Something happens to some cells and they start growing. They create a tumor, which is a collection of cells that shouldn't be there. Tumors can be benign or malignant. Malignant tumor is a form of cancer, and left untreated will destroy a part or all of the body, and often cause death. A benign tumor is not harmful in and of itself. However, they are usually removed because they are unsightly or because they can interfere with other functions of your body. For example, they could press against nerves or blood vessels as they grow. A doctor would have to evaluate if the tumor is dangerous and perhaps keep track of whether it is growing or not.

One particularly dangerous place to have a benign tumor is in the brain. My brother, Art, had one of these and had to have it removed. Had it kept growing it would have overwhelmed parts of the brain and caused all sorts of terrible effects. He had to have part of his skull removed for the operation and stapled back on. As a big movie fan, I think he rather enjoyed comparing himself to Frankenstein after the operation. He even took selfies. Within a few months you couldn't even see that anything had happened. It's pretty remarkable.

A doctor can suspect that a tumor is benign or malignant by looking at tests, but the only way you can know for sure is from a biopsy. Many women go through the discomfort of a breast biopsy because a mammogram is uncertain. In most cases it is benign, so don't get too upset if it happens to you. In a biopsy they examine a small sample from the tumor or suspicious area and see if it is benign or malignant. If the tumor is benign and they feel that they have removed all of it, then no further treatment will be needed, except to follow up after a period of time to make sure that it has not returned. If, on the other hand, it is malignant, It is dangerous, and there will likely be follow up procedures.

If the tumor is malignant, it is cancer and will attack the body. The biggest danger of a malignant tumor is that it might metastasize. That means that it will leave the place of origin and spread to other parts of the body. Once it has metastasized it becomes extremely difficult to isolate and kill it. The odds of success become much worse for the patient. In addition to the traditional radiation and chemotherapy, there are several new treatments, including ones that are more targeted at the tumor. The field is constantly changing, so if you are diagnosed with cancer listen to your doctor but also do some research on your own.

Odds of Success

How successful cancer treatment is depends on a combination of factors. The first is how soon it is caught. You may hear somebody say that they have stage one cancer, stage two cancer, etc. The higher the number the more advanced it is. If it's a stage one cancer it has been caught very early and the odds of a successful treatment are much better. That's why having regular, proactive screenings, such as mammograms and prostate exams, is so important. The worst is a stage four cancer. However, if you find out that you have a stage four cancer, that does not necessarily mean that it's a death sentence. I've known people who have survived stage four cancer.

The next factor is what part of the body is being attacked. Some parts of the body are easier to treat than others. If, for example, you have bladder cancer and it's caught fairly early, you have a very good chance of survival. On the other hand, if you have pancreatic cancer, your odds of recovering from that are not as good. Everyone was riveted by the stage 4 Cancer diagnosis of Alex Trebek, the TV host of Jeopardy, but he continued his work and looked great. Unfortunately he later died from his disease.

Though I suspect that perhaps his lovely hair might have been replaced by a wig. I don't know that for sure, but after all, cancer treatments often cause hair loss.

Finally, there are some factors that are not so quantifiable, such as genetics, general health, and attitude. Most people also feel that prayer helps. It couldn't hurt, unless the religion advocates prayer instead of treatment, rather than in addition to treatment.

Skin Cancer

One of the most common kinds of cancer is skin cancer. Skin cancers are generally classified as either basal or squamous cell carcinomas or melanomas. It's very common for people to have skin cancer because of sun exposure. When we were young we were encouraged to sunbathe to get a suntan and wore lotions that increased tanning, rather than protect you from the sun. There are also people who have used tanning beds for appearance. Those are a really horrible idea and very dangerous. When I was a little girl, there was a teenager next-door to us who used to spend the summer in a lounge chair in the backyard holding a reflector to get more sun on her skin to have a better tan. My guess is that she probably did not live to a ripe old age. When you go out and you're going to be in the sun for a while, be sure to wear good sunscreen. Many face creams have sunscreens as part of their ingredients and many people I know use them every single day year round. After all, in colder weather your skin is largely covered, but your face still gets sun exposure, even as you are driving. For the rest of your body check the spf number on the packaging and use one that is 30 or above. If you already have a sunburn raise the number and look for one that says sun block rather than sunscreen. Be especially sure to cover scar tissue.

If you find out that you have a basal cell carcinoma, which is very common, do not get too scared. This is probably the least dangerous kind of cancer there is. It does not tend to spread out of its immediate area. As long as it is caught fairly early on, it should be removed and that should be the end of it. Unlike cancer of an internal organ, you can see you have it. This is the only kind of cancer that Paul had. I had read a little bit about these things and knew to watch out for a wound that does not heal. I noticed that he had a scab on the corner of his forehead. I didn't worry about that, even though he didn't remember how he had gotten it. There's always a chance you could scrape against something or not remember it. However, when it came off and came back a second and third time I told him he needed to go to a doctor.

Sure enough, he had a basal cell carcinoma. It was a simple procedure to remove it in the doctor's office. No further treatment was ever needed. Of course, like anything else, there can be complications and I have a friend who had one removed from her nose and had problems with it not healing well. After a few weeks, though, everything was all right. Squamous cell cancers are also treatable if not too advanced.

If, on the other hand, you find out that you have a melanoma, *you do* need to be worried and you do need to have it taken care of immediately. This is a potentially deadly form of skin cancer that can kill quickly. Watch any moles that you have. You might want to go to a dermatologist once a year for a thorough exam where they check your whole body for moles. Moles in and of themselves are not dangerous, but if you have one that is black and irregular in shape be sure to mention it to a doctor. If you go to a dermatologist regularly they will be able to spot a melanoma immediately, though they will want to biopsy it to confirm it. Someone I know is very lucky that she knew a dermatologist and he spotted a melanoma on her when they were socializing.

Other Kinds of Cancer

Every woman hates mammograms, but you do need to have them once a year. I know they are painful, but it's possible that it could save your life. I think we all know somebody who has had breast cancer. It is that common today. If someone has breast cancer and they are lucky they will have a lumpectomy, which means just some lymph nodes in the breast will be removed, but in many cases they have to have a mastectomy, which means the entire breast is removed. Today, it is possible to rebuild the breast rather than just wearing a special bra. I have a friend who had breast cancer and elected to have the breast replacement happen immediately so that she woke up from the surgery with the breast already rebuilt rather than a flat scar area .

If you lose your hair because of radiation or chemo treatments, short hair can be stylish, and there are all sorts of stylish turbans and wigs available both human hair and synthetic. Natural looking synthetic wigs are only about $30 or $40 online.

I have spoken about prostate cancer in the urology section and colon cancer in the digestive system section, and you can refer to those there.

If you have a friend with cancer, one of the best things you can do for them is to offer to drive them to their doctors' visits, as they may have quite a few of them as they are following up. Of course, if anyone has any health problems it is best to simply ask in a sincere way what you can do to help. There is also a wonderful thing called Meal Train, where you can set up a schedule for someone to have friends bring them meals.You could also look into the program called Meals on Wheels for them. Also, if they are a senior, some senior services will deliver food to them. If they are not covered by Medicare for some reason and have medical bills, you could also possibly set up a GoFundMe account.

CHAPTER 31

Parkinson's Disease

This was one of Paul's many plagues, and one of the most serious. Paul had had shaky hands for several years and was told that it was a benign familial tremor, which could not be helped. When he was finally diagnosed as having Parkinson's it came as a bit of a relief to us to have confirmation of what we suspected and a name and cause for his problem. Little did we know how serious Parkinson's is.

What is Parkinson's?

I thought that Parkinson's was merely a tremor in the hands. I was so wrong. When, shortly after his diagnosis, Paul saw the doctor he was seeing about constipation and mentioned he had Parkinson's, the doctor said "Oh, no wonder you're having this problem". We thought that was an excuse for lack of success, but the same thing happened with every specialist he saw. It was annoying that none of them had ever suggested that he be checked for Parkinson's. I did a little research and found out that Parkinson's affects every single part of your body. It is a gradual deterioration of the nerves that control every aspect of it. It affects all kinds of things, such as digestion, and as we found out later, even vision. It can, in some cases, eventually cause death.

Some Effects

We finally learned that the reason that Paul was having so much trouble with reading, one of his greatest pleasures, was that there was a little shake in his eyes which was barely noticeable unless you were really looking for it. I was dreading some of the complications that I read could happen. For example, some people with Parkinson's lose some control of their face and cannot smile. Fortunately, it never got to the point where it affected Paul's face, and he always had a wonderful smile, when there was something to smile about, which became less and less frequent. However, he would sometimes look at me with love in his eyes, and I was very fortunate that that expression never changed.

Parkinson's also can affect walking. It can cause bent-over posture, and it can cause a condition where occasionally the legs freeze up on you for a moment, which can cause a fall. Paul did have problems with these things, but it was hard to tell how much was Parkinson's and how much was his arthritic back, periphery, or other problems that he had.

What Causes Parkinson's?

Parkinson's is caused by the lack of an enzyme called dopamine in the brain, so it is necessary to take drugs to compensate for that. Levo-dopa is the standard drug. Like most drugs it does cause some drowsiness and other problems. Parkinson's eventually does lead to death. But it progresses at really different rates for different people. The progress could be extremely slow, so that it takes years for the changes to take effect, or it could be relatively rapid. Michael J. Fox was diagnosed with an early onset case many years ago and has continued to act, so that is a hopeful example. However, even the rapid changes do not occur overnight. They occur over months rather than years. So I knew that the one doctor I talked to in a hospital about an overnight change in Paul's condition, who said Parkinson's causes changes, was unreasonable and not to be listened to. Art and I both think Paul had a small stroke that time and when the doctor examined him he sent him to intensive care.

Diagnosing Parkinson's

Diagnosing Parkinson's is not easy. There isn't a simple blood test, for example, that will tell you that a person has Parkinson's. The diagnosis is essentially behavioral. The neurologist will look at movements. For example, people who have Parkinson's generally do not swing their arms when they walk. A very early warning sign that you might be liable to have Parkinson's is lack of a sense of smell. However, there are other causes for that, now including COVID-19, so that is by no means definitive. Paul did not have a sense of smell from the time he was a child.

I just read online that the latest research is aimed at using smell to detect who has Parkinsons. They found that a person could smell it and they are working on an artificial nose to detect it. The hope is that they will be able to diagnose it before symptoms appear and that early treatment might help.

The Parkinson's Foundation lists the following as early warning signs of Parkinson's:

1. Tremor
2. Decreased size of handwriting
3. Loss of smell
4. Trouble sleeping and increased movement
5. Trouble walking
6. Constipation
7. Soft or low voice
8. A depressed look on your face
9. Dizziness or fainting
10. Stooping or hunching over

If I had seen this list, I would have taken Paul to a specialist and gotten him on the right drugs sooner.

Causes of Parkinson's

There are a variety of things that can cause Parkinson's, and it is not fully understood. However, there seems to be a genetic predisposition, so if someone in your family has Parkinson's you are more likely to get it. Paul's father did have Parkinson's, but he also had the second cause, which is head injuries. His father had been "a linesman for the county" when he was young, only it was really for Illinois Bell. He rode a motorcycle through the countryside checking telephone lines and had two major accidents. One time his motorcycle hit a pothole and he was thrown from it, and the other time he was up on a line and got electrocuted, but amazingly fell on a railroad tie and his heart was restarted. In both cases he had major injuries and was in the hospital for a while. We had been hoping that those injuries, not genetics, had been the cause of his Parkinson's.

Another possible cause is chemical exposure. This was proven by the number of first responders who got Parkinson's after working in the ruins of the World Trade Center after the 9/11 attacks. It was way, way beyond the normal percentage, so it appears to have been obviously due to exposure to toxic elements. While Paul disagreed with me, I always felt that his six years of developing photos six days a week in his one-hour photo shop affected his neurological health. So was it genetics or was it chemical exposure or a combination thereof? We'll never know and I guess that doesn't really matter, except to warn you to try to avoid chemical exposure without proper ventilation.

Help Dealing with Parkinson's

If someone is diagnosed with Parkinson's, be aware of some things that I was not aware of for quite a while. First, there are Parkinson's support groups. You can find them by Googling online, and I strongly suggest going to one of them. If your partner will not go with you, you can go alone, because support groups are not only for people who have a condition but also for the people who have to adjust around caring for someone with that condition.

The other thing that I really didn't check into very well is that there are Parkinson's specialists. Paul was already seeing a neurologist for treatment of his seizures, and we liked our neurologist very much, so we continued to go to him, but there are people who specialize in just Parkinson's. I actually found one later on, very close to the nursing home Paul was in. I asked if the doctor could come to the nursing home, since of course it was too far for his neurologist, but they wouldn't do that for a new patient.

Living with Parkinson's

If you are living with someone who has Parkinson's, you need to schedule a certain amount of time each day to help them. If you are a person with Parkinson's and you are living by yourself, it is going to become a growing problem. You will probably either need an aide to come in in the morning and at bedtime, or you will need to move to assisted living.

Someone first referred to me as a caretaker after I mentioned that Paul had Parkinson's.

I replied that it wasn't difficult for me because all I was doing was helping him button his shirts. After a little while longer I would say I was just helping him button his shirts and pouring his liquids. These are some of the things that you do have to do. As time goes on more and more tasks get added to the list.

For example, Paul was able at first to button his shirts with the help of a button hook, but that ability was lost after a while. I had to do other things, though it was never too burdensome. However, it was a concern if I actually had some work to do, such as a film shoot. I would have to think ahead and do things like button his shirt except for the top button so that he could put it over his head, or get a T-shirt ready that did not require buttoning. I would pour his liquids into a covered cup so he wouldn't spill when pouring, and prepare a plate of food for him to heat up, etc. After a while I also had to help him put on his socks. After a while it became a problem even to get a plate of food ready, because odds were that Paul might very well spill it while putting it in or taking it out of the microwave.

Some Items That Can Help

There are some devices that you can buy that will help someone with Parkinson's. If you are in a hospital and released, you can ask the occupational therapist if they will give you some of these items to take home, and they often will.

First, there are weighted utensils. It's very hard to eat when your fork, spoon, etc. are shaking and moving around. If you have weighted utensils they do not shake as easily, and so it's easier to keep the food on them. There are two kinds of weighted utensils. The first are utensils that have an extra thick handle and intrinsically weigh more. The second kind, which you can buy online, is weighted pieces that the silverware will slip into. You put the silverware in and then twist it so that the weighted handle stays on it. You then remove it to wash the silverware. They were very handy for us because they were easy to take to restaurants and you didn't have to worry about the weighted silverware being in the dishwasher and unavailable.

When we would go to eat out I would pack a bag. In it I would have either the weighted utensils or the handles to add to the utensils and a bib or full apron that ties or goes around the neck. Paul felt a little more dignified putting on an apron instead of a bib, so that is something to consider. I would also take a plastic bag to put the apron and utensils in after he was done eating.

The other things that I would bring, and that we also used at home, were cups with lids. It's very easy to spill liquids if you don't have a lid on the glass or cup. It's rather like what you have to do with a toddler. If you should forget your covered glass or cup, the restaurant may have some available because they may have them for children to avoid messes.

You can ask. However, those may be very small. I bought some full-sized ones at Dollar Tree. In fact, they had a variety to choose from. I think they are intended for picnics. The other thing that you might need to bring with you are straws. Restaurants always used to have straws available, but since there has been a movement against plastic and they sometimes do not have them, it is best to have your own. You can buy packages of those at Dollar Tree as well. You can purchase online metal reusable straws which you can take with you and rinse out, and then you don't have to feel guilty about plastic.

Another type of eating aid, which we did not carry with us but we did occasionally use at home, is the type of plastic bowls and plates that have suction cups on the bottom to keep them steady.

Some other aids that are helpful include button hooks to increase the amount of time of independence and the Carson e Z Reader that I talk about in the section on vision problems. With Parkinson's you may need a special prescription for glasses that is not the standard prescription, so that even if you have vision coverage, you may still have to pay a supplement. Of course, one of the aids that you will need is a walker or rollator, because of the unsteady gait and the possibility of falling. I also went to several stores before I found a universal TV remote with extra large buttons. Some cable companies now offer them with voice commands. I also found a flip phone that had buttons, not a touchscreen and had voice command for dialing. I went to Ebay to find one.

Of course, many people today have voice command aids, such as Alexa. I've been leery about getting one, but if Paul were still alive I would almost certainly get one for him. However, if you're considering it, be aware that there is some setup involved. For example, you need a piece to connect it to a lamp. I've also gotten used to voice commands with Siri and realize Paul could have used a smartphone. Of course that would have cost more. Since he only had the phone for emergencies and to call me, we just got an inexpensive prepaid plan from Tracfone for about $10 a month.

If you have short-term care coverage or you are willing to pay for it yourself, you can have someone come in to get meals ready and help when the patient first gets up and when they are getting ready for bed. As you can see, living with Parkinson's is a daily challenge. People can continue to lead an active life if they can manage to not be self-conscious about things like their hands shaking. It is important to continue getting out as long as possible to avoid losing mobility and getting depressed.

There are also exercise classes designed especially for people with Parkinson's. By the time I became aware of them Paul's back was too bad to participate and he didn't want to attempt it.

Hallucinations and Delusions

Many Parkinson's patients develop hallucinations and delusions. A hallucination is something visual that you see, rather like a mirage. Sometimes people see doubles of things. Several times Paul asked me if there were really two of something, or was there really such and such a thing there because he thought that it was unlikely that what he was seeing was true. It wasn't a real problem. *(Note: Double vision can also sometimes indicate concussion/traumatic brain injury to a cranial nerve; be sure to be seen by a doctor, especially if it comes on suddenly.)*

A delusion is not visual. It is an idea. For example, people who are delusional may be paranoid and think that somebody is out to get them or that other bad things are happening.

Ironically, Paul only began to have serious problems with these things once the nursing home suggested, and I was convinced to agree to, put him on a drug you see advertised on TV that is supposed to help with Parkinson's hallucinations. It actually caused some major, detailed hallucinations. While it did help to pass his boring time to watch the goings on at an airport or amusement park outside his window, I didn't want him divorcing from reality. I suspected that the drug might be the cause and looked it up online. I saw that there were lawsuits about it causing hallucinations and other mental problems. It took very concerted effort to get them to stop giving it to him. Once that was accomplished, he began to return to normal. Perhaps the drug would be helpful to you or yours, but I suggest that you monitor the reaction over the first several days if you try it. If asked to put someone on it, or really with any drug, make it clear to a nursing home or other facility that this is a week's trial, and you want to take them off of the drug after a week if they are not better.

It should be noted that we were dealing with Parkinson's and still getting out and enjoying life. The Parkinson's did not put Paul in the nursing home. It was the West Nile Virus that put him in first hospitals and then the nursing home. If it had not been for that we could have gone on for a considerably longer period of time with him living at home and still getting out and coping with matters.

Is There Hope?

Parkinson's is, at least for now, an incurable disease. However, there are a couple of organizations involved with intensive research on the subject. The first is the Parkinson's Foundation, which has been around for a long time. The second is the Michael J Fox Foundation, which was founded by the actor, who developed Parkinson's himself. Both of these organizations are working intensively on research on how to treat, and hopefully cure, Parkinson's. If you or someone you know has Parkinson's, I strongly suggest that you follow these organizations and get the latest updates. There is also rather thorough, focused research going on in Israel with some treatments that are not yet available in the United States, but hopefully could be soon. So I suggest Googling Parkinson's treatments in Israel for the latest updates.

Deep Brain Stimulation

The one treatment that has significantly bettered the lives of some Parkinson's patients is deep brain stimulation. This is a significant surgical procedure. In order to have this procedure you must first be evaluated, and your surgeon must decide that you are a good candidate for it. Not everyone can have it. Paul was approved for the procedure, but chose not to get it because he was uncomfortable both with the idea of having surgery taking place in his brain and the fact that there would be a wire coming out from his brain going to a transmitter in his body. Of course the decision had to be his. It is similar to the concept of a pacemaker for the heart, but isn't wireless like that.

Deep brain stimulation has been able to almost totally eliminate tremors in some patients. However there is no guarantee of that. Some people have the procedure with no improvement. In some other cases it helps for a short while and then stops. That is another reason that Paul chose not to get it. However, I suggest if Parkinson's is interfering with someone's life it would be worth investigating the procedure, talking with a specialist, and at least considering it.

Final Thoughts

I think it's important for someone who has Parkinson's to continue to feel useful. One by one, Paul lost the ability to perform simple tasks such as raking, doing laundry, or taking out the garbage. I always tried to find something for him to do. One job he kept was to load the dishwasher, because he could sit on a stool by the sink to do that. Yes, he occasionally dropped and broke something but I felt that it was worth it to avoid a feeling of helplessness. Also, while we did reduce the number of excursions as it became more of an effort, at my urging, we continued to get out for them on a semi-regular basis. Sometimes Paul objected, but he was always happy afterwards that he had done it.

If you or anyone close to you has Parkinson's, I wish you the best of luck.

CHAPTER 32

Infectious Diseases

Everyone became very conscious of the threat of infectious diseases when we were all worried about not catching Covid 19. Infectious diseases vary in two ways: both in terms of their origins and their transmission.

Origins of Infectious Diseases

Infectious diseases can be caused by fungi, protozoa, or worms, but most often, they are caused by bacteria or viruses. This is important to note because some people tend to think that an antibiotic will cure whatever disease they may have. However, antibiotics only work if the disease is bacterial. Sometimes doctors make their patients happy by giving them antibiotics for something that antibiotics will not cure. This is a terrible idea. Likewise, many farmers have done terrible things by giving antibiotics to animals that did not need them. What is wrong with this? The problem is when you use antibiotics on a routine basis to kill off bacteria, the only bacteria that are left are the ones that are very strong and resist those antibiotics.

So the germs just keep getting stronger and stronger as the weaker ones are killed off. That is the same reason why when you are prescribed an antibiotic, that is the one time where I feel you must take your medications exactly as prescribed. You will start to feel better after a day or two, and there's a temptation to not take the drugs longer, because they do affect people in different ways, including some negative effects. I remember one time I was on a strong antibiotic and it made me feel spacey, and I drove home from work after having put my purse on top of my car. I was fortunate that it was found and held for me. Still, you must take the antibiotic until the prescription is completely used up or the strongest germs will be left alive to multiply.

I try to buy meat that is antibiotic-free, if there's not a huge price differential. Also I do not use antibacterial soap under normal circumstances and do not use hand sanitizers. Of course, during the pandemic I did use some antibacterial soap. There's rarely a reason to use hand sanitizers. Soap works just as well or better. The one advantage hand sanitizers do have is that you can carry them with you to use in situations where you cannot wash your hands. Otherwise, they too are to be avoided. The more antibiotics we put into our environment the stronger the germs become. People in hospitals have been killed by superbugs that have developed that cannot be killed by normal antibiotics. I had great respect for my primary care physician, but was very disappointed in him one time when I called up and told him about a sore throat I had. He asked me if I wanted him to prescribe an antibiotic. I said no and went in to see him instead. Colds and sore throats are viral and will not be helped by antibiotics. The one time an antibiotic would help would be if you develop strep throat, which is a bacterial complication. Without an examination you cannot know that it is strep, so I went in to see him. I do not remember if I did have strep or not, but I don't think I did.

Viruses

Viruses are generally harder to treat than bacterial infections. Many viral diseases do not have a vaccine or effective treatment. When Paul's mysterious illness was finally diagnosed as West Nile Virus I was relieved, because I thought that once they knew what it was they could treat him. That hope was quickly dispelled when they said "but there isn't any treatment". Basically, all they could do was support him medically until his own body could conquer the virus.

Flu shots are one preventative measure that we do have for a viral infection, but we all know that flu shots don't always work and some years they are more effective than others. That is not to say that you should not get a flu shot. It's just to say that it isn't 100% guaranteed. The speed with which the Covid 19 vaccines were developed is unprecedented and only made possible by entirely new approaches to how vaccines are created and the investment of millions of dollars that would not be spent on less common diseases. While this speed saved millions of lives it also created unwarranted suspicion and hesitation about getting these historically safe shots.

Transmission

The other way that infectious diseases vary is in the method of transmission. Some diseases can be transmitted from person to person through contact but others are only blood transmissible.

There are hundreds of possible diseases one could catch, but here are some of the main ones.

West Nile Virus

West Nile Virus did not exist in the United States until 1999. When you look at the history of it, it began with a single person in New York State and then multiplied and spread throughout the country. It comes to my mind first because Paul had it and may have died from its long-term effects. It is a viral blood-borne disease transmitted by mosquitoes. It is only transmitted by a particular kind of mosquito, so the odds of you getting it are fairly low. However, it is something obviously that can happen to anyone anywhere outdoors. Therefore, if you're going to be outside for a while during mosquito season, you're going to want to either make sure that you have your legs and arms covered, or you want to use a good insect repellent, or both. If you do use an insect repellent be sure to shower it off later afterwards and launder your clothes; and be sure that as you are applying it you do not breathe it in. It isn't a healthy or pleasant thing, but it is better than catching the virus. In addition to wearing long-sleeved clothes, check your property to make sure that you don't have any place where there could be standing water. I was certain he got it just sitting on our front porch.

West Nile Virus, like Covid, has a wide range of ways it affects people. Someone who is young and healthy may just think that they've had a cold or a mild case of the flu. However, approximately 1% of the people who get it develop the more dangerous form, which is West Nile Encephalitis. Similar to Covid, you are most likely to get this if you are over 60 and have underlying health conditions. Of course, that certainly described Paul, and that is indeed what he did get. West Nile Encephalitis is an extremely dangerous disease. Encephalitis means that it infects the brain. This can result in immediate death or many other terrible effects. When Paul arrived at the hospital his fever was 105, and in a few hours he slipped into a state they referred to as "sleeping", which is just one step above unconsciousness. He was transferred to a larger hospital to check his brain activity. I worried, but did not panic because he had survived so many things and I thought this was just one more. He did gradually awaken and managed to gradually fully regain his memories and ability to speak, but not his ability to really walk or swallow safely.

When Paul was in the nursing home one of the nurses told us that someone down the hall from him was paralyzed from the neck down by West Nile. When Paul was making good progress recovering from the disease the first couple of months, I remember at a family meeting one of the staff members saying that the fastest he had seen anyone go home after developing it was five months, and that that was considered very fast. I kind of scoffed because Paul was making rapid progress at that time, but he plateaued after a while and never did get home. I feel that his death was indirectly a result of West Nile Virus, because while he did recover from the virus itself, I think it left him in a very weakened state. Being mostly bedridden also led to a serious bed sore and a couple of infections. His sudden death one night was never explained, but I think his weakened state, not to mention depression from not having any more progress, contributed to whatever at that moment killed him.

The one good thing about West Nile is that there is no person-to-person contagion. It is blood contagion only. So that means that when I went to visit Paul I could safely hold his hand or give him a kiss. The only time I was restricted was when he had an unrelated infection. A couple of times I even got into his hospital bed with him at the nursing home just to hug him and give him some comfort.

When I tell people that Paul had West Nile Virus they often ask me if he was hiking in the woods. This is because they're confusing it with Lyme disease. Since the only outdoor place he ever spent any time was our front porch he almost certainly got it there. The oddest question I've gotten is if we knew right away when he got it. Who pays attention to a mosquito bite?

Shingles

Shingles can be transmitted from person to person by touch; however, that is not what normally happens. Shingles is an unusual disease. People don't get shingles per se. What happens is that they had chickenpox as a child, and the disease stays alive, but dormant in their system and then recurs in the form of shingles, many decades later. This seems like a very odd thing to happen, but a similar thing has been known to happen with polio, where people who had polio as a child decades later get a kind of recurrence. So viruses can stay dormant in your system for a period of time, which would explain why it seemed at first as if some Covid patients who had recovered were being reinfected. They probably weren't actually being reinfected. The disease was just in remission and then re-awakened.

Shingles can happen at any age. I got it when I was 29. However, it most commonly does happen to older people. This has always been true, but it is especially true now, because younger people had a chicken pox vaccination when they were young, which makes it very unlikely that they will ever get shingles. Shingles, like a lot of diseases, can range from mild to severe. I was fortunate, having a brother for a doctor, that I mentioned to him the odd feelings that I was having and he suggested that I see a doctor and get tested for shingles. So I began treatment early on. Shingles can occur in various places in your body. The main symptom is that your skin becomes hypersensitive to touch. I found that it became extremely uncomfortable to shower, for example. You do also get a small recurrence of chickenpox-like blisters in a small area. The sensitivity generally travels along one nerve. In my case it went along the back. It can cause very bad skin inflammations, and some people get it in their scalp, which is what my mother had. As a result, she had to stop dying her hair. The funny part of the story is that she had always dyed her hair honey blonde. When she stopped dying her hair in her 70's, her hair came in brown, not gray and people were accusing her of dying her hair.

Shingles can be so uncomfortable and painful that people have been known to commit suicide from it. That's something that my doctor informed me of when he told me that I was over it. "Now that you're over it I can tell you that some people have committed suicide because of shingles." In my case I was lucky and had a mild case. I then said to him "Well, at least I don't have to worry about getting it later". He then told me to my surprise that no, it is one of the few diseases that you can get more than once. That was very disappointing. Fortunately, there is now a shingles vaccine. They developed one a few years ago, which I took right away; and they have developed an even better one now, which I also took. You would be very foolish if you were eligible for it yet did not take advantage of it, no matter what it cost. Like Lyme disease, the discomfort in some cases lasts for years, and it can also cause blindness. I recently ran across someone who felt guilty because she had given it to her young grandchild.

Coronavirus

We have all heard so much about this that I'm really not going to talk about it, except to say that it is a viral disease that affects multiple organ systems of the body, with an unfortunately high person-to- person contagion. That is why masks took on such importance. Many people who were not vaccinated in time became "long haulers" with effects lasting for months or even years.

The Flu

Early on during the pandemic, when people were, in ridiculous fashion, comparing the statistics of how many people had died within a few weeks of coronavirus versus how many people died in a full year of flu, there was something that I found very surprising. Besides the comparison being illogical, the surprising thing was finding out how many people die of the flu each year. I was pretty shocked, because I personally do not know anyone who has ever died from the flu. I think of it as an inconvenience that one has and gets over. However, perhaps because of other infirmities, thousands of people do die from it every year. Knowing that, if I ever had any reservations about getting a flu shot, they are now gone.

When you go for your flu shot, if you're over 60 you will be offered the enhanced version of the flu shot. The first year it was offered to me, I declined, thinking it was simply stronger. However, I found out that it's not the strength that is different, so much as it is the scope of it. There are a variety of different variations of the virus that can cause the flu, and the higher dosage vaccination covers more of them (4 strains instead of 3). The mutations of the flu explain why some years the flu vaccine is more effective than others. Getting a flu shot does not guarantee that you will not get the flu, but they say that even if you do get it, you'll probably have a milder case. I now do get the enhanced flu shot every year. It is covered by Medicare and almost every kind of insurance there is. In addition, sometimes drug stores or grocery stores even offer incentives to get the flu shot there rather than your doctor's office. They will give you a coupon towards your groceries or drugstore purchases. The shot is the same no matter where you get it.

A Couple of Common Sense Treatments

The old traditional treatments for flus and colds really do help. Chicken soup really helps. Hot liquids in general lessen virus symptoms and by relieving congestion may prevent the cold or flu from getting into the lungs and making it worse. Another benefit is avoiding getting chilled, because getting chilled makes it more likely that you will get sick. I once had a disagreement with Paul. He read that germs make you sick, not your body temperature. However, being chilled does make you more susceptible to those germs that surround us. Don't allow yourself to get chilled outside or in. Tamiflu is a treatment that is supposed to truly be effective. I do not have experiences with that to share because I have been fortunate not to have needed it since before it was invented. But it is supposed to genuinely help the severity and duration of the flu, especially if taken early on. Zinc lozenges, such as Coldceze used at the onset of a cold, help cut its duration. If you talk to your doctor these are some of the things to inquire about.

Bacterial Infections and Diseases

Bacteriological infections can be treated with antibiotics. There are not as many well-known ones as there are viral infections. Probably the main one to be concerned about is UTIs, that is, urinary tract infections. I talk pretty extensively about this in the section on urology.

Lyme Disease

I have found that people confuse West Nile Virus and Lyme Disease. We know mosquitoes are all over the place. We all get mosquito bites at certain times of the year. However, Lyme disease is not caused by mosquitoes. Thousands of people get this disease that was first identified in 1975. It is a bacterial infection caused by a tick bite and is usually gotten walking through a wooded area, though it can be gotten by contact with an animal, such as a dog, that has been in a wooded area. If you're walking through a wooded area, be sure to wear long-sleeved shirts and long pants and tuck your pants inside your shoes and use a repellent with DEET in it. When you get home examine yourself to see if you can find any evidence of a tick bite. Never touch a wild animal such as a deer, and never allow your pets to roam free. If you are rescuing a wild animal use a cloth or blanket, while wearing gloves, and do not touch them directly.

Lyme disease can cause body aches, fatigue, confusion, problems with memory and fever. The worst thing about Lyme disease is that the effects can last for years and come and go. Like most diseases, how severe it is depends on how early it is caught. One thing to watch out for is a rash. This will start in the area of the bite. Do pay attention to any rash you might find and report it to a doctor if you take an antihistamine and it doesn't go away in a day.

Pneumonia

Interestingly enough, pneumonia can be either biological or viral, which is quite unusual. Either one can cause mucus and congestion in your lungs. It seems that the lungs are a common target of infections. Just think about COVID-19. Obviously, not being able to breathe can be life- threatening.

Infections

Anything can become infected. I once had a spider bite that became infected. I did not want to seem like a hypochondriac or make too much of it, so I waited a while to go see the doctor. Avoiding getting care to not be perceived as a worry-wort or bother is more common for women, because we are raised to take care of others' problems. When I did go, he said it's a good thing I came in when I did and pointed out the red lines radiating out from the bite area. He prescribed an antibiotic and had me come back in a few days and said that if it wasn't better, he would actually have to do a small surgical procedure. Do not ignore anything that seems to be infected.

There are some types of infections that can be very quickly fatal. I remember the case of Jim Henson of the Muppets, who died within a couple of days of getting a bacterial pneumonia infection. Be especially concerned if your infection follows a hospital visit, as there are many superbugs around there. I talk about superbugs in conjunction with the reference to antibiotics earlier in this chapter.

You never know when a complication like this will arise after a medical procedure, so be on the lookout. We had a personal situation with this. Paul had an outpatient surgery on his wrist to just remove a plate that had been put in when he fractured it a couple of years before. it did not seem to be any big deal, and he was, as predicted, home for lunch. I went off to work and when I came home he complained about his arm hurting. I looked at his bandages and it seemed that they had been put on too tight. After a while I took him to the emergency room and it turned out the bandages were too tight because his arm was swelling up. When the doctor rewrapped the bandages Paul felt better, but the wise doctor said to wait a while before going home. The pain returned. He wound up being sent by ambulance to a larger hospital where his whole arm was opened to remove flesh-eating bacteria that was spreading up it. So scary. So if something feels amiss don't be stoic and ignore it.

Getting Help

When do you call your doctor? The fact that you have a mild case of a virus does not necessitate going to a doctor's office. Except in cases of emergency it's always best to call first anyway, rather than just showing up at a doctor's office or immediate care center. If telemedicine is available to you that can be the best for you and people you might infect. Generally speaking, if you have a low-grade fever of 100° or below and it doesn't last for more than two or three days, just ride it out. If, however, you have a fever of 101° or you ever, with or without fever, have trouble breathing, then you do need to contact a medical authority. If you have trouble breathing you need to do so immediately -- or possibly, if it's bad, even call an ambulance. Obviously, losing consciousness without known cause would be an emergency. Bad chills and shaking, which Paul had the evening of the night he went to the hospital for West Nile, are also bad signs.

Another thing to watch out for is the presence of a rash, even in a small area, with fever. That combination is usually a sign of trouble and can be seen with several diseases. When Paul was in the emergency room with West Nile, I had assumed it was a bad UTI, but a sharp doctor spotted a rash on the top of one foot when he removed his sock and said it looked like encephalitis or meningitis.

CHAPTER 33

Sleep Disorders

Sleep Problems - Behavioral Causes

Insomnia is more common in older people than in younger people. Some people have it chronically and it is hard to treat, but I want to give some ideas for those who have it occasionally. Many home remedies are helpful. For example, I have found that drinking hot milk really can help. However, I recently read an article that a classic hot bath doesn't help.

One cause of insomnia can be eating late at night, especially if there is sugar or caffeine involved. I have found many of my friends have commented that they have to cut off their caffeine intake earlier and earlier in the day as they age. Perhaps you can no longer drink regular coffee in the evening, for example. Keep in mind that coffee is not the only thing that has caffeine. Chocolate has both caffeine and sugar, so you may not want to have it after dinner, other than in very small amounts. You may have to cut off your caffeine intake as early as noon. While tea has less caffeine than coffee, it still has some. Even some herbal teas may have stimulating ingredients. Try chamomile or one that is labeled as being relaxing or for sleep.

Exercising during the day can help you sleep, but in the evening can stimulate your body and prevent sleep.

Napping can be an issue. It is healthy to take a nap in the afternoon, but set a timer and make sure that you do not nap for more than 20 minutes. To do so may affect your sleep at night.

Another influence can be the use of electronic devices late at night. There are some internet and phone companies that have become aware of this and offer the option of switching to a nighttime dimmer light on a timer late at night. Be sure to use this option. This changes the spectrum of light that your eyes receive and becomes less stimulating. There are also special blue light glasses you can order online that are supposed to help with this problem.

Nicotine is another stimulant to be avoided in the evening. Of course it should be avoided at all times, but especially then.

Set your alarm to get up at the same time 7 days a week.

You want to aim for 6 to 8 hours of sleep per night.

If you are having serious problems with insomnia, talk to a doctor to see if there is some underlying physical cause for the problem.

Mental Causes

There is a cliche about counting sheep. Why sheep? Perhaps because some shepherd came up with that idea. The point is, sometimes you can't sleep because you are thinking about something and that thought is stimulating. For me, I sometimes wake up thinking about things I want to write in this book. You could be thinking about something you're worried about. There is a cliché that if someone tells you not to think about a pink elephant, all you're going to think about is a pink elephant. What you have to do is focus your mind elsewhere. You have to focus on a positive, not a negative. You can't tell yourself not to think about something without finding somewhere else to focus your mind. If you're trying to get back to sleep, that thing probably has to be something boring. I sometimes count backwards from 100 to see if I can get back to sleep quickly and to distract myself. I also count in Spanish and French, which has a dual purpose of not only being repetitive and boring but also maintaining that knowledge. You also could keep a fairly boring book at your bedside, and if it doesn't disturb someone else you're sleeping near, read it (or if necessary, leave the room and read it).

Once again, you want your reading material to be something fairly boring.

I recently read a surprising tip. People who make their beds in the morning sleep better at night.

If nothing works try to think of the sleepless time as an opportunity you didn't have during the busy day to go over matters that need to be planned, and perhaps that positivity will relax you and help you sleep.

Environmental Causes

Environmental causes of insomnia can be fairly simple to solve. Experiment with adding or removing a blanket, opening or closing a window, changing the nighttime setting for your thermostat, or getting up and taking an over-the-counter remedy if you have some simple symptom. It is best for the temperature to be a little cooler before you get in bed. My dad used to say if you're having trouble sleeping, get up and take an aspirin because you might have something physically that's bothering you and that might take care of it. Maybe it's just the feeling of resetting that helps. In winter you might try adding a small humidifier in your bedroom or using a safe space heater near your bed.

I have one that looks like a small radiator near my bed, and I can reach over without opening my eyes and turn the dial up or down. A recent study said that painting your bedroom walls blue might help. If there are noises from roommates or neighbors interrupting your sleep, you might consider a "white noise machine" or soft radio. If the air quality where you live is problematic, indoors or outdoors, you might consider a HEPA filter.

If you tend to wake up too early in the morning, consider investing in room- darkening shades or blinds, instead of conventional ones. I have found that I have to close my closet door because of light coming in that window. Some people wear a sleep mask that covers their eyes.

You may or may not be comfortable with that. They can be purchased at a dollar store.

Medications and Sleep

Insomnia can also be caused by medications that you're taking for other things. One of the medications that Paul had to take for one of his chronic conditions listed as a side effect "vivid dreams". While they sometimes provided interesting stories for him to tell me about when we woke up in the morning, it could also cause movements that would wake both of us up. If the medication is essential there really isn't much you can do about that.

Do not take sleep medications, whether prescription or over-the-counter, on a regular basis unless it is an absolute medical necessity -- and then only as a last resort. A couple of tips for occasional insomnia: Never take the same medication twice in one week. Your body will begin to adapt to it, and it will lose its effectiveness. Second, when you buy sleep medications, you do not have to buy medications that are specifically for sleep. Many over-the-counter sleeping pills are simply antihistamines or Dramamine. You may have those in your medicine cabinet and can use those. A second tip would be to never buy capsules for use as a sleeping aid. Make sure you buy either pills or tablets. The ideal is a tablet that is designed to be broken in half. The reason for this is I would strongly suggest starting with the half pill of the medication and only taking the second half of the pill if you still can't get to sleep after half an hour or so. Taking too much medication not only has the possibility of becoming habit-forming but can make you dangerously drowsy the next day when you are out and driving. Some of these medications also tend to leave you dried out. Remember my rule of thumb that all medications have some bad side effects.

Because of the bad side effects of sleeping pills, some people prefer herbal remedies. Melatonin is the most widely touted alternative to traditional sleeping pills. However, people can have bad effects from melatonin as well. I just tried it a couple of times, and when I took a half a pill, it wasn't too bad, but when I took a full pill one time, the next day I found myself to be extremely drowsy. I also heard an expert on TV recently who said you would be better off taking magnesium. I have not tried it yet. Another herbal tea product designed to help with sleep is Easy Now tea, by Traditional Medicinals, which combines flowers and catnip. It is what my niece used to use for sleep after having used caffeine to stay up for final exams in college.

Other Sleeping Problems

Sleep Apnea

Sleep apnea is a condition in which you actually stop breathing while you are sleeping. This prevents you from getting a good night's sleep and affects your general health. Diagnosis is done by spending the night in a special sleep clinic where they monitor you and your breathing. People who are diagnosed with sleep apnea are given a special mask to wear attached to a machine used at night called a C-PAP. It isn't very comfortable, but it is a necessity for many people.

I saw an ad on TV for a new product that claims that with their device, you don't need a mask or hose. It's a new product, so I don't know how effective it is, but it would be great if it works. Check inspiresleep.com.

Involuntary Sleep

As we get older, we have more of a tendency to fall asleep when we don't intend to, sometimes for many minutes or many hours, and other times just for a second or less (episodes of which are called microsleeps). One problem that many people have is falling asleep while watching TV in the evening. This is a problem that I've had for a long time. It used to annoy Paul when I would fall asleep while we were watching a show together. He would then tell me to wake up, and I would then fall right back asleep. I told him, "Don't just tell me to wake up. Tell me to stand up for a minute." When I did that, it really did wake me up.

If you are home alone, you might want to keep an egg timer next to your chair and set it for every 15 minutes or so. If you have a smart watch or phone, you can tell it to set an alarm for a certain amount of time. One problem I used to have is that I would be very sleepy, and then I would go upstairs to wash up and get ready for bed, and that would wake me up, and I'd have trouble falling asleep in bed. What I've started doing is that about an hour before bedtime, I wash up and get into my nightgown and then go back downstairs and watch TV. Once I feel myself getting really sleepy, I can then just turn off the TV and get right in bed. I have found this to be very helpful.

While falling asleep at home might be annoying, it is truly embarrassing in public, such as when attending a concert or play. I know I can sometimes sit back in a comfortable seat in the darkened room and start to doze off no matter how good the entertainment is.

A few suggestions if you have this problem would be:

- Do not eat a heavy meal before attending a performance.
- Go with a friend who can poke you if you fall asleep, especially if you are snoring.
- Do not consume alcohol before the performance or during intermission.
- Bring some little chocolate or coffee flavored candies or a candy bar with you that you can nibble on during intermission to give yourself a sugar and caffeine rush or some fruit that isn't too messy such as grapes.
- Don't sit in the first couple of rows so you don't have to be embarrassed about the performers seeing you closing your eyes
- Sit forward in your chair.
- If there is music, subtly tap your toes to it.
- Get a little extra sleep the night before.

- Dress in layers so you don't have to be too warm. Make sure the top layer is one that can be removed easily and doesn't go over your head.

None of these tips are sure cures but they are helpful.

Narcolepsy

This is a less common disorder if you are otherwise healthy, but if someone refers to it, the term narcolepsy is used to describe someone who can suddenly fall asleep even during the day. That is dangerous, and if you suspect that problem in yourself or someone else, they should be seen by a doctor and not drive until the problem is solved.

CHAPTER 34

Memory and Brain Issues

Memory

Have you ever had trouble finding your keys? Have you ever walked into a room and forgotten why you had gone in there? Have you ever had trouble remembering the name of someone you haven't seen in a while?

If any of these things have happened to you every once in a while, don't worry. It is so common for seniors to have these kinds of problems that they are the fodder of comedians' routines. Having this happen to you occasionally does not mean that you have Alzheimer's. However, if it were to happen to you on a daily basis, you might want to talk to a doctor about it.

Here are some tips to help you with these common problems:

Remembering Names

I have always been bad at that. The funniest part is that while I can memorize a script well, I sometimes hesitate when it comes to saying a character's name because my brain tells me that I'm bad at names. I know that's pretty silly. When you meet someone new, try to repeat their name either in your head or out loud, such as "It's nice to meet you,

Phyllis." It also helps if you can associate them with something such as how they remind you of someone with the same name. You could also keep a notepad handy and write down their name. However, don't feel too bad about it. Anyone who is older themselves will understand if you've just forgotten their name and have to ask for a reminder. They may actually be relieved because they may have forgotten your name.

Keys

Try to have a specific place to put your keys every day. If you can't find them, check the pockets of whatever jacket you wore the day before. You can buy something called a Tile for about $20. This attaches to your keychain and enables you to send out a signal from your cell phone app to start a chirping sound if you can't find your keys. It also displays, on your linked cell phone screen, clarification as to whether you are getting closer or farther away. It's easy and handy. One thing that I do is I have a complete set of spare keys that includes both the house keys and the car keys. I keep those on a hook in the closet, and if I'm in a hurry I grab that set of keys and look for my main set when I get home. There are few things more stressful than being in a hurry to leave and not being able to find your keys anywhere. The more stressed you get, the harder it is to think, and the more unhealthy it is. This has solved that problem for me.

Cell Phones

If you have a landline and your cell phone has a number that is within its range, or if you have long distance, you can call your cell phone from your landline. My cell phone number is based outside my range, and I dropped my long distance service on my landline after Paul died, so I couldn't call my cell phone. I wasted time looking for it a few times and once called my brother and had him dial it. However, this is one of the benefits of my Apple watch. It has a little symbol I can touch and it will make my cell phone ping to help me locate it. There is a similar feature if you set up the Find my Iphone app, but this is easier. I imagine Android users have something similar available. Also, if you have a Tile, even though its main purpose may be to find your keys or another object via your phone app, it can be used in reverse to find your phone. You press and hold the button on the Tile for a couple of seconds, and your phone emits a sound to help you find it. All these techniques only work if the phone is fairly close by. If you have lost it while you are out, you either have to try calling the phone and hope someone answers, or use "Find my Iphone". I actually know someone who used that app from his computer to help the police locate the person who had burglarized him.

If you have an Android phone, there is probably a similar app. Be sure to ask and pair your computer and your phone.

Keeping Your Brain Sharp

Do daily activities that help your brain, such as doing the crossword, Jumbo, or other puzzles. Watch Jeopardy, Wheel of Fortune, or other game shows and try to beat the contestants. Be involved in activities and learn a new skill. Just keep your brain active.

There is a supplement that I see advertised on TV that is supposed to help memory. I haven't tried it and don't know if it does or doesn't, but it might be worth trying. Of course, you can talk to your doctor for suggestions. I reduced my Statin dosage to every other day, because I've heard that it reduces certain elements that the brain needs to function well and therefore affects memory. I did not totally eliminate it because heart health is so important.

Dementia and Alzheimer's

Sometimes I hear people using the terms Alzheimer's and dementia interchangeably. That is misleading. There are several kinds of dementia, and Alzheimer's is only one of them.

Dementia is any condition in which the patient becomes disconnected from reality. Unlike conditions such as bipolar disorder or schizophrenia, dementia usually occurs late in life. The symptoms can include noticeable loss of memory, hallucinations, changes in personality, and delusions. Some of the causes for this condition can be temporary. For example, many patients get hospital dementia. For some reason, being in the environment of a hospital gets them confused. Perhaps it is the lack of daily routine or the lack of a good night's sleep. They can become very confused and return to normal once they return to their home environment. Regular visits may help a bit with this situation. Other times dementia can be caused by medications. I encountered this with Paul once the nursing home suggested taking a drug that was supposed to combat Parkinson's hallucinations, such as double vision. He actually began to hallucinate more. When I insisted that they discontinue the drug, it did help. Some types of dementia can be permanent, but I would not assume so right away. If a loved one shows signs of dementia, I would insist on a complete medical evaluation to make sure that they do not have a tumor, change in medication, or other conditions that could be the underlying cause. My father never had dementia, but his memory was impaired by blocked carotid arteries that limited blood flow to the brain. Unfortunately, in his case, that was discovered too late to safely operate. He just called everyone he didn't see regularly, "Dear," and limited his conversation.

One difficult question is whether to humor a person's pleasant delusions and hallucinations or not. This is something that I dealt with with Paul. I felt that it would be best to tell him the real situation rather than going along with his belief that he had just missed a meal and was actually eating for example, but afterwards I wondered if that was the right thing to do if after all it made him feel better. This is a tough question and I don't know the answer. Another is knowing what to believe. When Paul was on that drug I could clearly see that there wasn't an amusement park outside his window. On the other hand, when he told me he could not sleep the night before because someone had their

T V blasting all night I doubted his story, but it was verified by others. I, of course, complained to management and apologized to him.

Alzheimer's, one of seniors' greatest fears, is a deteriorating disease of the brain. Its causes are not entirely known, but there is a hereditary tendency in some families. That does not mean that because one parent had Alzheimer's, that you will get it, but there is some increase in the odds. Alzheimer's usually doesn't begin until someone is in their 60s or 70s, but it can begin as early as in their 40s or 50s. That would be known as early-onset Alzheimer's. Patients with Alzheimer's gradually lose their connection with their memories and eventually may not recognize even those closest to them, which can be very frustrating. It actually causes more frustration for families than it does in the individual, who gradually becomes unaware of their problem. Some people with Alzheimer's become aggressive and unpleasant, but most seem happy and sweet. They sometimes have what is called sundowners syndrome, where in the evening they become agitated and aggressive. This can be a real problem.

Caring for someone with Alzheimer's requires expertise. When they have more advanced Alzheimer's, it may be impossible to leave them alone, as they may do things that are unsafe or wander off. It may be necessary to institutionalize them. If you do your research well and select the best possible facility, do not feel guilty about it .Just continue to visit them on a very regular basis. Sometimes you can't be sure what people are aware of. I remember at my aunt's final birthday party, it seemed as though she was totally out of it, but when I handed her a present she thanked me. Continue to be good to those with Alzheimer's even if they don't know who you are.

Seizures

Most often when someone thinks of seizures they think of epilepsy. However, that is only one cause of seizures. There are several different kinds of seizures and several different possible causes.

Epilepsy is a long-term condition where the brain fires incorrectly. It can start very early or late in life and can be genetic. It is even found in dogs. My cousin had a dog that had epilepsy. Sometimes when you go to a theater you will see a warning sign that strobe lights are used in the production. They have this warning because this can cause an epileptic seizure. However, epileptic seizures can occur at random times, especially if someone has not taken their medication.

Other problems that can cause seizures include a high fever. an overdose of medication, or injuries to the brain. Paul developed a seizure disorder when he was middle-aged, and it was explained to him that the cause was the blood clots that he had from two small strokes that he'd had. The blood clots interrupted the normal brain activity.

Usually, when we think of seizures, we think of grand mal seizures, which are also called tonic-clonic seizures. This is the kind that we may see sometimes on TV or movies where the person lies on the ground and shakes violently. Grand mal seizures are dangerous and on some occasions have caused death. However, some people do have them from time to time without ill effect. If you see someone having a grand mal seizure check to see if there is someone with them who is familiar with their condition. If they tell you not to call 911 don't do it. If there isn't anyone with them do call 911. Meanwhile, do not try to contain the seizures or hold them still. You may hurt them. What you can do to help is to place something, such as your coat, under their head to protect their head and turn their head to the side so that they don't choke.

There are other seizures that may go undetected. These are referred to as petit mal seizures, and there's more than one kind. One kind is absence seizures. When someone is having one of these, which is what Paul usually had, it may not be noticeable to other people. Basically they stare straight ahead and are unresponsive. Their thumb may twitch. If you suspect that someone is having one of these seizures, try saying their name and getting their attention. If they do not respond, just let them be, and after a few minutes, they will come out of it, though they may be confused and not make sense for a few more minutes. Once their brain is functioning normally, however, be sure to let them know what happened. They may not be aware of it, and they probably need to at least temporarily increase the dosage of their medication. If they are not on medication, they need to see a doctor right away.

Another kind of petit mal seizure is called an atonic seizure. This is more worrisome, because if someone has an atonic seizure, which Paul had once or twice, they suddenly lose consciousness and simply fall, which is why these are sometimes called "drop seizures". The effects are very short-term, but of course, they could get hurt by falling.

The medications for seizures are generally quite effective. It is important to get on medication, because the seizures can cause brain damage and erase memories. Once Paul got on the proper dosage of medication, which of course takes a little while to determine, he might go for weeks or months at a time without a seizure. If he did have a seizure he would take an extra pill each day for a couple of days until his body chemistry got back to normal.

People who have seizures should not drive unless they have been seizure-free for three months in a row. Sometimes people can tell when they're going to have seizures, and they need to be very aware of that if they plan to drive or operate heavy machinery. Paul was normally able to tell, but when he had a seizure at home without warning, he realized he could no longer drive.

Paul lost a couple of jobs because he had seizures which were not yet diagnosed. Once he had one while driving a forklift and crashed it. Once he had the diagnosis he was able to get Disability. He would have preferred working, given the choice; but it was too risky, and the person who interviewed him realized his medications would make it hard for him to learn new skills.

CHAPTER 35

Emergencies

Falls

Falls at Home

Falls are one of the most common problems that seniors have. Probably everyone knows someone who has had a fall and broken a hip. There are certain ways that you can lessen your chances of falling. If you have mobility problems or poor balance, you are going to want to use a cane or walker, no matter how it looks. If you are normally mobile, you want to watch out for certain things. The most dangerous place in the house for anyone to fall is the bathroom, because a wet floor is slick and the surfaces are so hard. Be sure to have a plastic mat in your shower or tub, if it has a smooth bottom, and be sure to have a rug with the rubber bottom that won't slip to step out onto when you come out with wet feet. Be sure to pick up that rubber mat when you're done so that mold does not grow underneath it. You're going to want to have a grab bar in the shower or tub no matter how able you are. I keep my Apple watch on because it is waterproof. If you have a safety device that isn't waterproof, put it within reach.

One place that is surprisingly hazardous and people don't think about is the bedroom. Making a bed can be hazardous because you can trip over the hanging linens. My cousin broke her ankle when she was only in her 30s because she simply tripped on a bedspread or sheet that was hanging down. So do watch out for that.

Kitchens are a possible place to fall because you may use a step stool or whatever to reach upper cabinets. I have a wide single-step unit that is secure to step on and a grabber I got from a catalog. The step unit has also proven handy for placing my laptop at the right level for Zoom exercise classes, etc.

Safe step unit with grabber laid across it.

For everyone it is a good idea to assess your house as to possible fall hazards. For example, do you have loose rugs that you deal with, rather than replacing, that move around?. If you are using a walker or wheel-chair, is there a threshold that creates a barrier; and if so, see if there is something that could act like a miniature ramp to get over that more easily. You can find things like that in catalogs. If you do have problems with getting around, you may want to add grab bars in the bathroom and difficult spots, as we did.

Falls Outside

When you are outside, try to leave early and allow extra time for walking so that you don't have to run or hurry. Try to keep your balance over your feet and not be in a forward-leaning running position where you are more likely to trip on a curb or raised sidewalk panel, as I have done. Make sure that you have shoes or boots on that do not have smooth surfaces. In fact, one of the things I look for when I buy shoes is that the shoes do not have a smooth surface even if they are only for indoor use. You never know when you will encounter slippery floors, and I have rejected many pairs of shoes that had totally smooth bottoms or felt slippery in the store.

If, as many people do, you live somewhere where there is ice in winter, you have to be very careful indeed. Everyone has friends who have slipped on ice and had an injury. While you can sometimes step around icy patches, there can be black ice which has discolored and isn't very noticeable. I slipped on black ice once while crossing the street and had a smooth spot on my boots and fell so hard my humerus broke in two. I have been much more careful since then. Some of my friends became snowbirds partly to avoid winter falls. Wear good boots with gripping bottoms. You can always bring fashionable shoes in a tote bag. You can also purchase cleats on a band that slip on and off your shoes or boots for added protection. I recently bought some at Dick's Sporting Goods. Of note: Any ice that is dangerous to walk on because of black ice can also be treacherous to traverse on wheels -- bicycles, manual or electric wheelchairs, scooters, cars....Some of the riskiest places are where ice is exposed to repeated changes of temperatures and melt and refreeze. This includes near doorways, under highway overpasses, on bridges over waterways, etc. My sister-in-law slipped on an icy welcome mat at a hotel that was being exposed to changes in temperatures when people opened the door. Also note that if you rely on a cane, walking stick, or any type of walker for mobility, the wheels or bottom surface of your mobility device can also slip on ice.

If you should fall, there are certain things to think about. First of all, take a moment to assess if you are seriously hurt or not before you get up. It often takes a minute or two to know that. The one possible exception to this might be what happened to me, which is if you fall while crossing the street. I knew at that time that my arm was broken and that you're not supposed to move when you have a broken bone. Indeed, I did find out why, since that caused much more extensive damage, but when you're lying in the street you do want to know if there is a car headed towards you. Actually, I shouldn't have worried about it because so many people came running to help me.

One thing you have to ask yourself is why you fell. In most cases, you will know you simply slipped or tripped. If you know the specific cause and if you are not seriously hurt, then it is not particularly worrisome, but if you don't know why you fell, or you have fallen more than once recently, you need to see a doctor and find out if there is a medical cause. There are many possible causes, such as atonic seizures, low blood pressure, etc.; and those should be addressed, to avoid future falls. In some cases, you will know the cause, such as with Paul, who often fell because his medications would make him dizzy. Of course, in that case, you want to talk to your doctor about whether there are any changes that can be made to avoid that situation. In some cases such as his, there is nothing that can be done about it, other than using a walker or other mobility aid.

Getting Up After Falling

Once you have fallen, it can be a problem getting up. Even if you were not hurt, it's possible that you may not have the energy or ability to get up. When you fall, never ask someone to help you up when you are on your back. They can hurt themselves doing that. You have to roll over onto your knees, so that you can grab something and pull yourself up. If necessary you may need to crawl to a solid object to hold onto to pull yourself up. If you need to do this and someone else is around, get a throw rug, as we used to do for Paul, and put it under your knees so that it doesn't hurt so much to crawl forward or even just push yourself up.

If you can't get up and the other person doesn't have the ability to get you up because you are bigger than they are, as sometimes happened with us, you have a problem. You then have two choices. Either you call some neighbors to come over and help, as we sometimes did, or if it is during the night or another time when you can't reach neighbors, you need to call 911. Paul sometimes objected to this for three reasons:

the embarrassment of having the first responders pull up with sirens blaring; the potential cost, and third, the fact that he did not want to go to the hospital.

None of these are real concerns. When I did call 911 I asked them not to sound their sirens, especially at night. I did this after the first time it had happened and a neighbor told me that his children were upset by an ambulance arriving with sirens blaring. Usually they will honor this request. As far as cost goes you will receive a bill anytime first responders come, but it is covered by Medicare and some insurance policies. You simply have to contact the number on the bill when you receive it and give them the insurance or Medicare information. As for the hospital, you can request that they only come to aid you in getting up and that you do not need to go to the hospital. If you know of the cause of the fall and are not hurt, they will honor that request. We did this a couple of times. If you are sick and have a fever, or if you fell for other reasons that are not likely to be OK, that is, of course, a different matter.

Other Emergencies

If there is ever an emergency, you are not going to be reading a book. Hopefully you will read these pointers now and file them in your memory.

Emergencies in Public

When do you call 911? You always call 911 if one of the following happens :

- If someone is unconscious, even if they regain consciousness.
- If someone is bleeding significantly. However, keep in mind that cuts on the face or anywhere else on the head tend to bleed more than they would in other parts of the body, because the blood vessels are so close to the surface. So some bleeding may not be particularly significant.

- If they have a grand mal seizure and are lying on the floor convulsing, and there is no one there to assure you that they know what to do or they're familiar with the situation.
- If someone hits their head and is then confused or dizzy.
- If a heart attack or pneumonia is suspected or they are having trouble breathing.
- If someone falls and you can't get them up.
- If someone shows signs of a stroke, such as slurred speech or confusion.
- If someone is unconscious, of course you're going to call 911 immediately.

Of note: If you have a landline, or if you have a cell phone with location on, 911 might be able to identify where you are, even if you are not able to name where you are. However, landlines are much safer than cell phones in this regard. The article below summarizes the risks of calling 911 from a cell phone. Short version: Keep your location on; know the address or street corners where you are and name it at the beginning of your call, in case the dispatcher can't discern it from your phone carrier. If you are using a Voice Over Internet Protocol in place of a phone, it will be even more important for you to be able to name your location. Your Smart Speakers cannot call 911 for you. However, if you have a new model of iPhone or a new model of Android phone, you can say, "Hey, Siri, dial 911" or "Hey, Google, dial 911" and your phone can call for you. This could save your life if you fall out of hand reach of your phone but within voice distance of it. Another option is to get a Lifeline necklace or comparable item worn around the neck with a panic button linked to a paid alarm service. Especially if you live alone and have lung, heart, or fall risks, this is a wise investment. Alternatively, see my chapter about Apple watches in Part One of this book.

A few tips about calling 911: See if there is a landline available. That will automatically give the location. If not, you can use any cell phone, even if it is not yours and is locked, to call 911. Just touch the screen and you will see that it says emergency on the bottom left. It may not give the location, so try to find out the address you are at.

If you are in a public place, look for someone of authority to help with the situation. Do not attempt to do CPR unless you have been trained in how to do it properly. CPR is only performed if that person has no pulse or breathing. You have to know what you are doing or you can actually kill them. While breathing into their mouth probably wouldn't do any harm, it is no longer recommended in most cases, and if you try to do compressions you can break off a fragment of a rib, which can puncture a lung.

You are actually safer using an A E D (Automated External Defibrillator), because those have instructions on them and will actually talk you through the process. They've become more and more common in public places. However, if you are in a public place and they do have one, the odds are there is also somebody who works there who has been trained in how to use them. Of course you would want to let them handle the situation.

As long as I'm talking about emergency situations I want to mention to you some situations that are not particularly age-related.

If there is excessive bleeding, especially gushing blood, it may be too late when an ambulance arrives, so you want to apply direct pressure. Ideally if you can find a cloth that's available, you can place it over the wound and press down. If there is no cloth available, you may have to just do it with your hands. In extreme cases, such as spurting blood, a tourniquet may be necessary until they can be treated. Tie a cloth around the leg or whatever it is, put something like a stick on top of the knot, tie again and twist. This is only for extreme cases as it cuts off circulation, which is dangerous.

If you are hurt and think that you may require stitches, you need to go to an emergency room or a good urgent care center fairly quickly. It's best if you get a ride if there is any possibility you might lose consciousness. There is a rule that stitches cannot be given after the first few hours from when the cut occurred. I once fell when I was pretty far from home, got bandaged by the EMTs and got tired of waiting in the ER and went home. I was going to wait until the morning to have it treated, but Paul insisted on taking me to the local emergency room, where they told me I almost waited too long. It has something to do with the germs that would be trapped. If you have a good doctor who performs the stitches, the wound will eventually fade. I was surprised to find that scar cream actually does help. You can get that over the counter at a drugstore and apply it as directed. You do have to be sure to apply sunscreen to scar tissue if you will be in the sun, or it will discolor.

In the case of choking, if you see someone who is choking, do not hit them on the back. I don't know why this is something that has been handed down generation to generation. It does no good and may actually push the food farther down the esophagus. If someone is coughing then they are still getting some air and are in less imminent danger than if they cannot speak at all. If someone is choking or if you are, the universal sign is to put your hand to your throat. I'm sure everyone has heard of the Heimlich maneuver, but may not be sure if they know how to perform it. It is actually not that difficult. To perform the Heimlich maneuver, grab the person around the diaphragm, clasp your hands, and sharply thrust up. The important thing is to do it around their diaphragm and not around their ribs. You can also bend them over the back of a chair to help. You want to call 911 first, but action must be taken immediately. You can even perform the maneuver on yourself.

The one exception to not hitting on the back is if you were dealing with an infant. For example, your grandchild is in your house, there's no one else around, and you see that they are choking. The thing to do is to grab them by the feet, turn them upside down, and then hit their back, but not too hard. Of course I hope this will never happen, and you want to always keep an eye on them. Not too long after I had taken a CPR course, I thought my then-baby son was choking. I performed this maneuver, and a penny popped out of his mouth. It all happened so quickly.

CPR courses are offered by the Red Cross, but hospitals and municipalities sometimes offer them for a lower cost. You do not need a class that provides certification if you are not going to use it in your job. Some classes are about babies only, some adults only, and some both. Be sure to check the details before registering. While my main interest was my grandson, I registered for one that covers both, because you never know when someone around you might need help.

Dealing with Emergencies at Home

You should have emergency information posted on your refrigerator. That is where the EMTs will look to check for your doctor, emergency contact and medical conditions.

When someone is ill or injured there are a lot of decisions to be made very quickly. If the situation is not very scary the first thing you want to do is call your doctor's office and explain the situation. Even if the doctor's office is closed, most will have an answering service and may page the doctor if the situation sounds as if it needs immediate attention. Sometimes you need to be insistent about that, if you are concerned. However, in some cases you need to do more than that. Your doctor may tell you to go to an urgent care center or if, for example, someone is bleeding and the doctor's office is closed, you're going to want to go to an urgent care center. If the situation is serious or past the hours of your local urgent care, go to the emergency room of your nearby hospital.

When do you call 911 and get the paramedics to come out? That is sometimes a difficult question. Paul and I sometimes went back-and-forth about whether to do that or not. Sometimes we made a tremendous effort and managed to get him to the doctor or an urgent care center when we really should have called an ambulance. Ironically, one of the ways you can determine whether to call an ambulance is whether the person is ambulatory. That is, if they are able to walk with minimal assistance to the car, then by all means take them to a doctor or urgent care center. However, if they normally can walk, but now they cannot stand up or walk without great assistance, then you should call an ambulance. When we managed to get Paul to an urgent care center with great difficulty, the first time he had pneumonia, they told me I should have called an ambulance. The reason being, that if somebody is having real problems breathing, not only is the breathing itself a problem and could cause fainting, but the effort to breathe puts strain on the heart and could cause a heart attack. Also if someone has a high fever over 101°, you can try calling your doctor, but if you cannot reach them you probably should call an ambulance. Another indication of a potentially serious situation would be the presence of a rash when there is a fever. It doesn't have to be all over the body. It could be in a small area. A doctor in the ER found a rash on Paul's foot when he removed his sock and said he thought he had encephalitis, which I didn't take seriously until it was confirmed days later. If there isn't a fever with the rash, just take an antihistamine and see if that reduces or eliminates it. As I talk about in the section on falls, if you have a fall and know the cause and are not injured, you can also call paramedics to help you up without going to the hospital.

Of course, the most important thing, if you do need to call 911, is to stay calm and give good information. Also, be sure to unlock your front door so that the paramedics can get in, and clear a path for them.

If you live close to more than one hospital, you can sometimes request a specific one. The paramedics may even ask your preference. Generally speaking, it is best to go to the one where your primary care physician practices, so that he can see the patient the next day if admitted. That may not be possible if they are full, but it is worth asking.

Another concern that Paul had was the expense of an ambulance. They are quite costly. It always seemed to me that they should be a municipal service, but they normally aren't. However, when you receive the bill later, just give them your insurance information. Some insurance policies do charge if you go to an emergency room and are not admitted, to discourage people from tying them up unnecessarily. If you arrive by ambulance that isn't likely to be a problem. Ambulances are normally covered by Medicare. In some areas, such as in Oregon, there may be programs such as "Life Flight" and "Fire/Med" that let you proactively pay a certain amount annually as a membership, and then cover or discount the portion of emergency medical transport not funded by your insurance, if you do not have Medicare and have medical problems.

If you have to go to the hospital, or even an urgent care center, be sure to bring your insurance information. In an emergency, a hospital cannot deny you treatment, but it does complicate things quite a bit if they don't have your insurance information, and you may have headaches to deal with later. Bring the list of prescriptions and dosages the patient is taking, which you should have ready in your wallet. Leave their valuables at home in case they are admitted. It isn't so much a matter of stealing as things being lost upon transfer. We have lost shoes and a hearing aid that way. If that should happen, ask the hospital to reimburse you. They did it for us both times, but it was a hassle. Also, bring reading materials and coins or small bills for vending machines, as you may be there a long time.

Your doctor should have an answering service or rotate being on call with another doctor, so call his or her number no matter what time it is. If they tell you to drive to the E. R., ask them to call there and tell them to expect you. We found this helped to get us seen right away. We would mention that the doctor had told us to go there and that they had called If you arrive by ambulance of course you get the highest priority.

When you get to the hospital, set up a family code. This is an easy word to remember that you will share with whomever you want to have access to the person's private medical information. Pick the word and make sure that you ask someone to enter it into the hospital records. Then let the family know. Otherwise HIPAA regulations will keep medical personnel from answering questions.

Urgent Care

Not all urgent care or immediate care centers are alike. Before you go to one you're going to want to call and ask some questions. If it is such an emergency, and if you were so concerned that you can't take the time to call, then that is an indication that you probably need to go to the emergency room. The first thing you want to check is their hours, which can vary greatly from place to place. The next thing you want to find out is what equipment they have. If you are only going because you have a cold or something like that, it won't be important. However, if you have suffered a fall, if you think there's a possibility of pneumonia, or if for other reasons, you think that you may want to have an x-ray, you want to find out if they have that equipment there. Some urgent care centers do; others do not. If you go to an urgent care center and then they send you on to an emergency room for an x-ray, then you have wasted a lot of time. Finally, you want to ask what their current waiting time is. Of course that can change in the 10 or 15 minutes it takes you to get there, but it will give you an approximate idea. One other thing is to check to see if they accept your insurance. Some places do not accept Medicare.

Your Own Emergencies

If you are worried that you may be having or had a serious condition such as heart attack, stroke, or TIA (mini-stroke), have a friend, taxi or whatever take you to the nearest emergency room immediately. Do not drive yourself. To use a cliché, "Better safe than sorry".

CHAPTER 36

Helping and Placing Loved Ones with Long-Term Medical Problems

Visiting Friends Who Are Ill

As we age, so do our friends and family, and the likelihood of one of them having a serious illness or operation increases. While a card is always appreciated, here are some suggestions for how to help when a good friend is hospitalized or in a nursing home.

Talk to the spouse/partner or closest relative and find out if the patient would like a visit. I regret that I did not ask people to visit Paul in the nursing home. Two people did visit, in addition to, of course, my immediate family, and Paul really appreciated those visits.

If you send or bring a card, try to find one with large print. The reason for this is that there's going to be very limited space on a table to place cards, and the card is likely to be taped up on a wall, fairly far from their bed. If they can't get out of bed, they can still see the large card, with a large picture and large letters, and enjoy that.

If you go to visit, ask what is appropriate to bring. For example, many ICUs will not allow flowers. While you may want to bring your friend a box of candy or other favorite treat, they may be on a special or restricted diet that would not enable them to eat it, and it could feel frustrating for them.

It is usually best to visit in the afternoon, as mornings are filled with doctors making rounds, and in the evening, the patient may be tired. However, you may want to ask them what they prefer.

When you approach their room, check to see if there is either a sign about contagion, or a box of hospital gowns right outside the door. If so, be sure to talk to a nurse before entering the room. You may have to don gloves, a disposable gown and/or mask. If you leave the room for any reason, such as to go to the bathroom or take a walk, be sure to leave the gown in the room and not wear it out of there. Even if their initial hospitalization was not for something contagious they may have picked up an infection in the hospital.

Try to be sensitive to the friend you are visiting and what they do or do not want you to do. For example, do not overstay your welcome. If they look tired, that might be your cue to leave. If a meal is served while you're there, you might want to ask if they would like help with eating the meal or not. If medical personnel enter the room, ask your friend if they would like you to wait in the hallway to protect their privacy. Most patients will prefer having privacy, and they will appreciate the consideration. Others might really want you to stay, in case they want to be able to talk to someone about their options and decisions. If the patient has started to have any kind of cognitive decline, or if English is not their first language, it might be particularly valuable for you to stay to help them. Simply offering them a choice is, itself, beneficial. It shows that you respect them, and it helps them remember they still have agency over their lives.

It would be a nice gesture to ask if there are any errands or chores that they would like you to handle, that they are unable to take care of.

When you select a card, be sensitive to the situation. A card that is optimistic,rather than sympathetic, if a person has a terminal disease, might only make them feel worse. If you go to a larger store, there will be a wider selection of cards, and you are sure to find something that is appropriate for the situation. If you are on a low budget, you might be pleasantly surprised by the variety of cards at some Dollar Stores. If you cannot find an appropriate card, it could be best to just write a personal note in a general note card. Another way to personalize a greeting is to find or print a photo, and write on the back of that or put a sticky note on it. What's important is for your friend to have a sense that someone cares how they are doing.

Becoming a Caretaker

The terms "caretaker" or "caregiver" have very broad implications. I remember the first time that someone referred to me as a caretaker. I commented that really, all I did was help Paul button his shirts and pour his liquids. Doing that only took a few minutes and really didn't impact what I did during the day. As time went on, tasks were added on a roughly monthly basis. There were more things that he could not do for himself, such as putting on his socks.

However it never got to the point where it kept me from leaving the house or doing things I wanted to do. It did restrict some of the things that we could do together, but not that many. We found a way to make it work.

There are situations, however, where someone becomes a full-time caretaker for a family member. This can be a real, full-time occupation. In New Zealand, they recently passed legislation to make it a paid position, as it probably ought to be; because if you're a full-time caretaker, not only can you not be out on your own, doing fun things, but you also can't be working outside the home. In Oregon, family members can become trained, paid caregivers through the Senior & Disabled Services office in their County.

It's understandable that people may want to do the caretaking themselves, either because of the financial burden involved in hiring help, or because they know that conditions in a nursing home or other institutions are usually less than desirable. Everyone became more aware of that with the pandemic, as nursing homes have been the epicenter of fatalities in the coronavirus outbreaks in the USA and it often became difficult or impossible to pay visits.

However, if you are a caretaker, it is essential that you have some time off. No one can have a job 7 days a week, 24 hours a day. Everyone needs time to themselves. There are many ways to accomplish this.

You can hire outside professionals to come in at a fairly reasonable fee. At one point, after Paul left a hospital, I did hire help for a few weeks. I only paid $20 an hour, with a 4-hour minimum. You might not be able to find a place that will help you for $80 a day, but you can look around. You can also hire someone directly, yourself, by advertising, especially if they don't need to perform medical tasks. If the person being cared for is tall or heavy, it might not be a good idea to hire someone who is petite, if they are going to be helping to lift or transfer them in any way. If any lifting or transferring is involved, you will want to look into professional training with gait belts and/or Hoyer devices, for the safety both of your assistant caregivers and your loved one. No matter whom you consider inviting into your home, be sure to get references -- both personal and professional -- and actually verify them. Especially if the person will be in your home alone with your loved one, and especially if your loved one has any cognitive or visual impairment , you should run a criminal background check. If you are hiring them through an agency, be sure to ask whether the agency runs criminal background and reference checks.

I recommend checking into short-term insurance. This is a newer product and only applies to home health care. It is not for use in a nursing home, nor for long-term care, but it can be used for a few weeks. It is surprisingly inexpensive. If you obtain this form of insurance, you can -- and, indeed, need, to hire licensed professionals. The coverage is quite complete; it covers almost any kind of home visit from a medical professional you might need. However, be sure to compare the different levels of coverage available. The least expensive level might not reimburse enough for a caregiver to be worth the expense. Mine reimburses a certain amount for prescriptions. Ask about that.

Another thing to look into is off-site respite care. If you find an agency that provides off-site respite care, that means that you can bring your loved one to spend some time at a specialized facility, just for the day. While it might not be accessible for someone who is bed-ridden, there might be such facilities in your area, specific to your loved one's diagnosis; such as for memory care. Be very specific with your terms, if you call around looking for such opportunities; because in the home health field, "respite care" means something completely different. Among home health workers, "respite" workers are those who come for an overnight shift to give family members who care for a loved one at home a day or a night off for leisure, travel, or simply to catch up on slumber. For logical reasons -- most importantly, avoiding caregiver burnout -- these are the most sought-after home health workers, and their overnight services and scheduling flexibility, especially for those who are "on-call" for last-minute shifts and most emphatically for those who work overnights (whether awake overnights or asleep overnights), generally are rewarded with a $1 to $5 an hour premium atop the pre-vailing wage. It will be worth it to you to budget for occasional respite care, if you do not have family members nearby who can assist.

If you live in a big enough municipality with varied enough social services; and if you have the funds or the top-tier insurance to pay for it; you might also look for specialized, short-term-stay facilities where you can bring someone for a period of time, so you can travel or have some personal time. A friend whose husband has Alzheimer's recently took a two-week vacation. She was really looking to get away for a week, but she found the facilities near her area had a two-week minimum to take someone and care for them, and she decided she might as well enjoy the full two weeks, as long as she was paying for it. She arranged for friends to drop in and visit her husband on an almost daily basis, and she was able to leave with a feeling of relative ease.

If someone qualifies for hospice care and is being cared for at home, Medicare will pay for them to go to a facility for a short stay while their caregiver takes a break. If this could apply to you, be sure to check into it. This is called a "Respite Care Benefit," if you want to see if your plan covers such.

Here's another thing to consider. A neighbor recently said that she could not join our Friday night gatherings on the block because she couldn't leave her mother alone in the house. She had help when she was away at work, but when she came home, she felt as if she couldn't step out and leave her mother alone. I suggested a baby monitor. The baby monitors today are much more sophisticated than they were years ago and include video feed. This enabled her to step across the street knowing that she would be able to return quickly if her mother got up or needed help.

Remember, in order to take care of someone else, you have to first take care of yourself. It's like when they give the safety warnings on a plane, and they tell you to put your own oxygen mask on, first, before you help anyone else. When Paul first entered the nursing home, I met his first roommate's wife, who always seemed to be there. She told me that she used to be there 24 hours a day and never left. I asked where she slept, and she told me that she slept in the chair she was sitting in. I was amazed at her self- sacrifice. She then went on to tell me that after a while, she was diagnosed with several stress-related disorders. After that, her son insisted on picking her up every night. While she was in her 80s and no longer drove and would not have been able to do much on her own, it still was not a good idea to be in one place all day and night.

Don't be a martyr. Take care of the caretaker. Contact your local hospital. Many have Caregiver Support Groups. You can find peers, share catharsis, learn valuable tips, and not feel alone during what can be some emotional, as well as logistical, transitions.

The final point I want to make is that sometimes you cannot be a caregiver. This could be an immediate decision at the onset of the illness or disability, or it could be that as the condition progresses it gets to be too much. You may not be able to do it physically, emotionally, financially, or because you have to work or the illness is too complex for home care. Perhaps they fall down a lot or cannot be left alone. Whatever the reason may be, as long as it's not because you don't care, you have no reason to feel guilty about it. You need to do what is best for both your loved one and yourself. This could mean just bringing in help at home; but it could mean that they need to move to a facility. If that is the case there are many decisions to be made, especially in the choice of facility. I was trying to figure out if there was some way to bring Paul home and care for him here, but his problems were too complex for it to be possible, and I had to accept that.

Types of Health Facilities

Assisted Living

To qualify for assisted living, someone must need help with daily tasks such as dressing and bathing but not need major medical care. If the person is not living alone it may be possible either for their partner to assist them or to have someone come in for a few hours a day. There are agencies that provide this kind of service, and the assistants even do light housekeeping and cooking. At least part of the cost will be covered by short-term insurance and possibly long-term insurance. The advantage is the comfort of being in your own home. The disadvantage is that the personnel will change from time to time, and after you've gotten used to a routine, you have to retrain someone as to what you want, where things are in your house, etc. My sister-in-law Judy has dealt with this several times.

If the person is living alone it may not be sufficient for them to have someone come in for a few hours. They may need 24-hour care. If they are frail and elderly and in danger of falling frequently, this becomes pretty essential. If you have someone coming in 24 hours a day, they will need a bedroom for them, and you may not have that. An assisted living facility may be more practical. Often couples will move to an assisted living facility together if they are concerned that they can no longer safely manage living by themselves. The criteria you want to use for selecting an assisted living facility are very similar to those for nursing homes. A couple of factors you have to look at are: What is the food like?

That is now even more important than in a nursing home. What will the facility do or not do? For example, when we were looking at assisted living facilities for Paul's sister Barbara, we found that they would not change a suprapubic catheter, so she did not qualify. All assisted living facilities should be able to provide help with medications, dressing, bathing, and be on call to assist in case of a fall. All of them should check on residents daily, and they should be safer than living alone.

If someone can qualify for assisted living, rather than a nursing home, it is preferable. Some assisted living facilities are quite nice and offer full apartments, rather than a room. Some accept Medicare and some do not, so be sure to ask about that before visiting. If you have long-term care insurance, you will probably be able to use it, but check with your company.

Memory Care

Memory care facilities may be one floor of a larger care facility or a separate facility. They specialize in dealing with patients with Alzheimer's or other types of memory loss, such as from dementia, stroke, or traumatic head injury. They try to provide a safe and stimulating environment, with locked doors and specialized activities.

Rehabilitation Facilities

These are often part of a nursing home. The difference is that the goal is to treat the patient for a limited time period and send them home. Many of the patients are recovering from a fall or surgery. They are conscious, not very ill, and can participate in therapy.

Long-Term Care Hospitals

I had never heard one of these until I was told that Paul would have to go to one. When he was beginning to heal from the virus, the hospital that he was at said that they no longer could keep him in the

ICU because he was no longer critical, but that it would take a long time for him to fully recover. They explained that the Medicare policy is that for a long-time recovery, someone has to go to a long-term care hospital. The stay at one of these hospitals is generally one month. After that month, they must be transferred to a nursing home. The long-term care hospital is somewhat like a midway point between the hospital and the nursing home. They don't have as intensive care as an ICU, but it is a hospital-like setting. They do provide a certain amount of rehabilitation. They have an ICU area in case someone, for example, develops an infection, as Paul did. He was in the ICU for a few days and then sent back to a regular room. At the end of the month he did transfer to a nursing home.

Nursing Homes

Nursing homes provide 24-hour care that could last for anywhere from weeks to the rest of someone's life, in a hospital-like setting. No one really likes being in a nursing home, but some are better than others. Private rooms are extremely rare. Most rooms are double, and there are even triple and quadruple rooms for Medicaid patients or those who are very short on funds. Most nursing homes do provide some activities, such as bingo, musical performances, etc.

Nursing homes do not have the same patient-to-staff ratio that hospitals do. You can sometimes spend a long time trying to find a staff member to take care of your loved one. If they're on lunch break or whatever, it could be a half an hour or more. Most nursing homes are not great places to be, but try to find the best possible one for your loved one.

Transferring from one facility to another

If you're dealing with discharge from a hospital or other facility to another, be sure to ask for the social worker and let them guide you as to which facilities would be the most appropriate for your loved one. Then be sure to visit those facilities yourself. Please read the section on "some things to look for". Do not let them rush you too much. Find out when the transfer will take place, so you know how to schedule your search. At one point I received a call from a hospital saying they were going to transfer Paul that day. I refused, because based on what I had been told earlier, I was still completing visits. They grudgingly complied.

It is very easy to lose items during a transfer. Try to be at the first facility shortly before the transfer and make a list of what items should be going. If there is something of value, you may want to take it yourself. Upon arrival, be sure to double check that all items are there. If you wait a day or so, the old room will have been cleaned and the item lost.

The social worker will make the arrangements for transport. You don't have to worry about that. You do have to check to make sure that all prescriptions and medical orders have been transferred. One problem I ran into was that Paul was due for a catheter change the day of the transfer. I pointed that out and they assured me the new facility was going to do it. I checked a couple of days later and the new facility didn't know anything about it.

Choosing a Nursing Home

At some point you may very well need to choose a nursing home for a loved one. It is a very challenging task. Anyone who needs one won't be in a position to do it themselves, unless they are simply looking for a place for rehab after upcoming elective surgery. Most of the time patients will transfer there from a hospital. Make friends with the social worker at the hospital and ask for their guidance in choosing a nursing home for your partner. In general they will not recommend specific institutions because of liability. However they can guide you to resources that will give you information about them and give you a list of appropriate facilities that are nearby.

Not all nursing homes are the same by any means. And that is not just referring to quality. Many nursing homes restrict the kinds of disabilities they will deal with. Not all nursing homes will take all patients.

For example, if someone is on a ventilator, or has even been on one recently, they will need a ventilator facility. Most nursing homes do not have the staff and equipment to cover that, so your choices will be limited. I was sometimes frustrated when I would ask about if anyone was familiar with a particular nursing home and people would say, "Oh you should check out such and such a place." That facility would not accept my husband if I wanted him to be admitted there, because he had a trach collar and most nursing homes will not accept a patient with one, so it was frustrating.

That greatly restricted our choices. The social worker was able to give me a list of appropriate facilities nearby. Be sure to visit them in person. You will be surprised at what you learn by visiting them. You can call and schedule a tour, but that is not required. You can drop by any nursing home at any reasonable time during visiting hours, and they have to give you a tour. Of course that may mean that you have to wait a while before someone is available to give the tour but it usually isn't very long.

Some things to look for include:

How many patients are in a room? Some of the facilities that I toured had some rooms that had up to four patients in them. I was surprised by this. Most facilities do not offer private rooms, except at a premium. However, the majority of them do offer double rooms rather than triple or quadruple rooms.

Another thing to look for is smells. It is inevitable that there are going to be some odors from people who have had accidents, but how bad is the smell? Is it just in one area they haven't got to clean up yet? Or is it throughout the facility?

How pleasant is it to be in that facility? Is it dark and dank or light and airy? While your loved one may be bedridden you hopefully will be visiting them frequently, and you want that visit to be as pleasant as possible. And if they are conscious they will be getting out of their room for therapy, etc. and a positive atmosphere encourages a positive attitude, which encourages healing.

Ask about the ratio of staff to patients and the kinds of staff members that they have. Do they have a doctor or nurse practitioner on staff?

Ask about physical therapy and ask to see the facilities. Ask how often they offer physical therapy to the patients.

Ask about activities. How often do they take place? Are they the kinds of activities that the patient will enjoy? For example, do they want to play bingo? Paul refused to do that, but others may love that. Will there be music? Etcetera.

Do they have outings? If so, who can participate in them?

Do they have a dining room for patients and/or visitors? What are the menus like? One problem Paul's sister Barbara had was that the nursing home would offer something like tacos, which she didn't eat, and it was hard to get a substitute, so she was undernourished.

How far and how difficult of a drive is it to get there? Will you be willing to make that drive often? Visits are very important to the patient.

What hospital are they affiliated with? Even if they have a doctor on staff the specialists will visit from a hospital. What do you know about that hospital?

What are the costs? The Medicare coverage will run out and you will be paying after 100 days.

How often do they do family conferences?

What is the reputation of the facility? Do you know someone who has had a family member there? You can look at online comments but bear in mind that there will always be a few negative ones.

If the weather is pleasant, you may find patients outside, and you can talk to them about what their experiences have been. I recommend waiting around until a visitor comes out. Most often this would be on weekends, and asking them about how happy they are with the care. Go online and check out government ratings and patient comments about the facility. One thing you have to look out for is the date for all of these, because conditions may have changed. For example, the facility we chose had a low rating from the government, but it was under new management, and there were some more recent good comments online.

Personnel You Will Encounter in a Nursing Home

One of the things that I found very challenging when Paul went into a nursing home was learning who does what. This is, in fact, one of the things that motivated me to write this book. You shouldn't have to figure it out for yourself, but don't expect a nursing home to give you an orientation. If you get one, consider yourself lucky. To complicate things further, the staff at nursing homes are much less likely than hospitals to have identifiable uniforms. Many of the personnel that work there are part-time, picking up extra work, and not full-time. Therefore, they are going to wear what they have with them.

RNs

Do not ask an RN Registered Nurse) to do things like change a bedpan or diaper. Nurses pretty much limit themselves to dispensing medication, checking vital signs, and seeing to the general status of the patients. If you're looking for an RN, look for a medications cart outside a patient room. Then you can assume that a nurse is in a room and you can then wait for them to come out.

Respiratory Therapists

Respiratory therapists are not found in every nursing home. If the patient is on a ventilator, or even if they just have a trach collar, they will be in a nursing home that does have a respiratory therapy staff. The respiratory therapy staff makes sure that the equipment that helps the patient to breathe is working properly. If the patient is not on a respirator, they will make sure that their airway stays clear by placing a tube in their throat and suctioning out phlegm. They will suction routinely so many times a day, but if the patient feels clogged up you can request that they come in and suction them at any time.

CNAs (Certified Nursing Assistant)

The CNA's job is to do all the things that the nurses do not or cannot take the time to do. They are the ones who will change a bedpan or diaper, bathe patients, and dress them. If the patient is not able to stand and walk by themselves but is not totally bedridden, they are trained to use what is called a Hoyer lift. A Hoyer lift is a mechanical lift that involves placing the patient in a sling-like device and then mechanically lifting them out of bed and into a chair or vice versa. It should be done by two people, not one.

Wound Care

Hopefully, you will not need a wound care specialist, but unfortunately we did and many other people do. If a patient is lying around a lot they can develop a bedsore. Bedsores can be extremely serious and the wound care team will treat bedsores, change bandages, treat rashes, etc. If the patient cannot move around a lot, be sure that they are on an air mattress that alternates the pressure on either side, and make sure the CNAs are changing their positions regularly.

Orderly

Orderlies do the most mundane tasks, such as moving beds around or wheeling a patient into a dialysis room. They do not have to be particularly skilled.

Maintenance Personnel

If going through channels doesn't work, look for these people yourself and be friendly. They can help if there is a problem with the television, the bed, etc.

Admissions Director

It's possible that in some places the admissions director is someone who only helps you select the facility and you don't have any more contact with them. However, for me, the admissions director was the person I went to when I was getting frustrated with not being able to find the personnel who were supposed to help me. She gave me her cell phone number when Paul was admitted, and if I was having a real problem I would give her a call. In most cases she was able to help me. Try asking the admissions director for their cell phone number.

Nurse Practitioners

A nurse practitioner has a status between that of a nurse and a doctor. While doctors visit several nursing homes, the nurse practitioner may be on staff at one particular home and get to know all the patients. If a nurse or a family member reports a problem, they will then coordinate with the patient's main doctor or an appropriate specialist to discuss the best course of treatment. When the doctors visit, they will generally make rounds with them. They have the power to order or remove prescriptions, which a nurse does not. It's a good idea to get to know your nurse practitioner well. They are the one to go to when you want to have medications removed.

Social Workers

The social worker should set up regular family meetings with relevant staff members to look at the patient's progress. They are the person to go to if you choose to transfer to another facility. If you are lucky they will help orient you upon arrival, but they are sometimes too overwhelmed to do it. They can also answer questions about Medicare, arrange follow-up care upon discharge, and generally help you advocate for the patient.

Therapists

Therapists help the patient to heal in ways other than with medication. Simply put, occupational therapists deal with tasks of daily living, which mostly involve the upper half of the body, and physical therapists deal with aspects of movement for the entire body. Occupational therapists may work on life skills such as cooking and doing laundry. Physical therapists work on walking, climbing stairs, etc. With daily work they can help patients make tremendous progress.

Speech therapists not only help people who have had strokes regain their normal speech, but also deal with swallowing. People with Parkinson's and some others may not be able to safely swallow without choking or aspiration into the lungs. The therapist may determine if they can have liquids, thickened liquids, or nothing orally. Paul, unfortunately, was sent to the hospital for a swallowing test when he wasn't feeling well and did not pass, despite the therapists' efforts to prepare him, and so had to remain on a feeding tube.

Northwestern University is at the forefront of research on swallowing, so if your loved one can't swallow, you may want to contact them to see if any of their developments may be of help. Ironically, I found out about this the day Paul died. I had the newspaper article about it in my purse to bring with me the next day. I did bring it with me when I went to pick up Paul's belongings a few days after his death and left it on the speech therapist's desk, in hopes of helping someone else.

A final tip: Be sure to know the full number of the patient's room, including if it is North or South, etc. You will need that information if you call and want to speak to their nurse, for example. Ask when you arrive if there is a list of which personnel are assigned to which area that day. It won't take long before you know the names of the regulars and know whom you should look for. I can't tell you how many times I approached a CNA and they told me that Paul wasn't their patient that day. Once in a while they would help anyway, but that was not the norm.

Being an Advocate in Nursing Homes

Having a loved one in a nursing home is very different from simply going to visit a friend who is in a nursing home. When you go, you are not only bringing them company, you are also going to wind up being an advocate for them. It becomes a part-time job. Even the best nursing home cannot notice everything a patient needs. You can. If they cannot talk, you will have extra responsibility to be their voice. It is all a grave responsibility. You know your loved one better than anyone who works there. Don't be afraid to speak up and advocate. Here are some things to expect and tips that will help you no matter what condition the patient is in.

If the patient is not fluent in English, you may need to serve as a translator and arrange someone to be there at least part of the time you cannot.

One very important thing to do is to make a friend or two in the administration of the nursing home. This could be the admissions person, the facility director, or even the receptionist. I found the receptionist at Paul's nursing home to be very helpful to me. The admissions director was my number one contact person, but when she wasn't there and I had a complaint, the receptionist, who liked me from our chats, would go and find the appropriate staff person for me. Be sure to get their cell phone numbers if there isn't an extension to reach your new friends directly. Also, get contact information for the social worker and other people that you might have to deal with.

The social worker should be setting up a "family meeting" at least once a month. Keep track of that and don't be afraid to ask when yours will be. The first month there may be one earlier than that. You can meet with staff and ask about status and plans.

Nursing homes tend to over-medicate patients. They want to keep them calm so that they will not injure themselves and so that the staff will not have to do a lot to deal with them. However, if they are medicated too much it makes it impossible for them to recover. This is a big danger of nursing homes and one do you always have to be vigilant about. At one point my husband was so over-medicated that you could not understand his speech, because he couldn't fully close his mouth to articulate. He also could not participate in physical therapy. After weeks of trying, I finally got his medications reduced, and these problems subsided. Another drug they recommend adding to his regular regimen caused hallucinations. Once again, it took me weeks of effort to get rid of it. You have to keep in mind that they don't know what is normal for someone the way you do. With not only Paul, but my mother-in-law and sister-in-law, when they went to a hospital or new facility, I would have to tell the staff that the confused state the patient was in was not normal for them. It would be for some people, after all. At least once a week it is important that you ask for a printout of their drug list. You may be surprised at what you find on it that you didn't approve or what is missing. These lists do change from week to week. It may take repeated requests to get it, but keep at it.

If the patient isn't able to get out of bed very much, they need to be rotated regularly to change the pressure points on their body and avoid bed sores. Bed sores, also known as pressure wounds, can go all the way down to the bone and can cause infections that can kill. Paul was hospitalized with one for a few days. They explained that it had gotten suddenly worse because he had a fever. It was treated superficially in the nursing home, but they scraped it out in the hospital and started the healing process. When it wasn't healing I should have pushed for him to go to the hospital sooner.

While I imagine actual abuse in nursing homes is rare, a certain degree of neglect is so common as to be almost universal. It is generally not intentional, but the problem is that nursing homes are chronically understaffed. It is hard to find people who want to do the kind of work that CNAs do for the pay they receive. Every time I would go into the nursing home, I would see signs up that they were hiring. They were never fully staffed. From what I've heard this is true at almost all nursing homes. Sometimes, I would plan on staying for two hours and wind up staying for three because I spent the last hour just looking for someone to put Paul back in bed, so that his back didn't hurt. Other problems include getting someone to change a diaper or get someone dressed. It's important that you see to these things because if, for example, they aren't dressed when they should be dressed, they cannot go to physical therapy. They must be dressed and in a wheelchair, and if they are not mobile enough to do that themselves, which most nursing home patients are not, you may have to make sure that the personnel do this. One problem that is solvable is that multiple people will go to lunch together at the same time, so no one is available to help. If you are running into problems like that, tell someone in the administrative staff.

One thing I did in the way of advocacy was reminding the staff to view and treat Paul as a person and not just a patient. There were a few ways I did this. One, suggested by my daughter-in-law, was to tape photos to the wall, including him at his best and not his worst. They often noticed and remarked about them. Another was when the staff had time to chat, I worked in a little background information about his interests and accomplishments. Finally, when the C.N.A.s were doing things like dressing him I reminded them, if needed, to talk to him about what they were doing and not just do it to him. That seems obvious, and I was told by an administrator I complained to, that they are instructed to do that, but sometimes the less caring ones didn't. A couple of times I saw someone come in and start turning or dressing him without saying a word. Our loved ones need us to advocate for respect for their dignity and humanity when they are not able to do so for themselves. This is also the kind of complaint that can be brought to an Ombuds. That term is short for ombudsman, who is someone whose job it is to investigate complaints against authority figures.

If the patient is able to use a computer, it can be a tremendous help. If you only have one computer and you need it at home, you can purchase a lightweight laptop at Best Buy or wherever for under $200. After the patient is discharged you can use it when traveling. There are so many things they can do with a computer, including Skyping with grandchildren who can't visit. Other possible things to bring include books, magazines, a radio with a CD player and some CDs, knitting, or other things they enjoy doing. Idleness leads to depression, which slows healing. Be sure to label everything with their full name, write up an inventory, and give it to management. Usually they have an inventory list, and it can be added to that. If you buy anything keep the receipts handy. Everyone I talked to had something disappear.

Does the patient have a suprapubic catheter? If so, you will have to keep track of the dates and remind them once a month that the tube must be changed. Sometimes a nurse will do this, but in other cases they have to arrange for a doctor to come in, so they will need a few days' warning. This is very important and something they are not likely to keep track of.

Some nursing homes may provide more guidance than others, but I found that the one that we were at provided very little orientation information about their facility, and I had to learn things on my own. So here are some things you need to ask about, so that you don't have to go through some of the same problems I did.

One problem we encountered was laundry. Limit how much you bring. Keep an inventory of every piece of clothing, and every other article that your loved one has with them in the nursing home. Use a permanent marker to put their first and last name on it somewhere inside all their clothing. Decide whether you want the facility to do their laundry or if you want to take their laundry home. I chose to take the laundry home, because my husband needed to use free and clear detergent as he had sensitive skin. I left a laundry basket in the closet, and I put up signs in the closet and in the room, stating that the family would do the laundry. We still lost some items, which may have been stolen, or simply lost in the facility's laundry. However if I had started keeping a list and doing our own laundry at the beginning, we would have lost fewer items. Be sure to file the inventory list with the facility as part of the admitting process. You may even want to take photos. Then if you need to buy a replacement for an item misplaced by or stolen from the facility, submit a bill with the receipt.

Talk to the activities director and discuss what kinds of activities your loved one would like to participate in. For example, do they like bingo? If not, like Paul, the activities director may stop thinking of them as a regular participant. If, however, they know that, for example, they only like musical performances, then they're more likely to bring them to those performances. It would be a good idea to keep track of the activities calendar and remind the activity staff the day before that this is something that the patient wants to participate in.

Every patient is assigned a doctor. However, that doesn't necessarily mean that you have to stick with that doctor. If you were having trouble communicating with that doctor, if they never come by to actually see the patient, or you have other reasons to be unhappy, you can request a change in their primary doctor. I wish I'd known this sooner. I didn't know, and I didn't switch Paul's primary until I'd dealt for months with a doctor I'd never met. Ask your friend in administration and patients' spouses for recommendations. Ideally, the doctor will visit once a week. Try to find out when that will be so you can consult with them. Get their office phone number in case you miss them.

If the patient is able to participate in physical therapy and leave the room, then I would suggest once in a while going to watch the physical therapy, so that you can have a better idea of what their progress is and offer words of encouragement. It helps to get to know the therapists by name. I found they could be helpful friends, too. If, for example, they came to get Paul, but he wasn't dressed, one of the therapists I got to know would see that that happened.

If your loved one is bedridden, then they still should be receiving physical therapy of some kind. Even patients who are unconscious should be receiving passive therapy. Passive therapy involves moving the limbs for patients so that they do not become stiff. This is also done to help prevent muscle atrophy (loss of muscle tone) and decubitus ulcers (pressure ulcers; bed sores). The next level of therapy would be bedside or restorative therapy, where they do not leave their room but they sit up and work on therapy while sitting on the bed. The most desirable therapy, of course, would be to actually go to a therapy room. There are two categories of therapy: occupational therapy, which involves activities, and physical therapy, which involves movement. These therapists may work together.

Physical therapy is crucial not only physically, but psychologically. Unfortunately, it is only covered for the 100 days of Medicare coverage. After that, the patient just receives restorative therapy in their room. However, there are some ways to extend complete therapy. First, if the therapists can show measurable, significant progress, they can ask for an extension. Next, if you have, as you should, Medicare Part B, you can get another month of free therapy. Our therapists offered to separate the physical and occupational therapy during the extension and do them consecutively, so Paul would have 2 months of additional coverage. One thing to be aware of, which I was not, is that every time there is a change in status, there is a break in time for new paperwork, etc. I was complaining unnecessarily about Paul not receiving therapy for a week because I didn't know this.

Some Quick Tips

If you get a newspaper, bring it with you. You can take turns reading sections, or if they are not able to read you can read it to them. Besides passing the time, it will help them to feel less isolated. Likewise, you can watch the news together. It will give you something to talk about besides medical issues.

If someone doesn't leave their room very much, and especially if they can't eat meals, it's very hard to keep track of time and distinguish 11 a.m. from 11 p.m. I looked online and found a 24 hour clock. Paul was in the military, so he knew how to read it, but some people may need a little coaching. I know you could also have a smart watch tell you the time, but that is too valuable an item to leave there.

If they have a feeding tube and cannot eat or drink, you should still be able to swab their mouth with some water. Ask for a few swabs to keep in a drawer so you don't have to always find someone to do that.

When you are leaving for the day, make sure that the call button, TV remote, and phone are within reach and the TV is facing towards them. If they are depressed, leave the T. V. on a channel they like.

If you are dissatisfied with the care, try speaking to someone in administration. If things don't improve, look on the walls near the desk or elevator and you will see the number of a state agency that you can notify. If you don't see that, tell them you want it. When you call, ask for the Ombuds, or Ombudsman, which would be the term for an advocate for patients in care facilities. If they say they don't have one, ask what their procedure is for reporting a problem with a nursing home.

Seeing to all this can be overwhelming, but it is essential that you take care of yourself and pursue your pleasures as well. If you are too stressed you are more likely to become ill and not be of any help. I limited my visits to a few hours a day and continued to act, shop, go to plays, etc. Paul understood and supported this. After the first few weeks of his illness, I worked out a schedule with my brother, Art, so that he would make the visit on whatever day of the week I was busiest, so I was only going there (about an hour and a half round trip) 6 days a week. Art, as a retired doctor, was also able to ask medical questions. Later, I began to ask my son, David, what day he would be going for his weekly visit (his work schedule was different every week), and skip that day as well. Paul still had a visit and a watchful advocate every day, and I had some free time and less stress. I didn't give up my second career as an actress, and so I was in a better position to continue on after Paul died.

CHAPTER 37

Legal Matters

End of Life Decisions: DNR's, Palliative Care, and Hospice

I was surprised to find how little I knew about this area. I'd heard of DNRs but thought it was an all or nothing matter. That isn't true. DNR stands for Do Not Resuscitate. That means that you feel that the quality of life that would be achieved by resuscitating someone whose heart has stopped is not worth the effort. However, there are actually different levels of DNR that you can choose from. For example, you can specify that you do not want chest compressions, which can break the ribs, but you do want the person's heart to be shocked if it stops. Be sure to discuss your options with someone on the staff of the hospital or nursing home. Be sure to discuss this with the patient if they are conscious. If not, have your power of attorney available, and you will be allowed to make the decision rather than the hospital deciding.

Palliative care I thought was only to manage pain and help someone who is in hospice. This is not true. Palliative care is appropriate for anyone with either a fatal or simply chronic illness. We could have benefited from palliative care starting a few years back when my husband was diagnosed with Parkinson's disease. Palliative care means that you get a monthly visit from a specialized nurse who will help guide your medications and other medical decisions. This can be very helpful because each doctor prescribes for their specialty and often doesn't step back to see how their drugs can duplicate or interact with the drugs of other doctors. The palliative care nurse can fight on your side if you feel your loved one is being over-medicated or under-treated.

I also thought that hospice was only for those in the last few weeks of life. Hospice care in the hospital often is for those who are actually dying, but you can receive hospice care at home if you are not expected to live more than six months. If you are still alive at the end of the six months, hospice care can be renewed. I know of someone who was in and out of hospice care for a few years. It is of great comfort to families to have someone to help make end-of-life choices and comfort easier. I was very impressed to find out that if someone is listed as being in hospice care, Medicare will pay for all equipment necessary for them to be cared for at home, such as a hospital bed or even a Hoyer lift, which is a mechanism to lift a person in and out of a bed or a wheelchair when they can't do it themselves. However some residential hospice centers are very pleasant and have activities, not just medical care. The focus of hospice care is comfort, not healing, so it is an important decision. If someone is in hospice care a nursing home will just make them comfortable and not send them to the hospital if they get an infection or have other problems. Palliative care, on the other hand, should not affect those matters.

Ethicists

Finally, there is a group I just found out about. Ethicists help you make the big decisions, such as whether to give up on cancer treatments, or whether someone should enter hospice, or whether life support should be ended. They can give an objective view to emotional topics when you need guidance about medical decisions. Your hospital will have an ethics committee (if you watch Chicago Med you have seen them mentioned many times), but there are also private ethicists you can consult with, or you can do an online search. They will sometimes recommend other doctors or facilities for treatment. It is reassuring to have someone who is not involved with the case take a look at it.

Doulas

You may have heard about birth doulas. I just learned recently about end of life doulas. The decisions around this topic are so complex it could be hard to know what to do. Doulas perform some of the same functions as ethicists, but they will also help with things like filling out forms, finding resources for day to day help, etc, help you plan funerals, etc. They work independently and are not covered by Medicare, but are generally just a few hundred dollars. It seems to me it would be well worth it to have someone to lean on for the small decisions and not just the large ones when dealing with this difficult situation. One source is doulagivers.com.

I also strongly recommend getting the workbook "My End of Life Decisions" from compassionandchoices.org. It is free and can be downloaded from their website or you can request a hard copy be mailed to you. It will help clarify your wishes not only for others but even for yourself.

Returning From a Hospitalization

If you were hospitalized for more than one night, you will need time to recuperate when you get home. Being hospitalized tends to take a real toll on people. I've heard it said that for every day of hospitalization, you need three days to recuperate. Of course, this will vary from individual to individual, but it gives you an idea of what to expect.

Why is this? It's not just the lingering effects of whatever was put into you in the hospital, but it's also the hospital itself. First of all, even if you do have therapy for an hour a day, you are still less active than you normally would be at home. At least for most people. And you are spending much more time than normal on your back, so the muscles that support the body are not being used enough. Secondly, your sleep patterns have been disrupted. There are probably people coming in at all hours to check on you and a strange environment that does not allow for good sleep. Third, you have probably been given medications that you don't ordinarily take. Fourth, in some cases you may have been catheterized, which takes a toll on your system. I have a whole separate chapter on those people who are catheterized and cannot get off of it.

Many hospitals have an inpatient rehabilitation floor. This floor is intended for people who are not ill, but are either injured or recovering from illness. If you have been in the hospital for more than a couple of weeks, this could be a good option for you to help prepare you to go home. If you are recovering from an injury such as a broken hip, this is also an excellent option. The atmosphere is a little less like a hospital and a little more like a nursing home, in the positive sense. The patients are not linked to their rooms by equipment such as IV's. They can leave their rooms in a wheelchair, and in some cases, they will be offered a dining area, rather than eating in their rooms.

If you feel that this would be a benefit to you, you may want to ask about it and see if there is a room available, which is sometimes a problem. It took quite a bit of persuasion to get Paul to do this after his heart complication, because after being in the hospital for a long period of time, he was anxious to get home. However, this is a much better option, if it is deemed medically appropriate. You don't have to worry about going out for therapy, and you don't have to worry about scheduling someone to come in and see you occasionally. I was relieved when he agreed, because going right home puts a lot of pressure on the caretaker. On the rehab floor of a hospital, you are right there in the facility, with the skilled care and daily rehab. Of course, at some point, you will be ready to go home, and you will have to think about what you're going to need. In many cases, if you have been using equipment, such as a walker, in the hospital, Medicare will allow you to take it home with you. Do not hesitate to ask. Also, therapists can offer, when asked, other devices, such as weighted spoons. Pretty much anything that you've used personally that isn't heavy equipment is liable to be covered by Medicare. Do not hesitate to ask.

Once you are home, if you are on Medicare, you will automatically have a nurse coming to check on you a few times a week, until you are better, and physical therapy if you need it. This is very helpful, but it does not provide you with a day-to-day caretaker. If you have a spouse who can take care of house duties, this may not be too much of a problem; but if you live alone, or if your spouse is not in good shape, this is a significant problem. You will probably have to hire a caretaker to come in for at least a few hours a day. If you contact a local agency that provides home helpers or caretakers, you will find that not only will they perform essential tasks, such as giving you your medicine and helping you get in and out of bed, but they will also do light house cleaning and cooking. If you have to go to a doctor or rehab, they can take you to your appointments (though you might have to supply or arrange the transportation). The price for this is typically $20-$40 per hour. Most private agencies have a four-hour minimum per shift. You can hire someone to come in for four consecutive hours, or you could hire someone to come in in the morning to help you get ready and at night to help you get ready for and into bed, each within two-hour shifts. If your needs are more substantial and continuous, you could hire someone to live in. This would probably be two people in 12-hour shifts, but you can also find people who will stay with you around the clock, if it's going to be for a long period of time. If they live in, they can count on that for their room and board, in addition to their salary. Both my aunt and my mother had wonderful women who moved in with them, took care of them, and remained friends with the family for months, even after the people whom they supported had died.

Depending on what condition you are in, you may need specialized medical equipment when you get home. Here are some types of equipment that may be helpful. Some of them can be rented short-term, if you think you only need them for a while. Others are inexpensive, or you may be using them for a long time and you'll want to purchase them. Some things, such as mobility devices, such as wheelchairs, which I cover in a separate chapter, may be covered by Medicare. Always ask about that before purchasing anything.

Medical Equipment

When someone is recovering from an accident or injury, one of the most common needs is for durable mobility equipment ("DME"), such as canes and wheelchairs. See my separate chapter on mobility issues. There are other items, however, you should know about. As the population ages, more and more companies come up with products to help senior citizens at home. All you have to do is look up one product on the Internet and you will soon be inundated with catalogs and other sales offers. I'm going to talk about some aids and do it by room.

The Bedroom

If a person is truly incapacitated, you can rent or buy a hospital bed. A hospital bed allows you to raise or lower its level, raise the head, raise the feet, etc. This would only be something you would want to do if the person were very seriously ill and was going to be for an extended period of time. I looked on the Internet and I did see a hospital bed from Progress Mobility that was only $845. However, you have to keep in mind that it is a single bed, and if you've been sleeping in the same bed as each other for years, you have to think about where the other person would sleep.

Something that even some people who are not particularly ill like to have is a bed that will raise the head up to help you get out of bed. These are for sale at ordinary furniture stores. It does not have to be a medical equipment store. If you're going to buy one of these, I strongly suggest you buy the kind where each side of the bed can be raised independently, rather than raising both people's heads at the same time. Someone may not be ready to get up. They are usually called adjustable beds or power base beds.

A quick and easy aid for people who just need a little help getting out of bed, perhaps because they have a bad back or are weak, is a bed rail. There are two major kinds of bed rails. First, there are bed rails that go along the entire side of the bed, to keep someone from falling out of the bed. This is similar to what many young children have. Of course these have to be hoisted up and pushed down to allow a person to get in and out of the bed. Then there are smaller ones that are sometimes called assist rails. These can serve a dual purpose. First, it may help prevent someone who is a restless sleeper from falling out of bed. Second, you can grab onto it and help get yourself out of bed. We ordered a free-standing one with legs on the floor, but couldn't get the height right and wound up returning it. We were very happy with the one pictured. What we had was a little curved grab bar, in essence, that Paul could use to help him get out of bed. This reduced the strain on his bad back. It has long ribbons that slip under the mattress to keep it in place. It's very important that you put the straps that go underneath the mattress all the way across, and that you make sure that the bed rail is in a secure position and will not slip off the bed when you grab it. If you set it properly, it is secure.

Bed-Rail

It disassembles pretty easily, it is lightweight, and it has a cloth case, so we were able to take it on trips. As a bonus, we have a dimmer switch on the light on the nightstand, and it would often be hard to find. The solution was to wrap the cord around the rail. It all worked out well enough that it was the one medical aid I kept in place after Paul died.

Bathrooms

Bathrooms are the most difficult room in the house to deal with. They are small, which makes it hard to maneuver in them. And they are slippery and have hard surfaces. Bathtubs can be difficult to get in and out of. Even just sitting on a toilet and getting up can be difficult.

Here are some things that can help. If you are having a new toilet installed, I recommend that you buy what's called a highboy. Toilets do come in different heights, and a highboy makes it easier to sit down and stand up, because you don't have to go so far. Our downstairs toilet had to be replaced, and that is what we got. Now, when I use the one upstairs, it feels so low. The odds of you needing or wanting to replace your toilet, however, are low, but there are alternatives. You can buy a special seat. There are two kinds of these toilet seats. The first one is merely a thick, fairly soft plastic seat that clips on to your toilet's seat. The second has that, plus it has handlebars to grab onto to help you get up. This can be a good solution. However, you have to check to see that you have enough space between your toilet and the sink or whatever is next to it in order to use one of those. We did not have enough space to do that. So, when Paul first came home from the hospital and needed to regain his strength, we just got a seat without the railings around it. Then we had a grab bar installed on the wall across from it, for him to grab onto to help him stand up. Obviously where you would put something like that would depend on the configuration of your bathroom.

Taking a bath or shower can be very difficult for someone who isn't agile. There are a couple of possible solutions. If you want to do actual remodeling, you can purchase a step-in shower, which is easy to get into and has a built-in seat. There are even roll-in showers, designed for wheelchairs. If you do not want to do anything so expensive and extensive and that may take a while to arrange, you can simply buy a shower chair. Shower chairs are inexpensive, purchased at a drugstore or from a catalog, and allow you to sit rather than stand while showering. I strongly recommend that if you don't already have it, you have a shower hose attached to your shower head, so that you have the flexibility of holding that in your hand and using it where you can comfortably sit, rather than having to position yourself directly under the shower head. You don't want to fall off your shower chair reaching for anything. However, if you invest in a dangling showerhead, you need to either leave it dangling, or make very, very sure of 2 things: (1) That where you have it hanging is somewhere that everyone using the shower and/or the caregivers assisting them to bathe can reach; and (2) That it is secured sufficiently that it won't fall and bonk someone on the head.

Make sure everything is all lined up before the person gets in the tub or shower. Shower chairs come with or without backs. We ordered from a catalog, and we ordered one with the back. It was fairly easy to assemble. Having the back obviously gives you more support and makes it less likely that you might fall off the back. It's worth a few extra dollars. Very important: If the chair is in a bathtub, do not attempt to step in and then sit down. Put your butt on the seat, and then lift your legs in. Repeat in reverse when you get out, and make sure that you have a good bath mat or rug to step onto that won't slide. Most hotels have a couple of shower chairs available. Call ahead and reserve one. Ask for a handicap room. The cost is almost always the same, but the bathroom is larger, and it has other pluses.

If someone is using a wheelchair, it may be difficult to get it into the bathroom; and depending on their mobility, they may be able to go from the wheelchair to the toilet, but perhaps not. If a person cannot make it to the bathroom for whatever reason, you can get a bedside commode. Someone would have to then empty and sanitize the bucket under the seat every time someone goes to the bathroom.

If a person cannot get out of bed at all, then they'll probably be using adult diapers and chux (moisture-wicking bed coverings) and will probably receive a sponge bath. There are wipes you can use instead of sponges or washcloths, so you don't have to worry about getting the bed wet. There are also powders that can be used instead of liquid shampoos, if someone who does not leave bed still has hair to shampoo. In nursing homes, if someone cannot get out of bed they use something called a Hoyer lift to get them up and into a wheelchair. A Hoyer lift is a sling that is placed under and around the body of the person who needs to be transferred from bed to chair. There are two versions of Hoyer lifts: manual and electric. Each has its pros and cons. An electric Hoyer can be operated by someone of lesser strength, but it is much larger to store, does not fold down as small, and is much more expensive. Ironically, it is also harder to push and position. A manual Hoyer takes physical arm strength and back flexibility to pump, but is much, much smaller, lighter, and more foldable for storage, and easier to push once someone is lifted, because the structure weighs so much less. But Hoyer lifts are heavy, they are expensive, and they are supposed to be used by two people together; so, it is unlikely that you would ever have one in your house, unless you have substantial home health care benefits, possibly including a live-in caregiver.

Kitchen

See my Parkinson's chapter for information on specialized utensils. If someone is eating in bed, get a bed tray, and raise them up with pillows, if nothing else.

One Thing Few People Know

Perhaps the best thing I can tell you is that there is a newer product on the market that almost no one I talk to knows about. That is short-term care. Long-term care has a couple of restrictions. One is a period of elimination (waiting) before it kicks in. The other is that the condition itself must be something that is expected to be of long duration. For example, if you break a leg and are unable to work for a month or two, you would not be eligible for long-term care, even if you go beyond their elimination period, because you are expected to recover.

So, what do you do? If you are working or own a business, you may want to purchase disability insurance to cover lost wages. However, if you are retired, that wouldn't apply. Also, disability will not pay for nursing or therapy.

Ask your insurance company what they would cover. If you are concerned, I recommend looking into short-term care coverage. Up until a few years ago, I had never heard of this product. It will cover your care during the elimination period. A plus or a minus, depending on your circumstances, is that it is designed only for home care (or at least the policy I have is). It will cover skilled nursing care, therapy, etc. It is true that Medicare will cover some of that, but not on a daily basis; and knowing that it is covered provides me with peace of mind. If you live alone, who will do things like prepare your meals and help you to the bathroom? With this insurance, you can have a caretaker come in to do that.

One of the great things about the policy we have is that it is inexpensive. If you have multiple prescriptions, it offers partial reimbursement for some of those. Be sure to have a box or envelope to accumulate those little receipts the pharmacy gives you with each prescription, and mail them in once or twice a year. The insurance company then sends a check for partial reimbursement up to a certain yearly limit. The premiums for the policy come out of my checking account each month, and I barely notice them.

Our policy is with G T L. I admit to not having done comparison shopping in this area, so you may want to do so, but I have been happy with them.

CHAPTER 38

Our Health Odyssey

This chapter is the most personal of all. I have been surprised to get reactions to my Facebook posts that tell me that people actually do want to hear about what Paul and I went through. If you don't want to know, you can always skip this chapter. It is my hope that by reading about all the many difficulties Paul and I dealt with, you will realize that there is a possibility of dealing with whatever you may face. I am not going to cover every medical problem Paul had in detail in this chapter, both because it would make a book in itself, and also because I have talked about many of them in previous chapters. I am simply going to give you a list of what they were and then talk about just a few of them in more detail.

In some cases I am not sure of the exact number of times things happened over the years, because unfortunately I cannot find the medical notebook where we started to keep track, and we never completed it, anyway. So that would be a recommendation to you: Keep your records on your computer (and backed up), rather than in a notebook, so that you cannot lose them. Include notes about every time you or your partner have a significant health problem. Be sure to include the diagnosis, the date, the doctor, and the treatments or prescriptions involved.

The list is very overwhelming. When I look at it I wonder how we ever coped with it all; but of course, it did not all happen at once. It happened over a period of years. We would learn to deal with something, and then another thing would be added on or replace it. When I look at the list, I realize that it's not surprising that one of the problems Paul sometimes had was depression. Sometimes he asked, "Why me?" However, I pretty successfully endeavored to keep him going, getting out, and staying interested in life until he got West Nile Virus.

Here's a list of conditions we faced, in no particular order:

Two strokes; frontal lobe seizures, of 3 different kinds; peripheral neuropathy; varicose veins; irritable bowel syndrome; mononucleosis; tinnitus; dizziness; arthritic back; slipped disc; heart arrhythmia; 4 heart cardioversions; hearing loss in both ears; a stroke, resulting in total deafness in one ear; bad hay fever; recurrent depression; extremely irritated skin, especially in winter; food allergies; no sense of smell; leg skin discoloration; prostate enlargement and surgery; a stomach ulcer; basal cell carcinoma; gallbladder removal; broken wrist; panic attacks; SAD (seasonal affective disorder); Parkinson's disease; repeated falls; swallowing problems; West Nile Encephalitis; mobility problems; pneumonia four times; being intubated (put on a ventilator); having a tracheotomy; having to relearn to speak; open heart valve surgery; Dressler's syndrome; atonic (failed) bladder; suprapubic catheter; catheter blockages; fungal infections at incision sites; multiple urinary tract infections; congestive heart failure, twice; cataracts; glaucoma; memory issues; and hallucinations.

I met Paul in 1978, and we married in 1980. When we married, Paul's health was pretty good. He had a few health problems. He had tinnitus, and he put his back out once, carrying a big pumpkin upstairs. Not much. After we were married he developed some digestive system problems. He had an ulcer and at one point had to have his gallbladder removed. He developed irritable bowel syndrome, which turned out to be primarily food allergies. Once we had to eliminate a segment of a vacation because he was, strangely, diagnosed with mononucleosis, a contagious disease which is more often gotten by teenagers. Other than that, his health was pretty good. From about 1986 to 1993, he owned and operated a one-hour photo shop, where he did developing and mixed chemicals every day.

In 1994, in the fall, everything changed. He had an episode where he was acting strangely, and he kept asking the same questions over and over and was very confused. I immediately took him to a nearby health clinic. It was late in the evening, and there wasn't much open. The doctor there said that he had a panic attack. I told the doctor that I didn't believe that, because I'd read about panic attacks, and his situation and symptoms did not seem to fit what I had read. The doctor assured me that panic attacks can take many forms. He prescribed a drug and said we should see a psychiatrist to deal with the panic attacks. That's what we did -- with 3 different psychiatrists, for almost 2 years, without much success. I should have sought a second, different kind of opinion, but did not. I was not assertive enough. This is a teachable example of what not to do. This was a very stressful time in our lives, because Paul would panic because he didn't know what had happened; and he would sometimes call me at work, and if I couldn't calm him down, he would insist that I come home. A couple of times, he called the campus security, because it was an easy number to remember, and they got me out of class. One time I had to leave a field trip. It was quite stressful.

At the end of this time, after telling the psychiatrists that there were some odd things happening with Paul, and even one of those instances happening during a session, one said that since he had not been able to help, we should go to another psychiatrist. When we met with the next one, and I once again told him some of the things that I was experiencing with Paul, such as his sometimes not responding when I called his name, he responded with, "Well, if you're suggesting that he has a seizure disorder, which I don't think he does, let's try this approach for six months; and then, if he still not better, take him to a neurologist."

I thought that was ridiculous. When Paul had his next panic attack, I called the doctor, and the doctor actually yelled at him over the phone. Then a week or so later, Paul had an episode where he didn't know what month it was, and he was very confused. I decided not to wait any longer and took him to a neurologist. I should have taken charge sooner. Please don't ever be intimidated by doctors against your better judgment. You know yourself and the people you live with best.

The neurologist that my brother recommended did a scan of his brain and said that he saw two blood clots, which indicated that Paul had had two small strokes. They were misdiagnosed because they were not in the part of the brain that deals with movement. Instead, they were in the part of the brain that handles memory and speech. The doctor then said that the clots in the brain were probably causing seizures. A quick EEG did not show one, but the doctor, smartly, had him take a 24-hour EEG, and the repeated seizures showed up. He then prescribed an anti-seizure drug. At this point, Paul was having several of these episodes a day. After a couple of weeks on the anti-seizure drug, the episodes went down to about once a day; then, once a week; then, a short cluster once a month; and eventually, only rarely. Once he knew what was happening and the seizures were getting under control, he never had a panic attack again.

Paul never agreed with me, but I always felt that one of the reasons he had so many health problems is because he spent six years owning and operating the one-hour photo shop, where he dealt with chemicals every day and did not have any ventilation. Neither one of us thought about it at the time, but in retrospect I thought that that was certainly at least a contributing factor.

Once Paul was on the anti-seizure medication, his seizures were under control, but the drugs had a sedating effect, and he went on disability. He could tell when he was having a good day or bad day, and what his chemical balance was, and whether he would have a seizure or not. So he would drive only on those days that he felt all right. One day, however, he had an unexpectedly unusually long and stressful day, and he was trying to navigate through a strange area at night; and he suffered a seizure while driving. While I don't normally believe in miracles, I do believe that what happened to him was a miracle, and that one of our ancestors grabbed the wheel. He was in an extremely crowded residential area, yet he did not hit a person or another car. He only knocked down a fence and went into a strangely empty lot. Not only that, but the car then changed direction, and headed towards an odd, solitary brick wall in the field. The bricks collapsed around the car and stopped it before it continued on to a wrought iron fence with busy State Street on the other side of it. The next day I met an insurance adjuster there, and we figured out what had happened. The area where he entered the field was blocked by cars when we were there. On top of all that, there was a police station nearby, and an officer saw the car suddenly accelerate and was there to help right away. Paul only spent one night in the hospital, and he had only a minor fracture to one of his vertebrae. We were very lucky this one time.

After that Paul only drove locally during the day. Then one time, when he had a seizure at home when he didn't feel it coming, he decided it wasn't safe to drive anymore and gave up his car. In retrospect, I'm surprised that none of his doctors told him to stop driving.

Other health problems followed. He began to have trouble climbing the stairs at night to go up to our bedroom. He went to see a cardiologist and found that one of his valves was leaking and needed to be replaced. He then had open heart surgery, because it was the kind of valve that required that kind of operation. Some valves, depending on their location, can be replaced laparoscopically, but not all. As it turned out, they were able to do a repair, rather than replacement. I talked about this in another chapter. He actually recovered from the open heart surgery much more quickly than I expected, and it went quite smoothly. We were both surprisingly calm about it, and the wound healed amazingly fast.

However, as bad luck would have it, he developed a complication to the procedure, called Dressler's syndrome. This caused fluid to build up in his heart sac and lungs, which had to be repeatedly drained. He wound up spending a total of three months in the hospital! After a few weeks, I asked if I could have a parking discount, and I got it. A tip to remember. Even worse, he actually was sent home twice during that time. The first time, he got up the stairs and collapsed on our front porch. We managed to get him inside and dealt with it for a day or two.

I was learning to be more assertive, and I remember calling the doctor, who said it would take a while to recover, and saying "It's not that it's taking him a while to get better. He's getting worse." The doctor was a bit dubious but told me to bring him for an exam. At the end of the exam, he was sent immediately to the emergency room and readmitted. The second time he was sent home and was getting worse, I called the doctor and he had him go straight to the emergency room. Thank goodness, the third time was the charm. Of course, he needed physical therapy both before and after going home to get him back in shape.

Another problem that he had was pneumonia. He had pneumonia three or four times. Sometimes he was hospitalized, and sometimes not. A couple of times were memorable. The first time he got it, we did not know to recognize it and waited too long for treatment. He was in Intensive Care and unconscious for several days, developed a heart arrhythmia, and had his first cardioversion. It was scary when the doctor called and said he wanted permission to restart Paul's heart. Fortunately, I was able to pass the ball to Art to talk to the doctor and make the decision. It was a bad time in more ways than one. After being on a catheter for several days, his bladder gave up, and that is when he wound up with a permanent catheter.

One time he was even hospitalized with pneumonia when we were on vacation in California. He could barely walk, and we were in a hotel, in a room quite far from the elevator. We got innovative, which is what you sometimes have to do. He sat in the rolling desk chair, and I rolled the desk chair out to the elevator. Some employees helped me get him into the car and returned the chair. I drove him to an immediate care center. After they examined him, they called 911 to have him taken to the hospital. They explained that it was because pneumonia puts a strain on the heart and therefore can be very dangerous. They were also concerned that, since I was not familiar with the area, I might have trouble finding the hospital. Paul and I actually shared a bit of a laugh as about a half dozen paramedics arrived and we agreed that it looked like a scene out of Chicago Fire. It seemed like overkill, but better safe than sorry. He spent several days in the hospital in Torrance, California, but he was conscious and not in as bad a shape as the first time he had pneumonia.

The third time, we caught it early, and Paul was able to just get an antibiotic. The doctor would have liked to have hospitalized him, but he agreed to outpatient treatment. The fourth time, he did go to the hospital for a few days, and I asked a doctor there why he kept getting pneumonia. He told me that, looking at his X-ray, he could see scar tissue in one lung. Apparently, when they were draining his lungs because of the Dressler's Syndrome, they nicked his lung, and scar tissue developed. The scar tissue would then catch phlegm and hold it in place, causing the pneumonia to develop.

That's when I had an epiphany. I realized that, as so often happens, one health problem leads to another and has a cascading effect. Because he had the valve repair, he got Dressler's syndrome. Because he had Dressler's syndrome and his lung got nicked he wound up having pneumonia four times. And it probably also damaged his heart and resulted in the congestive heart failure he dealt with two or three times later on. Because he was hospitalized with pneumonia, he developed heart arrhythmia problems and had the first of what wound up being four cardioversions. Also because of the bad bout of pneumonia he had the first time, he wound up with a suprapubic catheter. Because he had a suprapubic catheter, he wound up having several visits to emergency rooms to get the catheter unblocked and one for a fungal infection of the incision. Also because of the super pubic catheter, he tended to get UTI's. The UTIs caused falls, though fortunately none of those caused serious Injuries. He did, however, have to go to the hospital more than once to treat his UTI;s. I also wondered if his death was in some way caused by an untreated blockage in his catheter that I knew happened the day before.

Another example of one thing leading to another was when he slipped on ice while he was walking a dog and the dog pulled him. He broke his wrist in the fall. A couple of years later, he had pain and went to the doctor and found out that because his bones grew well, there was not enough room in his wrist for the plate that they had inserted. He had to have an outpatient procedure to have the plate removed. When he had the plate removed he developed an infection. He wound up having emergency surgery and having his whole arm opened up.

Isn't there an expression about when troubles come they come not in singles but in droves or something to that effect? Once you start getting serious health problems, one thing leads to another

Because he had a stroke, he developed seizures. The seizures plagued him for years. and caused him to lose a couple of jobs, because when he had them and didn't know what had happened, he had panic attacks. He also crashed a forklift during one.

Likewise, his Parkinson's affected almost every function of his body, such as digestion; and combined with the West Nile, his swallowing.

When you look at things this way, the incredible number of health problems he had becomes less incredible.

This was all getting to be rather overwhelming, of course, but the thing that made these things tolerable is that while Paul might be ill or in the hospital for a while, he would also have pretty long periods where, other than being tired from taking medications he was pretty much OK.

The worst things that happened to him were Parkinson's, the suprapubic catheter and West Nile Virus, but I discussed those previously.

Dealing with the West Nile Virus was exhausting, because it went on for 7 months. The nursing home was an hour-and-a-half round trip away, I was trying to balance my almost daily visits and advocacy with continuing my acting career, and the emotional ups and downs were also exhausting. He would get better and then have a setback several times before his sudden death. The first time that was particularly hard was when he was sent to the hospital with an infection, and the doctor said that if Paul didn't recover over the weekend, which he didn't think he would, and if it were a family member of his, he would "let him go". So I was thinking he might die. It was the first time I began to consider the possibility that he could die. He did recover and went back to the nursing home.

The second depressing time was when I realized he had hit a plateau. He was no longer making progress in physical therapy, and he had failed the swallowing test. That meant he could not eat or drink anything. All I could do was swab his mouth with a bit of water. Because he was a big person, the nurses were afraid to try to help him stand, so he had to wear a diaper and be lifted in a sling to sit in a chair, which is pretty humiliating. It was alright when we thought it was temporary, but when I realized he had stopped improving I thought the future was very bleak. I remember wondering if he would be stuck in a nursing home for years, a fate I knew he considered worse than death. I even looked into installing an elevator to get into our house, but he really had so many health problems at this point, including a serious bedsore and needing repeated suctioning because of his trach collar, that it really wouldn't have been possible. I thought about how he always said he didn't want to die in a nursing home and didn't know what to do. In some ways it was a blessing for him when it ended suddenly one night. That's especially true since he died the year before Covid hit and no one could visit their loved ones to comfort and advocate for them.

CHAPTER 39

Dealing with a Death

When your spouse or someone else you are responsible for dies, the number of things that you have to think about may be overwhelming. Here is a list of some of them you can refer to. I hope that this helps.

The Day Of

Sometimes people die suddenly when they are young, and no one is prepared for that. But by the time you are a senior, you should realize that there is a possibility that something could happen to your spouse or other loved one, and you should be prepared for that.

While some people do die at home or with family at their side, many people do not, and so it's possible that someday you will get the call. What is the call? You will either be told the person is dead or dying, or that they are being administered CPR. That is the call that I got, that they were administering CPR. I knew that they only do that if the person has stopped breathing.

So what do you do immediately? The very first thing you do is call the person who is your greatest support and lives in the area. Also call the immediate family members who should be there. In my case, I called my brother, Art and my son, David and asked them to meet me at the nursing home.

The second thing that you do, which fortunately I thought to do, is to grab any papers or your spouse's wallet that relate to their possible demise.

After you have done those two things, if, and only if you feel that you are capable of driving safely, head for the facility that your loved one is at. If you do not feel that you can safely drive, which is a definite possibility, you need to either call someone to drive you or call a taxi. If you're going to call a taxi, or use a rideshare app such as Lyft or Uber, you can do that before you grab the relevant card or papers.

My brother Art, my son David and I all arrived at the nursing home at the same time. We had some trouble getting in because it was after hours, but after some phone calls we did finally get inside and were told that Paul was dead. The paramedics were still there. I identified him. Then I got the inevitable question of, "What do you want us to do with the body?" This is something you need to think about ahead of time. While it is true that any hospital or nursing home will have a cold storage facility where they can place the body until the next day, it is best if you don't have to think about that question. In my case, I simply handed them the membership card in the Neptune Society cremation service and did not have to do anything after that. They took care of everything. It is best to know ahead of time, so you don't have to go home when you're grieving and start calling funeral homes or other services. If you don't have this decided, it's possible the facility may have places that they recommend.

After this, go home and grieve. Let your support person call those who need to know immediately, such as out-of-town close relatives. Call and talk to someone if you want to, but do whatever makes you feel best.

The Next Day

You're going to want to call someone you can count on to help you with handling tasks. Have them tell the people who were notified that they are to call them and have them filter the phone calls and take the messages for you. With the exception of close family members, you do not want your phone ringing constantly and people contacting you. You may not feel like talking. If you want to talk to someone, you can always call them. So have a close family member or close friend manage the calls for you, both outgoing and incoming. If the deceased was expected at work or anywhere else, let them know not to expect them.

The next thing you'll have to deal with, of course, will be funeral or memorial arrangements. Hopefully, this has been planned ahead of time and it's simply a matter of following through on the plans. In an earlier chapter, I talk about having a cemetery plot purchased. See my chapter about funerals for some ideas. You will have to contact both the funeral home, if you use one, and any clergy you want to use, to check their schedules. You don't have to have the restaurant, if you use one, settled and placed in the notice. You can announce it at the service or tell friends who ask. The decisions you will have to make include not only what casket, if you have a burial, but if it will be open or closed, who will speak, etc. Be sure to only have a few speakers and to give the speakers a time limit.

The funeral home or cremation service will almost certainly ask you how many copies of the death certificate you want to order. It's worth the modest charge to have more than you need, because they are more difficult to get later, and some companies will insist upon an official certificate and not just a photocopy. I would get at least a half-dozen.

A very immediate concern is to contact close friends and relatives and the place where your loved one worked, as well as where you work/worked. You should also notify very quickly any congregation that you or they belong to. The congregation may be of significant help in this difficult situation.

You will need to place a death notice in the paper with the details of the funeral or memorial arrangements. Think about not only your city newspaper, but any local newspaper in the deceased's community. The death notices in large papers are fairly expensive, so you will want to take some time to word it carefully. Look at examples in the paper to remind you of things that you're going to want to include in the death notice , including if you want to include religious and other symbols that are sometimes included. You may want to write a longer death notice for the local paper, since in my experience there generally isn't any charge for them. I had a long column with a photo of Paul that went into the local paper for free. The funeral home can help you and may even handle placing the notices. If you are going to include an address for shiva or condolence calls, you will need to ask a friend to stay at the house during the funeral. Sadly, there have been cases where houses have been burglarized during the service by people searching those notices.

Planning and Preparing for a Funeral

I started writing this book during the pandemic. At that time the only safe possibility for funerals was to stream them and have people watch on Zoom or other platforms. Besides safety, the advantage is that you can include people who are in remote locations. Normality is returning, and so I am writing largely on that basis, though many of these pointers apply either way.

When someone dies suddenly, the family may feel at a loss about what to do. It is best to discuss these things ahead of time. Fortunately we did, and I knew what Paul wanted. Arranging a funeral is one of the most challenging tasks that there can be, because of the time pressures involved. Jewish funerals require the shortest period of time, but all funerals generally take place within a week or so of the death of the person. That puts a lot of pressure on whoever is making the arrangements. When selecting the date of the funeral, you have to consider whether there are people who must fly in from out of town and when they are available. There is also the availability of the clergy, or other officiant, and the funeral home involved. The next question for Christians is the timing of a wake or visitation before the funeral.

Many today are doing a graveside service, rather than holding a funeral in a funeral parlor. This can be fine, but personally I prefer a traditional ceremony, because when you go to the graveside it can be muddy, raining, or otherwise unpleasant. Also, there may be handicapped people who have difficulty walking through the cemetery to get to the gravesite. However, this may be an economic necessity for some families, and I understand that. During the pandemic, it may be that a service held outdoors at the grave site is the only way people can safely congregate to bid farewell to their loved one. Recently I did attend a memorial service in a church with strictly limited attendance and numerous precautions. However, I was still a bit uncomfortable. They did also stream the service to those who did not want to attend in person. Indeed, I imagine this may continue, even after the pandemic is over, as a service to those who are far away, or who, for whatever reason, cannot attend.

The next question is who will speak at the funeral? It is a good idea to determine ahead of time 1 to 3 people who will speak, and to let them know the time limit for how long they speak. It is also important that the clergy or officiant consult with the family about what they are going to say. This is especially important if the clergy or officiant didn't know the deceased well. I remember one family being very upset because they thought the remarks showed a real lack of knowledge of the deceased.

The next issue that you will have to deal with is what happens after the service. Will there be a luncheon or other reception? If so, will it be at the congregation, or will it be at a restaurant? There are restaurants that specialize in funeral luncheons. This is a challenging situation, because you cannot predict the exact number of people who will be at the luncheon. There are banquet halls, as well as some restaurants, that are used to dealing with the situation. If you have never been to one of those for a funeral luncheon, I suggest googling under funeral luncheons and seeing who is prepared to do that. The meals traditionally have been served family-style, rather than plated; check with your intended location to see if this process has been altered during the pandemic.

Another possibility, and what Paul requested I do, is a memorial luncheon or event. The memorial luncheon may take place a week, a month, or more after the actual death of the person. That allows time for more planning and to find out how many people are coming. A memorial event tends to have a more upbeat atmosphere than a funeral and is considered to be more of a celebration of the person's life rather than mourning of their loss. Many people call them "Celebrations of Life" for that reason. One actor I knew, who died suddenly, was memorialized at a movie theater, where they showed clips of his film work. That is pretty fantastic.

We had Paul's luncheon a couple of weeks after he died, so there was time for Mike and Pat and others to arrange to fly in. I had a table full of photos that people could look at and played music that he liked as people entered. Of course, some people have photos out during wakes, as well. I like that tradition very much. I had a short, prepared, mostly light hearted speech and opened up the floor for a couple of other comments. In the death notice, I gave the date for the memorial and asked for people who wanted to attend the luncheon to contact me and I would get back to them with the location. I was then able to check out a few different restaurants, give a count to the restaurant, and have a plated meal. I chose the place because I liked the food and the layout, and it was right across the street from where Paul's photo shop had been.

After the memorial luncheon we then had a short service at my temple. Paul was not religious, but I don't think he would have objected, because he respected my religion of Reform Judaism, and it was a comfort for me and several other family members. There were also several people who attended the service even though they chose not to attend the luncheon. So the final arrangements are best to be a balance between the dead and the living.

You definitely should talk to your spouse about burial. If the person is cremated, there's a question of what to do with the ashes afterwards. In our case, Paul considered several possibilities and finally decided that, rather than having his ashes scattered somewhere, he would like to have them placed in my grave when I die. I still haven't figured out what I'm going to do with this box of ashes while I'm alive. It's just sitting in a corner of the den now. I do not feel an emotional attachment to it, but some people feel differently.

Memorial Plaques

Partly because Paul will not have a headstone until I die, I decided to purchase a memorial plaque in the nearby park where he used to walk our dog every night. This is actually an idea I suggested to him a couple of years ago and that he liked very much. Besides the wording of the plaque itself, there are other decisions you will want to think about if you do something like this. I worked with someone in the Park District to walk around the park and select what I consider to be the ideal location. I did not want something in the middle of the park, because it would be difficult for my sister-in-law or anyone else with mobility problems to get to it. I wanted something close to where a visitor could park. I also wanted a tree that was old enough to look impressive but young enough to be there for many years. I like flowers, so I chose a crab apple, even though it was smaller than some other trees. There are many different kinds of places, such as museums and botanical gardens, that also offer such plaques.

Paul's tree and plaque in the northwest
corner of Taylor Park

After the plaque was installed, I held a little ceremony that substituted for a headstone dedication, which is normally done in Judaism. I invited family and those who had sent me unsolicited contributions with their condolence cards. We met by the plaque to see it, and I talked about why I had chosen the wording. We then went to a restaurant next to where Paul's shop had been for a luncheon.

Attending as a Guest at a Funeral

I was appalled recently when someone told me about a funeral that they had attended. Someone came up to one of the bereaved and asked, "So who's going to get the house?" This was in terrible taste. When you attend a funeral, shiva, or wake, you are there simply to offer your condolences, and not to pry. They probably haven't made any decisions yet, anyway. The bereaved may also enjoy sharing memories with you.

The Jewish tradition is what's called *shiva*. Shivas are held at a family member's home, rather than a restaurant. People go and keep the family member company and eat and talk together. The time is much more open-ended than in a restaurant, where you have to be out in a couple of hours. Shivas often take place over two or three days, and even if you cannot make the service you can make what is called a "condolence call" and stop by. If you would go to a shiva house, it is traditional to bring a food item with you, such as a dessert. However, don't worry too much if you cannot, or if you forget the item at home, because there will be so many other people who bring food there is usually too much food. The idea is that everyone can comfort the grieving family. As you enter the home, if you're coming directly from the cemetery, you will be asked to wash your hands before you enter the house, and a bowl will be provided. If you are the host, there will usually be a group of people from the Temple who will help prepare your house for company and help to arrange the food and clean up. Even if you are not Jewish, you may want to do some aspect of this. I actually regret that I didn't.

One point I want to mention is that if you are attending someone else's funeral outside of the family, you may want to send flowers. That's very nice, but do not do it if the deceased was Jewish. It is discouraged because it is felt that it might be depressing to watch the flowers die. If you organize a funeral with flowers, there is the question of what happens to them afterwards. There are organizations that will pick them up and distribute them to nursing homes and hospitals. Your funeral director may know about them. If not, you could try Googling them. I remember the pleasure when donated flowers arrived at the nursing home.

What Comes Next

One of the tasks that you will have to deal with is what do you do with the possessions of the deceased. Hopefully they have left a will to deal with the financial matters. If so, then you don't have to worry too much about that, other than actually filing the will with the county. Hopefully, all property and accounts have both your names on them. If so, you automatically control them.

The big dilemma comes with the person's possessions. You may have been in your house for many years and may have accumulated a lot of possessions. It's possible that some of them may be of enough value to be worth selling, but most of them will not be.

The first thing that you want to do is contact immediate family and close friends and ask them if there are any possessions that they would particularly like to have. I know in my case, I was a little disappointed to find out that no one wanted much of anything. It is a common problem that people have so much of their own possessions that they don't really want to add to them. Don't be surprised. It doesn't mean that they did not care for your spouse or whoever it might be. I know when my mom was moving from her condo to a retirement home, she was disappointed that I would not take her furniture, but I had enough furniture already and no room for more. Young people today, as a rule, do not like a lot of possessions.

So you have to think about whether you're going to attempt to sell, which is a lot of work, or simply donate and take a tax deduction if you itemize. If you donate, what organization do you want to donate to? Do you support their cause? Will they pick things up? Are they nearby? etc. Start working on it soon, but do not be in a rush to get rid of everything. You may be sorry.

When Paul died, I was more than happy to donate all his medical equipment, such as walkers, to our senior services lending closet, a service which allows people who need medical equipment to borrow it for as long as they need it. I certainly did not have any positive emotional ties to anything medical. I was lucky about the one item of significant monetary value. I had a checkup at our local hospital and told the valet who had always helped Paul when he went for his doctors' appointments why he wouldn't be seeing him again. After he expressed his sympathy, he immediately asked what I was going to do with his "wheelchair", meaning the mobility scooter he often admired. He said it would help his mother-in-law. I sold it to him for less than he expected, and we were both happy.

Other things may have some emotional value. You may be surprised at your reactions. I immediately bagged up a whole bunch of Paul's clothes to donate for an Amvets pick up. However, I thought about a couple of particular items of clothing that I really liked, ran out to the porch, and brought them back in to hang in the closet. It's totally irrational, but I really didn't want to give away the new jeans he bought and really liked and his favorite shirt. I kept one or two outfits of Paul's and gave away the rest. If you give things away, you cannot take them back. If you are on the side of being cautious, you can always donate something later. So start small, but do start on the process as soon as you are emotionally able to do so. Take photos of anything you liked but are giving away. Be sure to get tax donation forms for anything you contribute.

Make it a habit to put in a bag or donation box, perhaps one item a day until you feel you don't want to get rid of anything else. Hopefully, if you give yourself that modest goal, you will see other things to get rid of, as well. It's hard to start if your goal is to do everything.

One bit of advice that I heard from several sources, with which I would agree, is don't make any major decisions for two years. That is, such things as if you were going to sell your house and move. It probably would take you that long to sort through everything anyway. What you can always do is start thinking about whether you are going to move in two years, and start thinking about what changes you would need to make to your house. What would you want to get rid of? What would you want to keep? What needs to be fixed or improved? You may find that after you have made the changes that are necessary to make your house more marketable, that you are enjoying it more and don't want to move. That happened to some neighbors. They fixed up their house to sell it but removed the listing after a couple of weeks and stayed another 4 years or so. Of course, you may want to move, and now you only have to worry about packing and not repairing.

The exception to this general advice would be if you were not capable of managing to live by yourself and maintain the residence by yourself. If you have a situation where your spouse was helping you significantly with day-to-day tasks, it may be that you may need to move to assisted living, or at least to a building with an elevator, and/or with a modified bathroom, or whatever other amenities you need to live more independently. If, on the other hand, the only reason you would consider moving is because you do not feel you were capable of doing the chores that are necessary to maintain a house, then I would suggest that you simply start looking around for a good handyman. If you were to move to a condo, you would be paying monthly fees, and in the long run you would probably be paying less if you pay for a handyman, land-scapers, or whatever else you need. You can always look for a high school or college student to do things like mow your grass or shovel your snow. That alone is probably not enough of a reason to move, but of course you have to do what feels right for you.

If, at the end of the 2 years, you feel that you want to move because you want to be closer to family or friends or to be in a different location, or you feel like your house is too big for one person, or whatever, you now have a ready-to-market house that should sell fairly easily. If you are moving to an apartment, you don't have the pressure of trying to figure out the timing of both selling and buying. Personally, if I were ever to sell my house, I think I would move to an apartment in a building with an elevator. Then if something happened to me, I could move to assisted living without dealing with the hassle of selling a condo.

Those are the big things that you have to think about early on. Once you are over the initial things that have to be dealt with, there are still a lot of things that you have to do. So, here is a simple list of some of the tasks you will have to attend to if you have a spouse who has died.

When the spouse dies, you want to go to your county authority and file the will. I made a mistake and tried to file my will, but at least in Illinois, what you do is you file the will of the deceased person. If you do not have the original, then you can file the copy, but you have to fill out additional forms, and this is more work.

- If you do not have a Trust, and there is less than $100,000 that was inherited, fill out an Affidavit of Small Estate and keep it handy. For some reason, this does not get filed. Please note: When determining the amount of an inheritance, anything that is in both your names, or which, such as an IRA lists a beneficiary, does not count towards the total.
- Contact any life insurance companies right away. Paul had 3 small policies. He had too many health problems for too long to get a big one. I found some required a death certificate and other paperwork, while others, such as Mutual of Omaha, paid right away. All did pay.
- Contact the companies that handle your own insurance policies and change your own beneficiary.
- Contact frequent flier and frequent stayer programs to see if the points can be transferred to you before you close the accounts. They often can be.
- Notify Social Security. They will have someone set up an appointment to call you and tell you if you are eligible for spousal benefits and if so, how much it will be. If nothing else, they will give you $255 towards the funeral expenses. If you forget to call them right away, you will have to return any payments they send and possibly face consequences.
- Keep the deceased's name on any joint account for at least two years. If you get a check made out to them, do not sign it. Have it stamped at the bank. It is possible that a company may send you a check made out to "The estate of ...". This happened to me, and I was unable to deposit it. So, either you have to open an estate account, or simply call the company and have them reissue

it made out to either one of you ("To spouse A and/or spouse B"). That is what I did.

- Notify utilities so there won't be any issues someday when you sell, and keep track of anything that comes in the mail in their name. However, if you have a landline, you may want to keep the listing and answering message in both names, because some people prey more upon the widowed. I personally like landlines because they are quickly available during an emergency, and because if you keep your landline corded, rather than transferring it to your cable system, it will work during a power outage.

- Notify credit card companies, if your spouse was the primary cardholder, but do not close the accounts until you have gotten any accumulated rewards transferred or redeemed. If it is in both your names and you are not just an authorized user, you can continue to use the account.

- If they were receiving a pension, contact the company and find out if there are survivor benefits.

- Change your tax status with any pensions or other payments you are receiving.

- Contact a lawyer to file a transfer-on-death form if you own a home or condo, so your heir does not have to go through probate.

- Make sure you have your Power of Attorney forms accessible to whoever would handle your emergencies.

- If you are now living alone, get an Apple Watch or some other form of emergency alert system. Even if you are healthy, you could fall.

- Notify any schools attended to list for their alumni association.

- Notify your car insurance company. Your rate may be lower as the sole driver.

- Check your "Just in Case" list to see if there are other companies you have to contact.

- Transfer IRAs and other accounts to your name.

- Examine the will to see if there are bequests you've forgotten about.

- Send a copy of the death certificate to one of the 3 credit bureaus. This will prevent anyone from opening an account in the deceased's name. Almost 2 years after Paul died someone filed for unemployment in his name. That's when I found this out. If you notify one they will notify the other 2. I sent it to Equifax; P O Box 105739; Atlanta Georgia 30345-5139.

If You Live Alone

Most of my advice is related to people who have lived with someone, such as a spouse. However, there are many people who live alone. If you are the person who would be in charge of their estate, by designation or by default, hopefully you have made sure you have a house key. There are several things you have to think about and do.

- The first thing is to remove and place any pets where they can be cared for. While you probably know if they had a dog or cat, you might not be aware of other pets, such as fish. For mammals, look around the house carefully and take all their objects such as beds and toys. They are going to be traumatized by both the loss and the move and familiar items will be comforting. Just coming in to feed and walk them will not take care of their emotional needs.
- The second thing you want to do is go to the post office and fill out a change of address form. You do not simply want to have the mail returned marked deceased. You want to receive all their mail, at least for a few months. You never know what might be in there. There could be important correspondence, bills, or insurance statements. In fact, even though it's a bit of a pain, I would suggest that you keep their mail coming for a year. There are some bills, for example, that only come once a year, such as some life insurance bills. You want to be sure to get those, in case there is a payment due to someone else, or a payout owed to you. You also want to make sure that utilities are not shut off for non-payment.

You need to keep those going so you don't deal with frozen pipes, so you have electricity when the house is being shown, etc.

- If they were living in an apartment, notify the landlord about the death and a likely move-out date. Ask if you are responsible for sub-letting and how the deposit will be returned.
- If they were living in a home or condo, begin clearing it out and preparing it for sale. You can hire a service to do this. Check the display ads in the local paper, if you don't know a realtor to give you an appraisal and list it.
- If it is a house, you will have to make sure the grass is mowed and/or the sidewalks and drive shoveled, and that someone is picking up any fliers that are dropped off.
- If they were living at home, introduce yourself to a neighbor or two, give them your contact information, and ask them to notify you if they see any suspicious activity or problems.
- Be sure to stop any newspapers that may be delivered. If you don't know what papers they are getting, just check back at their place of residence every few days to make sure they are not piling up. You don't want to have someone breaking into the residence.
- In that regard, you want to be sure ahead of time that you know any information about any burglar alarm they may have in their residence, and you want to continue to set that. Even if they have moved out of their house, you still don't want someone breaking into the residence and causing damage before you sell it.
- If they were residing in a facility, such as an assisted-living facility or a nursing home, you will want to inquire about any down payment that they made when entering that facility. It may take a while to get the payment back, because they want to be sure that there are no more bills coming from Medicare or whatever, but you do want to initiate the process and let the facility know that that payment has not been forgotten. It could be thousands of dollars. Some facilities, frankly, would be very happy if no one claimed it. Others want to return it but may not know where

to send it. Also ask for all personal possessions, and see if there is anything to be passed on or anything to be donated to other residents who need them.

- Hopefully, you have the password for their computer, if they have one. If so, you should check their computer and see if there is a list of important information. You want to put a notification in the vacation response option of their email (an option that is typically listed under "Tools"), if you have the password, so that anyone who contacts them knows what has happened.
- You need to find a copy of their will and see that all provisions are met.

If you are the person who is most responsible for the deceased, you should have made arrangements to get all the information that you need as to what their final wishes are, so you can fulfill those wishes.

Grieving

While a funeral is a very emotional time, especially if the death was unexpected, many people find the days after the funeral to be even harder. Immediately after the death, you were probably surrounded by a lot of people and a lot of activity, and you had a lot of tasks to accomplish. Once the tasks are done with and the people are gone, there is a huge letdown. Many people get extremely blue at this time. That is normal. I suggest that you immediately do a search for a grief support group. Grief support groups are sometimes run by religious organizations, hospitals, or local health organizations. Do a search and ask your clergyman if they are familiar with any. Make sure you talk to someone, and don't just go based on an online presence. For example, I thought that one grief support group that was meeting at a church was merely using their facility; but when I spoke with the person in charge, she said that they use readings from the New Testament, which would not have been comfortable for me. In my case, my inquiry to my rabbi finalized something the clergy had been talking about, and they began a grief support group for the first time.

It may be a while before the grief support group you select begins. Try to keep yourself occupied during that period of possible let down. While you don't want to resume a lot of frivolous activities immediately, you could always get together with some close friends, do projects around the house, and set various goals for yourself. If you have a goal you are trying to achieve, you are less likely to sit around thinking about how sad you are. Yes, you need to allow a certain amount of time for grieving; but you don't want it to occupy your entire day. Do not feel guilty if, while watching a movie or TV, you laugh or enjoy yourself. That's OK, and your loved one would not want you to despair. Everyone grieves in their own way. That's one thing I learned in the grief support group that I joined. Some people cry every day, but others very seldom. Everyone is different, and you have to accept your reactions as normal, no matter what they are.

My grief group developed a lovely bond. We all had similar ages and situations in many ways. We decided to stay together after the formal meetings were over, and now we get together every 2 or 3 weeks, either in a park, on Zoom, or whatever.

I just read about a new movement called death cafes. Strangers gather to talk about death. Some are grieving, some just looking ahead and want to converse about it. If you would prefer that, you could google to see if there is a group like that near you or online.

There are also many, many books that deal specifically with grief. For example **Good Grief** by Westberg. You may want to ask friends for recommendations.

Different Sources of Grief

In this book, when speaking about loss, I focused primarily on the loss of a spouse, because that is what will touch most of us. However, loss and grieving can be related to many causes. People can be very closely emotionally tied to other family members, such as a sibling or a very close friend. There are also very strong ties that sometimes develop with a pet. The loss of a friend, relative, or pet can also involve substantial grieving. I have one friend who marks the anniversary of the death of her pet much as one would observe the yahrzeit (death anniversary) of a family member. We have to both recognize grieving, from various causes, in ourselves, and respect it in others. I've heard that there are special support groups for those dealing with the loss of a pet.

I remember Paul telling me one story of regret from his youth. When he was a teenager and working part-time, one of his coworkers was grieving the death of a dog. Paul and a couple of friends bought the person a sympathy card as a joke. Fortunately, the person didn't realize it wasn't sincere and appreciated it very much. At the time he thought it was funny. When we were married and had our own dog, he understood how serious that attachment was, and we both grieved at the loss of our dog we had for over 15 years. We saved a lock of her hair and her collar and put them together in a photo frame with a nice photo of her and hung that on our wall. We also often talked about her, and I chose to mention her on Paul's memorial plaque. We actually buried her ashes in the urn in which we were given them underneath the tree where she liked to lie. If anybody ever excavates our yard, they're going to wonder what that little urn is. So, it's nice to honor the memory of pets, as well as of people.

Religion as a Guide for Dealing with Grief

About midway through Paul's illness, we experienced a weekend when he was hospitalized with an infection. The doctor said that he probably would not survive. At the time, my focus was simply on the question of whether he would recover. When he did recover and was returned to the nursing home, it dawned on me that I really didn't know what to do if he were to die. I met with my rabbi, and we talked about the process of what one does once the funeral is over. He told me that the traditional rules did not apply in my case, both because Paul was not Jewish and because he was being cremated and not having a traditional funeral. However, he told me a little bit about the Jewish traditions, which have been developed over thousands of years, and I think they are a good guideline or starting point.

In Judaism, there are three stages of mourning: the first week, the first month, and the first year. Each of the stages has a Hebrew name, but I will give a rough equivalent to them. During the first week, the focus is on the death and the support that is given to you by friends and family. Of course, funeral arrangements must be made, and friends and family not only help you with the immediate aftermath of the funeral, but also help prepare your house and help you make changes. In the remaining three weeks of the first month, you gradually resume day-to-day activities, such as work and shopping, but refrain from frivolous ones, such as going to parties. Once the first month is over, you resume a normal schedule as you are comfortable, every few months attending a special service, "Yizkor," where the dead are remembered.

On the first anniversary of the death, the "Yahrzeit," you have a simple ceremony with family, where you dedicate the person's headstone in the cemetery. You then go out to lunch and remember them and other matters. The period of mourning is now at an end. Each year, on the anniversary of the person's death, you light a Yahrzeit candle, which is a 24-hour candle designed especially for the occasion. This candle serves as a reminder of their life, and you say a prayer for their soul and then take a little time to remember them. Their name is read in the temple during the weekly service.

I like this tradition, and I think even if I were not Jewish, I would think about observing it. Yahrzeit candles only cost about a dollar and can be found in any major grocery store in the Kosher section. They come in a glass and are safe to light and keep lit, but I keep them on the stove to be extra safe.

You may want to develop your own family traditions. It doesn't have to be a candle, but I think it's nice to know that you will be remembered at least once a year after you are gone. Maybe you want to have a family lunch in honor of them or whatever other tradition you create.

Holidays

Don't spend holidays alone. I've heard from other people that holidays are especially difficult, but what came to my mind were the big family holidays, such as Thanksgiving and Christmas. I did not expect that smaller holidays would bother me as well.

The first holiday after Paul died was Passover, and Art and Judy and I were invited to Beverly's family's house for a Seder. We missed Paul and toasted him, but overall, it was a lovely, warm, family evening. The next holiday that came was Memorial Day, which didn't seem that significant to me, so I really didn't think much about it ahead of time. But as I sat there alone in my house, it felt very lonely. I went out to the River Forest Memorial Day parade, and that did help, especially since it was very nice out. However, I wished I had planned ahead and planned to do something with family or friends.

Don't wait for an invitation to join anyone. It may or may not come. Start new traditions. Think about somebody else who is alone, and see if they want to get together for the holiday. If you have your family nearby, make plans with them. If your family is out of town, you're going to really have to work ahead of time to plan to visit them or invite them to visit you. If you don't have family, look for a friend who is also alone, with whom you can spend time. When we are safe to no longer have to be socially distanced, throw a party, if you think you can handle it, or meet someone in a park or restaurant. Plan ahead and do something nice, so you can't sit around and be blue. The highest rate of suicide is during the big holidays such as Christmas and New Year's, because people miss their past traditions and associations so much. Try to create something that can become a positive new tradition.

Talking as a Coping Mechanism

If you are not used to living alone, the quiet in the house may be very disconcerting. Playing music or having the TV on does help, but it isn't the same as being able to talk about your feelings. I found my conversations with Paul, whether at home or in the nursing home, to be among the things I missed the most. Sometimes you can talk to a friend or relative, but not every day. So what do you do? Here are some ideas that might help.

I also sometimes talk to myself. That doesn't mean that I'm crazy. I don't want to do it too often, because then I might get in the habit so much that I do it in front of other people, which would be weird. However, while I don't talk to myself constantly, I find it very helpful as a focusing mechanism. If something occurs to me that I need to do or want to do, for example, I say it out loud. For example, "Do the laundry", or "I'm putting the keys on the kitchen table". If I say it out loud, I am much more likely to remember it than if I let my mind wander into the next area of thought or do something without thinking. It also does break the quiet.

If you join a grief support group, the main benefit will be the opportunity to talk to others in the same situation. Sometimes, with other people, you are not sure if they want to hear about your loss. When our formal sessions were coming to an end I suggested that we continue to get together. Over 2 years later we still meet at a park or restaurant about once a month. We enjoy each other's company and it is mostly social, but we also feel comfortable talking about long term recurring grief we experience.

There are all kinds of grief. The amount of grief you feel will be influenced by factors such as whether someone had a full life or not, whether their death was expected or not, if they were suffering prior to death, how close your relationship was, your own personality and circumstances, and even unpredictable factors. Everyone grieves differently and for different lengths of time. Losing a spouse you are living with and who has been a part of your daily life for decades is an especially difficult loss and change in your lifestyle and status, and requires major adjustments. While you have to find what works best for you, here are some experiences I can share.

Here is something that I've worked out for myself. When meeting people I didn't know or didn't know well, when they would say something like "How are you?'" or "How do you do?" in just a polite way, it seemed wrong to say, "Fine," but I didn't think it was appropriate to bring up the death if they didn't know about it, so it was the easiest thing to say. I found if I said, "Fine," but later worked in a reference to my "late husband," that avoided having to explain the situation. Of course, the first month or so, it would not be appropriate to say you were fine, unless it was someone you were only talking to in passing, and with whom you were making polite conversation . If it were someone you knew and just hadn't seen in a while, you would need to say something along the lines of "I don't know if you heard but..." A stranger doesn't need to hear about it.

You may want to consider a grieving journal for yourself, and/or a blog for others. I find Facebook to be an outlet to express my thoughts.

Or, write a book as I have.

Shortly after the activities involved with planning Paul's memorial were over, I sat down one day and realized that I had no obligations in my life. I don't have a regular job, my son is married and living an independent life. I have no one depending on me to care for them, my mortgage is paid off, and I have a pension. So there is nothing I have to do, no schedule to keep. It was a surprisingly unnerving feeling. I felt as if I were adrift without an anchor. There was no particular direction to my life, and nothing I had to do. I realized logically that most people would really envy my position. I had no pressures in my life and was living a modest life, with no financial worries. But I needed to do something. No one can just sit around.

The first thing I realized was that it was important to maintain a regular schedule. This is something that I read about later during the pandemic. it's important to set that alarm clock, even though you don't have to go to work, and to keep yourself going on a regular basis, and not drifting. You also need to set some goals for yourself, something you want to achieve, even if it's just cleaning up at the house or doing some other task you've been meaning to do.

Success in acting would be great, I thought; and in fact, the most exciting casting of my life came a little over a month after Paul died. I got a small role in the TV show, "Better Call Saul," and was flown out to Albuquerque to shoot it. The casting, the shooting, and the whole experience were really wonderful and took my mind off of things for a few days. When it was over, though, for a while acting didn't seem so important.

The pandemic made everything more difficult for everyone, but I regularly got together with friends and family on my porch or deck, or by Facetime or Zoom, so I didn't feel so alone. Now, of course, I am resuming activities such as going to plays with friends that make things feel more normal.

Grief will never entirely disappear but it does ease a bit over time and becomes easier to deal with. After awhile try to focus on the good memories.

How to Deal with Someone Else's Loss

We all have been put in the situation of not knowing quite what to say or do when someone experiences a loss. A couple of tips for dealing with a friend's recent loss from my perspective and experiences:

- Don't ignore it. Very shortly after Paul's death I actually asked someone who didn't say anything, "Do you know that Paul died?" They responded "Yes, but I thought it would be best not to bring it up." No matter what the occasion or situation, if it's the first time you've seen someone since the loss occurred (even if you sent a card - it can be hard to remember who sent them), you should at least say, "My condolences about..," "I was sorry to hear about....," or similar. The second sentence could be something like, "How are you doing?" Then, if they want to talk about it, they can, and if they don't, they'll just say something quick and move on. If you know the person well, a hug, if you aren't social distancing, is usually good, but you have to judge your relationship. Actors tend to be very used to and comfortable with hugs. Of course, the pandemic has changed that dynamic. If it's the second time you see them, ask how they're doing. The third time, just move on unless they bring it up.
- Be specific. I must have had at least 50 people say, "If you need something, if you want to talk", etc. Those sentiments are truly

appreciated, but I often didn't know how to respond. However, if you live nearby, better would be something along the lines of, "How about if you come over to my house for dinner?" or "I'm going to ... would you like me to pick you up to go with me?" A surprise gift of some food would be nice, too.

- Follow up quickly: Someone did ask me if I'd like to go to their house for dinner, and I said yes. They weren't able to set the date at that time, and now I don't remember who it was. I'm sure they don't remember about it now. I also got 2 invitations to people's houses the one weekend I was out of town and assured them I'd like to go any other time but never heard from them again. It's too awkward to remind them.

- A donation in someone's honor to any good cause is always appreciated.

- Be understanding if things like thank-you notes are late or absent. It is amazing how much there is to deal with after a loss, especially if the loss was of a spouse.

- Don't avoid someone because you don't know what to say. I don't know of this happening in my case, but thought I'd mention it.

- Allow others to deal with grief in their own way. Don't impose your ideas of what and when. There is an exception to this, however. If you notice that the person is not getting out after a couple of weeks, it could be a sign of serious depression. Try and get them to do something with you, or drop by with a pie or whatever, and see if they want to invite you in for a talk.

- Don't offer unsolicited advice, especially if you haven't been through a similar situation. Just say you have some ideas, and they should let you know if they want to hear them. Even if you have been in the same situation, ask if they want to hear how you handled it; don't just tell them, as if it's the only right way to do it. Be a good listener.

- Don't assume that because someone seems to be handling things well, that they don't need anything. If you have lived with someone else for years, and now you are alone, it is bound to seem lonely at times. Don't be a pest, but once a month or so ask if they'd like some company.

- Don't bring it up the first several months, but if they seem to be adjusting and you know an appropriate person, you can ask how they feel about being fixed up. Warning, they may be offended if it's less than a year, but they may appreciate it. I think I'd like it.

Moving On

A few suggestions about moving on with your life:

Grief can come and go for years, depending on what is going on in your life. If you are still working, that can keep you busy. If you are not, it is more challenging. Think about whether there are any activities you've been wanting to try, or places you've wanted to go, but it was too difficult to do before, especially if your spouse had health problems. Look at the Opportunities presented in the first part of this book for some suggestions.

Old friends can be a great comfort when you're mourning. However, you may find that the friends you had when you were half of a couple are not the same friends you want to have now. If your friends always do things as a couple, you may feel like a fifth wheel if you do something with them. You may have to find friends who are either pretty independent or single. If you involve yourself in various activities, you will naturally make some new friends.

You may even want to get a job, even if you don't have the financial need. Some people enjoy working because of the regularity of the schedule and the socialization. Of course, so many people today are just working out of their houses, so there is no socialization involved.

Do something totally frivolous to give yourself a treat about once a week. Before Covid hit, to brighten my days alone, I treated myself to things such as, once-a-week, stopping and having a sundae or going to a movie whether with a friend or alone.

Dating Sites

After a few months, when you feel you are ready, you might want to experiment with a dating site, such as match.com. Match also has a subsidiary that's aimed at just older people, referred to as Our Time. Look at people's profiles carefully. Don't just look at their photos, but see if you have common interests before contacting them. Never give anyone even a penny of your money, nor any financial information. One guy asked me, in an initial conversation, if I lived alone and how many bedrooms my house had, and that was it. I hung up on him. If you think you might possibly be interested in somebody, the best thing to do is to meet them in a public place for a cup of coffee. Then if you don't like them, you just leave, no harm done. If you can't meet them in a public place, then talk to them on the phone or Zoom with them. It isn't the same as meeting someone in person, but at least it's something. I found that the majority of the people I've seen on Match don't interest me, but I have talked to some nice men with common interests, and perhaps I will meet them someday. There's nothing wrong with meeting someone on a dating site. It has become quite acceptable, and in fact, both my son and my nephew met their wives online. My nephew met his wife in a chat room, and my son met his wife on a dating app. However, it's best to look at it as a way to meet a friend or have some company for lunch or coffee.

If you encounter anyone trying to get money from you or exhibiting other suspicious behavior, report it to the website administrators. They do respond and block people.

You can also do a search on meetup.com to see if there is an over 50 singles or widowed group in your area. Don't be surprised if you go to an event and it is predominantly female, but that isn't so bad. I recently made a new friend that way

Remember that, especially if you are healthy, your life is not over. You have just moved on to a new chapter of it. One that you have more complete control over. If you have lost a loved one, my condolences. It is very rough, but it does get easier with time and new interests.

CHAPTER 40

Some Final Thoughts

Choose Your Own Adventure

You don't necessarily have to wait for a diverting opportunity that someone else has created to present itself. You can create your own. I was feeling bad that I was not getting new acting roles and that my old films were not being submitted to festivals by the directors. I decided to take matters into my own hands and submit a film I was in to some festivals myself. I wound up traveling to festivals in California, New York and even Cannes, France. I hesitated about the last but then I had enough miles for a free trip from the credit cards I talked about in the travel section of this book, so I thought Why not? The whole festival experience has been pretty exciting.

The Big Picture

No one quite knows what it's like to be a senior until you are one. Every year, and sometimes every day brings a new experience. Some of them are exciting and full of potential. Others are full of challenges. Many times I've wished I had a personal guide to help me know what to do next. Hopefully this book has given you some ideas about what you can do. I have enjoyed sharing my experiences and thinking that some of them may be of help to others. I appreciate you reading about them and hope you have found that it has helped you in some way. If you have comments, you can email me at joycekporter@yahoo.com.

I have also set up a Facebook page for this book.

https://www.facebook.com/profile.php?id=100086241203346

You can go to it to make comments, see updates about the book or share tips from your experiences. I look forward to hearing from you. Of course comments on Amazon are appreciated as well.

CPSIA information can be obtained
at www.ICGtesting.com
Printed in the USA
BVHW050306281222
655044BV00010B/234